# STUDY GUIDE

# FOUNDATIONS OF FINANCE

## THE LOGIC AND PRACTICE OF FINANCIAL MANAGEMENT

# STUDY GUIDE

SECOND EDITION

## Arthur J. Keown
*Virginia Polytechnic Institute and State University*

## J. William Petty
*Baylor University*

## David F. Scott, Jr
*University of Central Florida*

## John D. Martin
*The University of Texas at Austin*

# FOUNDATIONS OF FINANCE
## THE LOGIC AND PRACTICE OF FINANCIAL MANAGEMENT

**Prentice Hall**
**Upper Saddle River, NJ 07458**

Acquisitions editor: Paul Donnelly
Associate editor: Gladys Soto
Project editor: Richard Bretan
Manufacturing buyer: Ken Clinton

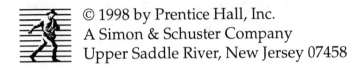 © 1998 by Prentice Hall, Inc.
A Simon & Schuster Company
Upper Saddle River, New Jersey 07458

Printed in the United States of America

10   9   8   7   6   5   4

ISBN 0-13-673377-8

Prentice-Hall International (UK) Limited, *London*
Prentice-Hall of Australia Pty. Limited, *Sydney*
Prentice-Hall Canada Inc., *Toronto*
Prentice-Hall Hispanoamericana, S.A., *Mexico*
Prentice-Hall of India Private Limited, *New Delhi*
Prentice-Hall of Japan, Inc., *Tokyo*
Simon & Schuster Asia Pte. Ltd., *Singapore*
Editora Prentice-Hall do Brasil, Ltda., *Rio de Janeiro*

# CONTENTS

**Supplementary Materials**

# PREFACE

The objective of this *Study Guide* is to provide a student-oriented supplement to *Foundations of Finance*. There are several ways in which we have attempted to accomplish that end, these being:

1.  A condensation of each chapter in the form of a detailed sentence outline. This overview of the key points of the chapter can serve both as a preview and quick survey of the chapter content and as a review.

2.  Problems (with detailed solutions) and self tests which can be used to aid in the preparation of outside assignments and in studying for examinations. The problems were keyed to the end-of-chapter problems in the text in order to provide direct and meaningful student aid. Also, both multiple-choice and true-false questions are used to provide a self test over the descriptive chapter material.

3.  A tutorial on capital budgeting. The tutorial helps the student work through this important topic on an individual basis at his or her own pace.

4.  A teacher's note on understanding the rationale and logic of the internal rate of return. Students frequently learn the procedure for computing a project's internal rate of return but fail to grasp the meaning or the "why" of its computation. This brief note helps the student better understand this important concept and tool of finance.

5.  A complete article appearing in *Financial Practice and Education* that demonstrates the use of a variety of financial calculators. Students have found the article extremely helpful in getting started at using a financial calculator.

6.  In addition to the tables giving compound sum and present value interest factors, we now have tables showing how to compute the interest factors using a financial calculator.

The foregoing material provides what we believe is a valuable learning tool for the student of financial management. Best wishes in your study of finance.

# CHAPTER 1

# An Introduction to the Foundations of Financial Management—The Ties That Bind

Orientation: This chapter lays a foundation for what will follow. First, it focuses on the goal of the firm, followed by a review of the legal forms of business organization, and a discussion of the tax implications relating to financial decisions. Ten axioms that form the foundations of financial management then follow.

I.  Goal of the firm

    A.  In this book, we will designate maximization of shareholder wealth, by which we mean maximization of the total market value of the firm's common stock, to be the goal of the firm. To understand this goal and its inclusive nature, it is first necessary to understand the difficulties involved with the frequently suggested goal of profit maximization.

    B.  While the goal of profit maximization stresses the efficient use of capital resources, it assumes away many of the complexities of the real world and for this reason is unacceptable.

        1.  One of the major criticisms of profit maximization is that it assumes away uncertainty of returns. That is, projects are compared by examining their expected values or weighted average profit.

        2.  Profit maximization is also criticized because it assumes away timing differences of returns.

    C.  Profit maximization is unacceptable, and a more realistic goal is needed.

II.     Maximization of shareholder wealth

    A.      We have chosen the goal of shareholder wealth maximization because the effects of all financial decisions are included in this goal.

    B.      In order to employ this goal, we need not consider every price change to be a market interpretation of the worth of our decisions. What we do focus on is the effect that our decision *should* have on the stock price if everything were held constant.

    C.      The agency problem is a result of the separation between the decision makers and the owners of the firm. As a result, managers may make decisions that are not in line with the goal of maximization of shareholder wealth.

III.    Legal forms of business organization

    A.      The significance of different legal forms

        1.      The predominant form of business organization in the United States in pure numbers is the sole proprietorship.

    B.      Sole proprietorship: A business owned by a single person and that has a minimum amount of legal structure.

        1.      Advantages

            a.      Easily established with few complications

            b.      Minimal organizational costs

            c.      Does not have to share profits or control with others

        2.      Disadvantages

            a.      Unlimited liability for the owner

            b.      Owner must absorb all losses

            c.      Equity capital limited to the owner's personal investment

            d.      Business terminates immediately upon death of owner

C.	Partnership: An association of two or more individuals coming together as co-owners to operate a business for profit.

1.	Two types of partnerships

    a.	General partnership: Relationship between partners is dictated by the partnership agreement.

        (1)	Advantages

            (a)	Minimal organizational requirements
            (b)	Negligible government regulations

        (2)	Disadvantages

            (a)	All partners have unlimited liability
            (b)	Difficulty of raising large amounts of capital
            (c)	Partnership dissolved by the death or withdrawal of general partner

    b.	Limited partnership

        (1)	Advantages

            (a)	For the limited partners, liability limited to the amount of capital invested in the company
            (b)	Withdrawal or death of a limited partner does not affect continuity of the business
            (c)	Stronger inducement in raising capital

        (2)	Disadvantages

            (a)	There must be at least one general partner who has unlimited liability in the partnership.
            (b)	Names of limited partners may not appear in the name of the firm.
            (c)	Limited partners may not participate in the management of the business.
            (d)	More expensive to organize than general partnership, as a written agreement is mandatory.

D. The corporation: An impersonal legal entity having the power to purchase, sell, and own assets and to incur liabilities while existing separately and apart from its owners.

    1. Ownership is evidenced by shares of stock.

    2. Advantages

        a. Limited liability of owners

        b. Ease of transferability of ownership, i.e., by the sale of one's shares of stock

        c. The death of an owner does not result in the discontinuity of the firm's life

        d. Ability to raise large amounts of capital is increased

    3. Disadvantages

        a. Most difficult and expensive form of business to establish

        b. Control of corporation not guaranteed by partial ownership of stock

IV. Federal income taxation

A. Objectives of federal income taxation

    1. Provide government revenues

    2. Achieve socially desirable goals

    3. Stabilize the economy

B. Income taxes for sole proprietorship

    1. All income and expenses for the business are reported on the owner's personal income tax forms.

    2. Taxation of the business income is the same as for the owner's personal income.

C. Income taxes for partnerships

    1. Partnership tax return reports every transaction that has a tax consequence and allocates the transactions as specified by the partnership agreement.

    2. The individual partners report their portions of the partnership income within their personal tax returns.

D. Income taxes for corporations

    1. A tax return must be filed and the resulting taxes paid by the corporation.

    2. Taxable income is basically determined as income less allowable exclusions and tax-deductible expenses.

    3. Seventy percent of any dividends received from another corporation are tax exempt.

    4. Dividends paid by the corporation to its stockholders are not tax deductible.

    5. Corporate rate structure:

| | | | |
|---|---|---|---|
| 15% | $0 | - | $50,000 |
| 25% | $50,001 | - | $75,000 |
| 34% | $75,001 | - | $10,000,000 |
| 35% | over | | $10,00,00 |

There is an additional surtax of 5% for income between $100,000 and $335,000.

There is also an additional surtax of 3% on income between $15 million and $18 1/3 million.

    6. It may be that some of a firm's income originates in a foreign country. If so, the tax rates, and the method of taxing the firm, frequently vary. The financial manager would obviously want to minimize the firm's taxes by reporting as much income as possible in the low tax-rate countries and as little as possible in the high tax-rate countries. Of course, other factors, such as political risk, may discourage your efforts to minimize taxes across national borders.

7. Depreciation

   a. For assets acquired prior to 1981, two depreciation methods, among others, may be used for tax purposes.

      (1) Straight-line
      (2) Double-declining balance

   b. For assets acquired in 1981 or later, the Accelerated Cost Recovery System (ACRS) should be used.

8. Net operating loss: If a corporation has an operating loss in any year, the loss may be applied against the profits in the 3 prior years. If the loss has not been completely absorbed by the profits in these 3 years, the loss may be carried forward to each of the 15 following years.

9. If after deducting all capital gains and capital losses, the company has a net capital loss, such losses may be carried back for 3 years and forward for 5 years to offset any capital gains occurring during these periods.

E. Implications of taxes in financial decision making

   1. Taxes and capital investment decisions

      a. When a plant or equipment acquisition is being considered, the returns from the investment should be measured on an after-tax basis using the marginal, not average, tax rate in the computations.

      b. The depreciation method will have an impact on the timing of taxes.

      c. The estimated salvage value also may have a tax impact; the greater the anticipated salvage value, the less the amount of annual depreciation charges.

   2. Taxes and the firm's capital structure: The tax deductibility of interest payments gives debt financing a definite cost advantage over preferred and common stock financing.

   3. Taxes and corporate dividend policies: The differential tax treatment for the firm's common stockholders might influence the firm's preference between stock price appreciation, i.e., capital gains for the investor, and dividends, i.e., ordinary income for the investor.

V.  Ten axioms that form the foundations of financial management.

    A.  Axiom 1: The risk-return tradeoff—we won't take additional risk unless we expect to be compensated with additional return. Almost all financial decisions involve some sort of risk-return tradeoff.

    B.  Axiom 2: The time value of money—a dollar received today is worth more than a dollar received in the future.

    C.  Axiom 3: Cash--not profits--is King. In measuring value, we will use cash flows rather than accounting profits because it is only cash flows that the firm receives and is able to reinvest.

    D.  Axiom 4: Incremental cash flows—it's only what changes that counts. In making business decisions, we will concern ourself only with what happens as a result of that decision.

    E.  Axiom 5: The curse of competitive markets—why it's hard to find exceptionally profitable projects. In competitive markets, extremely large profits cannot exist for very long because of competition moving in to exploit those large profits. As a result, profitable projects can be found only if the market is made less competitive, either through product differentiation or by achieving a cost advantage.

    F.  Axiom 6: Efficient capital markets—The markets are quick, and the prices are right.

    G.  Axiom 7: The agency problem—managers won't work for the owners unless it's in their best interest. The agency problem is a result of the separation between the decision makers and the owners of the firm. As a result, managers may make decisions that are not in line with the goal of maximization of shareholder wealth.

    H.  Axiom 8: Taxes bias business decisions.

    I.  Axiom 9: All risk is not equal since, some risk can be diversified away, and some cannot. The process of diversification can reduce risk, and, as a result, measuring a project or an asset's risk is very difficult.

    J.  Axiom 10: Ethical behavior is doing the right thing, and ethical dilemmas are everywhere in finance. Ethical behavior is important in financial management, just as it is important in everything we do. Unfortunately, precisely how we define what is and what is not ethical behavior is sometimes difficult. Nevertheless, we should not give up the quest.

## Study Problems

1.  A corporation had $145,000 in taxable earnings. What is the tax liability?

    SOLUTION

| Income | | Marginal Tax Rate | Tax Liability |
|---|---|---|---|
| $ 50,000 | x | 15% | $ 7,500 |
| 25,000 | x | 25% | 6,250 |
| 25,000 | x | 34% | 8,500 |
| 45,000 | x | 39% | 17,550 |
| $145,000 | | Total tax liability = | $39,800 |

2.  A corporation has earnings before interest and taxes of $86,000, dividend income of $8,000, and interest expenses of $9,000. Also, a contribution to a university was made in the amount of $1,000. What is the corporation's (a) taxable income and (b) tax liability?

    SOLUTION

    (a)

| | | |
|---|---|---|
| Operating income | | $86,000 |
| Dividend income | $8,000 | |
| Dividend exclusion | | |
| 80% x $8,000 | (6,400) | |
| Taxable dividend income | | 1,600 |
| Interest expense | | (9,000) |
| Contribution | | (1,000) |
| Taxable income | | $77,600 |

    (b)

| | | | | | |
|---|---|---|---|---|---|
| 15% | x | $50,000 | = | $ 7,500 | |
| 25% | x | 25,000 | = | 6,250 | |
| 34% | x | 2,600 | = | 884 | |
| | | $77,600 | | $14,634 | = Tax liability |

3. The M. M. Roscoe Corporation is a regional truck dealer. The firm sells new and used trucks and is actively involved in the parts business. During the most recent year, the company generated sales of $4 million. The combined cost of goods sold and the operating expenses were $3.2 million. Also, $300,000 in interest expense was paid during the year. The firm received $5,000 during the year in dividend income from 1,000 shares of common stock that had been purchased three years previously. However, the stock was sold toward the end of the year for $100 per share; its initial cost was $80 per share. The company also sold land that had been recently purchased and had been held for only four months. The selling price was $55,000; the cost was $45,000. Calculate the corporation's tax liability.

SOLUTION

M.M. Roscoe Corp.—Corporate Income Tax

| | | |
|---|---|---|
| Sales | | $4,000,000 |
| Cost of goods sold + operating expenses | | (3,200,000) |
| Operating profits | | $800,000 |
| Dividend income | $5,000 | |
| Less 70% exclusion | (3,500) | 1,500 |
| Interest expense | | (300,000) |
| S-T capital gain | | |
|   Selling price | $55,000 | |
|   Cost | (45,000) | 10,000 |
| L-T capital gain | | |
|   Selling price | | |
|   (#shares)(price/share) | | |
|   1,000 x $100 | $100,000 | |
|   Cost | | |
|   (#shares)(price/share) | | |
|   1,000 x $80 | (80,000) | 20,000 |
| Taxable ordinary income | | $531,500 |

Tax liability:

| | |
|---|---|
| $50,000 x .15 = | $7,500 |
| 25,000 x .25 = | 6,250 |
| 456,500 x .34 = | 155,210 |
| | |
| Surtax: | |
| $235,000 x .05 = | 11,750 |
| Total taxes due = | $180,710 |

4. The A.K.U. Corporation had sales of $5.5 million this past year. The cost of goods sold was $4.6 million, and operating expenses were $125,000. Dividend income totaled $5,000. The firm sold land for $150,000 that had cost $100,000 five months ago. The firm received $140 per share from the sale of 1,000 shares of stock. The stock was purchased for $100 per share three years ago. Determine the firm's tax liability.

SOLUTION

A.K.U. Corporation—Corporate Income Tax

| | | |
|---|---|---:|
| Sales | | $5,500,000 |
| Cost of goods sold | | (4,600,000) |
| Gross profits | | $900,000 |
| Operating expenses | | (125,000) |
| Dividend income | $5,000 | |
| Less 70% exclusion | (3,500) | 1,500 |
| Ordinary income | | $776,500 |
| Plus capital gains | | |
| Land: | | |
| Sales price | $150,000 | |
| Selling price | (100,000) | 50,000 |
| Stock: | | |
| Selling price | | |
| (#shares)(price/share) | | |
| 1,000 x $140 | $140,000 | |
| Cost | | |
| (#shares)(price/share) | | |
| 1,000 x $100 | (100,000) | 40,000 |
| Taxable income | | $866,500 |

Tax liability:

| | | |
|---|---|---:|
| $50,000 x 0.15 = | | $7,500 |
| $25,000 x 0.25 = | | 6,250 |
| $25,000 x 0.34 = | | 8,500 |
| $235,000 x 0.39 = | | 91,650 |
| $531,500 x 0.34 = | | 180,710 |
| $866,500 | | $294,610 |

TRUE-FALSE

_____ 1.  Profit maximization is considered to be a more appropriate goal than shareholder wealth maximization because it considers the timing of the expected returns of the firm.

_____ 2.  Shareholder wealth maximization considers the effects of the riskiness of a prospective earnings stream.

_____ 3.  Many businesses are formed as corporations because of the ease of establishment.

_____ 4.  Two major criticisms of the profit maximization goal are that it does not deal adequately with the uncertainty and the timing of returns.

_____ 5.  The income from a partnership is reported by the partners on their personal tax returns.

_____ 6.  Interest and dividend payments made by a corporation are both tax deductible by the paying corporation.

_____ 7.  In general, the less risk a firm is willing to assume, the higher the expected return will be from a given course of action.

_____ 8.  Ethical considerations are not relevant in the financial management.

_____ 9.  Product differentiation helps reduce competition and thereby allows for larger profits.

_____ 10. In order to employ the goal of shareholder wealth maximization, every stock price change should be considered to be a market interpretation of the worth of our financial decisions.

_____ 11. The agency problem is a result of a separation of management and the owners of the firm.

MULTIPLE CHOICE

1. The long-run goal of the firm is to

   a. hold large quantities of cash.
   b. increase sales regularly.
   c. maximize earnings per share.
   d. maximize shareholder wealth.

2. Maximizing shareholder wealth means maximizing the

   a. value of the firm's assets.
   b. value of the firm's cash.
   c. value of the firm's investments.
   d. value of the firm's profits.
   e. market value of the firm's common stock.

3. Advantages of the corporation include:

   a. transferability of ownership.
   b. unlimited liability.
   c. ability of the corporation to raise capital.
   d. double taxation of dividend income.
   e. a and c.
   f. a and b.

4. Disadvantages of the partnership are:

   a. expense of formation.
   b. lack of permanence.
   c. double taxation on income.
   d. unlimited liability.
   e. b and d.
   f. a and d.

5. Profit maximization is not the proper objective of a firm because

   a. it is not as inclusive a goal as the maximization of shareholder wealth.
   b. it does not consider the uncertainty of the return.
   c. it does not consider the timing of the returns.
   d. all of the above.
   e. none of the above.

6.  The market price of a share of stock is determined by

    a.  the New York Stock Exchange.
    b.  the Federal Reserve.
    c.  the company's management.
    d.  individuals buying and selling the stock.

7.  Which of the following forms of business organization is the largest in number?

    a.  Corporation
    b.  Partnership
    c.  Sole proprietorship

8.  The agency problem

    a.  is associated with insuring the firm.
    b.  is no longer important.
    c.  invalidates the goal of maximization of shareholder wealth.
    d.  is a result of the separation of the decision makers and the owners of the firm.
    e.  is all of the above.

# CHAPTER 2

# The Financial Markets and Interest Rates

Orientation: This chapter considers the market environment in which long-term capital is raised. The underlying rationale for the existence of security markets is presented, investment banking services and procedures are detailed, private placements are discussed, and security market regulation is reviewed. Further discussions cover rates of return over long periods and recent periods, interest rate determinants, and theories of the term structure of interest rates.

I.    The mix of corporate securities sold in the capital market

    A.    When corporations raise cash in the capital market, what type of financing vehicle is most favored? The answer to this question is corporate bonds. The corporate debt markets clearly dominate the corporate equity markets when new (external) funds are being raised.

    B.    We know from our discussion on the cost of capital and planning the firm's financing mix  that the U.S. tax system inherently favors debt as a means of raising capital. Over the 1981-95 period, bonds and notes accounted for about 75.5% of new corporate securities sold for cash.

II.    Why financial markets exist

    A.    Financial markets consist of institutions and procedures that facilitate transactions in all types of financial claims.

    B.    Some economic units spend more during a given period of time than they earn. Some economic units spend less than they earn. Accordingly, a mechanism is needed to facilitate the transfer of savings from those economic units that have a savings surplus to those that have a savings deficit. Financial markets provide such a mechanism.

C. The function of financial markets, then, is to allocate savings in an economy to the ultimate demander (user) of the savings.

D. If there were no financial markets, the wealth of an economy would be lessened. Savings could not be transferred to economic units, such as business firms, which are most in need of those funds.

III. Financing business: The movement of funds through the economy

A. In the *financing process*, financial institutions play a major role in bridging the gap between savers and borrowers in the economy.

B. In a normal year, the household sector is the largest net supplier of funds to the financial markets. We call the household sector, then, a *savings-surplus* sector.

C. In contrast, the nonfinancial business sector is a *savings-deficit* sector. In recent years, the federal government has become a "quasi-permanent" savings deficit sector.

D. All in all, within the domestic economy, the nonfinancial business sector is dependent on the household sector to finance its investment needs.

E. The financial market system includes a complex network of intermediaries that assist in the transfer of savings among economic units.

F. The *movement of savings* through the economy occurs in three distinct ways:

1. The direct transfer of funds.

2. Indirect transfer using the investment banker.

3. Indirect transfer using the financial intermediary.

IV.	Components of the U.S. financial market system

    A.	*Public offerings* can be distinguished from *private placements*.

        1.	The public (financial) market is an impersonal market in which both individual and institutional investors have the opportunity to acquire securities.

            a.	A public offering takes place in the public market.

            b.	The security-issuing firm does not meet (face-to-face) the actual investors in the securities.

        2.	In a private placement of securities, only a limited number of investors have the opportunity to purchase a portion of the issue.

            a.	The market for private placements is more personal than its public counterpart.

            b.	The specific details of the issue may actually be developed on a face-to-face basis among the potential investors and the issuer.

    B.	*Primary markets* can be distinguished from *secondary markets*.

        1.	Securities are first offered for sale in a primary market. For example, the sale of a new bond issue, preferred stock issue, or common stock issue takes place in the primary market. These transactions increase the total stock of financial assets in existence in the economy.

        2.	Trading in currently existing securities takes place in the secondary market. The total stock of financial assets is unaffected by such transactions.

    C.	The *money market* can be distinguished from the *capital market*.

        1.	The money market consists of the institutions and procedures that provide for transactions in short-term debt instruments which are generally issued by borrowers who have very high credit ratings.

a. "Short-term" means that the securities traded in the money market have maturity periods of not more than 1 year.

b. Equity instruments are not traded in the money market.

c. Typical examples of money market instruments are (1) U.S. Treasury bills, (2) federal agency securities, (3) bankers' acceptances, (4) negotiable certificates of deposit, and (5) commercial paper.

2. The capital market consists of the institutions and procedures that provide for transactions in long-term financial instruments. This market encompasses those securities that have maturity periods extending beyond 1 year.

D. *Organized security exchanges* can be distinguished from *over-the-counter markets*.

1. Organized security exchanges are tangible entities whose activities are governed by a set of bylaws. Security exchanges physically occupy space, and financial instruments are traded on such premises.

a. Major stock exchanges must comply with a strict set of reporting requirements established by the Securities and Exchange Commission (SEC). These exchanges are said to be *registered*.

b. Organized security exchanges provide several benefits to both corporations and investors. They (1) provide a continuous market, (2) establish and publicize fair security prices, and (3) help businesses raise new financial capital.

c. A corporation must take steps to have its securities *listed* on an exchange in order to directly receive the benefits noted above. Listing criteria differ from exchange to exchange.

2. Over-the-counter markets include all security markets except the organized exchanges. The money market is a prominent example. Most corporate bonds are traded over the counter.

V.    Using an investment banker

    A.    The investment banker is a financial specialist who acts as an intermediary in the selling of securities. He or she works for an investment banking firm (house).

    B.    Three basic functions are provided by the investment banker:

        1.    He or she assumes the risk of selling a new security issue at a satisfactory (profitable) price. This is called *underwriting*. Typically, the investment banking house, along with the underwriting syndicate, actually buys the new issue from the corporation that is raising funds. The syndicate (group of investment banking firms) then sells the issue to the investing public at a higher price (hopefully) than it paid for it.

        2.    He or she provides for the *distribution* of the securities to the investing public.

        3.    He or she *advises* firms on the details of selling securities.

    C.    Several distribution methods are available for placing new securities into the hands of final investors. The investment banker's role is different in each case.

        1.    In a *negotiated purchase,* the firm in need of funds contacts an investment banker and begins the sequence of steps leading to the final distribution of the securities that will be offered. The price that the investment banker pays for the securities is "negotiated" with the issuing firm.

        2.    In a *competitive-bid purchase*, the investment banker and underwriting syndicate are selected by an auction process. The syndicate willing to pay the greatest dollar amount per new security to the issuing firm wins the competitive bid. This means that it will underwrite and distribute the issue. In this situation, the price paid to the issuer is not negotiated; instead, it is determined by a sealed-bid process much on the order of construction bids.

3. In a *commission* (or *best-efforts*) offering, the investment banker does not act as an underwriter. He or she attempts to sell the issue in return for a fixed commission on each security that is actually sold. Unsold securities are simply returned to the firm hoping to raise funds.

4. In a privileged *subscription*, the new issue is not offered to the investing public. It is sold to a definite and limited group of investors. Current stockholders are often the privileged group.

5. In a *direct sale*, the issuing firm sells the securities to the investing public without involving an investment banker in the process. This is not a typical procedure.

D. The negotiated purchase is most likely to be the distribution method used by the private corporation. It consists of several steps.

1. The security-issuing firm selects an investment banker.

2. A series of pre-underwriting conferences takes place. Discussions center on (1) the amount of capital to be raised, (2) the possible receptiveness of the capital markets to a specific mode of financing, and (3) the proposed use of the new funds. These conferences are consummated by the signing of a *tentative underwriting agreement*. The approximate price to be paid for each security is identified in this agreement.

3. An underwriting syndicate is formed. The syndicate is a temporary association of investment bankers formed to purchase the security issue from the corporation. The syndicate's objective is to resell the issue at a profit.

4. Most new public issues must be registered with the SEC before they can be sold to final investors. This involves filing a lengthy technical document called a *registration statement* with the SEC. This document aims to disclose relevant facts about the issuing firm and the related security to potential investors. Another document, the *prospectus*, is also filed with the SEC for examination. It is a shortened version of the official registration statement. Once both documents are approved, the prospectus becomes the official advertising vehicle for the security offering.

5.      A selling group is formed to distribute the new securities to final investors. Securities dealers who are part of the selling group are permitted to purchase a portion of the new issue at a price to the public. A *selling-group agreement* binds the syndicate and the members of the selling group.

6.      A due-diligence meeting is held to finalize all details prior to taking the offering to the public. The price at which the issuing firm will sell the new securities to the syndicate is settled. Usually, the offering is made to the public on the day after this meeting.

7.      The syndicate manager (from the investment banking house that generated the business) is permitted to mitigate downward price movements in the secondary market for the subject offering. This is accomplished by the syndicate managers placing buy orders for the security at the agreed-upon public offering price.

8.      A contractual agreement among the syndicate members terminates the syndicate. In the most pleasant situations, this agreement is made when the issue is fully subscribed (sold).

VI.    Private placements

A.      Each year, billions of dollars of new securities are privately (directly) placed with final investors. In a private placement, a small number of investors purchases the entire security offering. Most private placements involve debt instruments.

B.      Large financial institutions are the major investors in private placements. These include (1) life insurance firms, (2) state and local retirement funds, and (3) private pension funds.

C.      The advantages and disadvantages of private placements as opposed to public offerings must be carefully evaluated by management.

1.      The advantages include (1) greater speed than a public offering in actually obtaining the needed funds, (2) lower flotation costs than are associated with a public issue, and (3) increased flexibility in the financing contract.

2.    The disadvantages include (1) higher interest costs than are ordinarily associated with a comparable public issue, (2) the imposition of several restrictive covenants in the financing contract, and (3) the possibility that the security may have to be registered some time in the future at the lender's option.

VII.   Flotation costs

A.    The firm raising long-term capital typically incurs two types of flotation costs: (1) the underwriter's spread and (2) issuing costs. The former is typically the larger.

1.    The underwriter's spread is the difference between the gross and net proceeds from a specific security issue. This absolute dollar difference is usually expressed as a percent of the gross proceeds.

2.    Many components comprise issue costs. The two most significant are (1) printing and engraving and (2) legal fees. For comparison purposes, these, too, are usually expressed as a percent of the issue's gross proceeds.

B.    SEC data reveal two relationships about flotation costs.

1.    Issue costs (as a percent of gross proceeds) for common stock exceed those of preferred stock, which exceed those of bonds.

2.    Total flotation costs per dollar raised decrease as the dollar size of the security issue increases.

VIII.   Regulation

A.    The primary market is governed by the Securities Act of 1933.

1.    The intent of this federal regulation is to provide potential investors with accurate and truthful disclosure about the firm and the new securities being sold.

2.    Unless exempted, the corporation selling securities to the public must register the securities with the SEC.

3.   Exemptions follow from a variety of conditions. For example, if the size of the offering is small enough (less than $500,000), the offering does not have to be registered. If the issue is already regulated or controlled by some other federal agency, registration with the SEC is not required. Railroad issues and public utility issues are examples.

4.   If not exempted, a registration statement is filed with the SEC containing particulars about the security-issuing firm and the new security.

5.   A copy of the prospectus, a summary registration statement, is also filed. It will not yet have the selling price of the security printed on it; it is referred to as a *red herring* and called that until approved by the SEC.

6.   If the information in the registration statement and prospectus is satisfactory to the SEC, the firm can proceed to sell the new issue. If the information is not satisfactory, a *stop order* is issued which prevents the immediate sale of the issue. Deficiencies have to be corrected to the satisfaction of the SEC before the firm can sell the securities.

7.   The SEC does *not* evaluate the investment quality of any issue. It is concerned, rather, with the presentation of complete and accurate information upon which the potential investor can act.

B.   The secondary market is regulated by the Securities Exchange Act of 1934. This federal act created the SEC. It has many aspects.

1.   Major security exchanges must register with the SEC.

2.   Insider trading must be reported to the SEC.

3.   Manipulative trading that affects security prices is prohibited.

4.   Proxy procedures are controlled by the SEC.

5.   The Federal Reserve Board has the responsibility of setting margin requirements. This affects the proportion of a security purchase that can be made via credit.

C. The Securities Act Amendments of 1975 touched on three important issues.

    1. Congress mandated the creation of a national market system (NMS). Implementation details of the NMS were left to the SEC. Agreement on the final form of the NMS is yet to come.

    2. Fixed commissions (also called fixed brokerage rates) on public transactions in securities were eliminated.

    3. Financial institutions, like commercial banks and insurance firms, were prohibited from acquiring membership on stock exchanges where their purpose in so doing might be to reduce or save commissions on their own trades.

D. In March, 1982, the SEC adopted "Rule 415." This process is now known as a shelf registration or a shelf offering.

    1. This allows the firm to avoid the lengthy, full registration process each time a public offering of securities is desired.

    2. In effect, a master registration statement that covers the financing plans of the firm over the coming two years is filed with the SEC. After approval, the securities are sold to the investing public in a piecemeal fashion or "off the shelf."

    3. Prior to each specific offering, a short statement about the issue is filed with the SEC.

IX. Observed rates of return in the financial markets. Ibbotson and Sinquefield examine the realized rates of return for a wide variety of securities spanning the period 1926-1995. They have found the following:

A. The average inflation rate (the "inflation-risk premium") was 3.2% for the period.

B. The default-risk premium for long-term corporate bonds was 0.5%.

C. Common stocks earned 6.5% more than the rate earned on long-term corporate bonds (12.5-6.0), and small firms earned 5% more than the total population of common stocks.

X. The effects of inflation on rates of return

   A.  The real rate of interest is the difference in the nominal rate and the anticipated rate of inflation.

   B.  The notion of a real rate of interest can be thought of as the "price for deferring consumption."

   C.  Letting the nominal rate of interest be represented by $K_{rf}$, the anticipated rate of inflation by IRP, and the real rate of interest by $K^*$, we can express the result by the following equation:

   $$1 + K_{rf} = (1 + K^*)(1 + IRP)$$

   or  $$K_{rf} = K^* + IRP + IRP\ K^*$$

   For example, if the real rate, $K^*$, is 5% and the expected inflation rate, IRP, is 4%, the nominal rate, $K_{rf}$, would then be 9.2%, computed as follows:

   $$K_{rf} = .05 + .04 + (.05)(.04)$$

   $$= .092 \text{ or } 9.2\%$$

XI. The term structure of interest rates

   A.  The relationship between a debt security's rate of return and the length of time until the debt matures is known as the *term structure of interest rates*.

   B.  The term structure reflects observed rates or yields on similar securities, except for the length of time until maturity, at a particular moment in time.

   C.  Three theories have been suggested to explain the term structure of interest rates.

       1.  The *unbiased expectations theory* says that the term structure is determined by an investor's expectations about future interest rates.

       2.  The *liquidity preference theory* suggests that investors require liquidity premiums (addition returns) to compensate them for buying securities which expose them to a greater risk of fluctuating interest rates.

25

3. The *market segmentation theory* is built on the notion that legal restrictions and personal preferences limit investment choices to certain ranges of maturities, and, therefore, affect the rates of return required in each range.

## Study Problem

1. If the expected inflation rate is 4%, and the real rate of interest is 8%, what is the nominal interest rate?

SOLUTION

$$\text{Nominal rate, } K_{rf} = \left(\begin{array}{c}\text{Real} \\ \text{rate}\end{array}\right) + \left(\begin{array}{c}\text{Inflation} \\ \text{rate}\end{array}\right) + \left(\begin{array}{c}\text{Real} \\ \text{rate}\end{array}\right)\left(\begin{array}{c}\text{Inflation} \\ \text{rate}\end{array}\right)$$

$$= 8\% + 4\% + (4\%)(8\%) = 12.32\%$$

## Self Tests

TRUE-FALSE

_____ 1. A share of IBM common stock is a real asset.

_____ 2. Capital formation in underdeveloped countries might be assisted if those countries' financial market systems were more extensively developed.

_____ 3. General Motors is a typical example of a financial intermediary.

_____ 4. The Money Market is housed at 11 Wall Street, New York City.

_____ 5. Common stocks are money market instruments.

_____ 6. Price quotations on organized security exchanges have been facilitated by the existence of NASDAQ.

_____ 7. The Banking Act of 1933 separated the activities of commercial banking and investment banking.

_____ 8. In a negotiated purchase, the price the investment banker pays the security-issuing firm for the new issue is negotiated between these parties.

_____ 9. Underwriting syndicates are prohibited by the Securities Act of 1933.

_____ 10. Life insurance companies are major purchasers of privately placed securities.

_____ 11. Secondary markets reduce the risk of investing in financial claims.

_____ 12. Equity instruments are traded in the money market.

_____ 13. The capital market includes those securities that have maturity periods extending beyond one year.

_____ 14. Trading in currently existing securities takes place in the primary market.

_____ 15. When new funds are being raised in a typical year, corporate equity markets are favored over corporate debt markets, in terms of dollar volume.

_____ 16. The U.S. tax system favors debt as a method of raising capital in comparison to equity instruments.

_____ 17. A life insurance company is an example of a financial intermediary.

_____ 18. "Crowding out" refers to the use of debt vs. the use of common stock to raise new funds.

_____ 19. Flotation costs for debt generally exceed those of common stock.

_____ 20. In general, flotation costs are inversely related to the size of the security issue.

_____ 21. Inventories represent a category of financial assets.

_____ 22. Financial markets allocate savings in the economy to demanders of those funds.

_____ 23. Financial intermediaries issue their own financial claims called direct securities, and invest the money obtained in indirect securities, the financial claims of other economic units.

_____ 24. The U.S. government is the largest savings-surplus sector in the economy.

____ 25.  Financial markets provide a mechanism to facilitate the transfer of savings from those economic units that have a savings surplus to those that have a savings deficit.

____ 26.  The New York Stock Exchange, American Stock Exchange, and Midwest Stock Exchange are the only three <u>national</u> exchanges in the U.S.

____ 27.  There is an inverse relationship between the total flotation cost per dollar of funds raised and the amount of the security issue.

____ 28.  The primary objective of the Securities Act of 1933 is to provide potential investors with accurate and truthful disclosure about the firm and the new securities being sold.

____ 29.  Long-term corporate bonds are more risky than common stocks from the investor's point of view.


MULTIPLE CHOICE

1.  Which of the following is *not* a benefit provided by the existence of organized security exchanges?

    a.  A continuous market
    b.  Helping business raise new capital
    c.  Keeping long-term bond prices below 8%
    d.  Establishing and publicizing fair security prices

2.  What is it called when an investment banker agrees to sell only as many securities as he or she can at an established price?

    a.  A private placement
    b.  A direct placement
    c.  A privileged subscription
    d.  A best-efforts agreement
    e.  An upset agreement

3. Which of the following security distribution methods is least profitable to the investment banker?

   a. Negotiated purchase
   b. Competitive-bid purchase
   c. Commission basis
   d. Privileged subscription
   e. Direct sale

4. A prospectus resembles most closely

   a. a registration statement.
   b. a red herring.
   c. a selling group agreement.
   d. a letter of credit.

5. The purpose of financial markets is to

   a. lower bond yields.
   b. allocate savings efficiently.
   c. raise stock prices.
   d. employ stock brokers.

6. The maturity boundary dividing the U.S. money and capital markets is

   a. an arbitrary classification system.
   b. set by the Federal Reserve Board.
   c. periodically reviewed and altered by the SEC.
   d. determined by the U.S. Treasury.

7. Flotation costs are highest on

   a. bonds.
   b. preferred stock.
   c. common stock.

8. Insider trading is regulated by

   a. the Banking Act of 1933.
   b. the Glass-Steagall Act of 1933.
   c. the Securities Act of 1933.
   d. the Securities Exchange Act of 1934.

9. Which of the following methods for the distribution of securities bypasses the use of an investment banker?

   a. Negotiated purchase
   b. Competitive-bid purchase
   c. Direct sales
   d. Best-efforts basis
   e. Privileged subscriptions

10. The difference between the gross and net proceeds from a given security issue expressed as a percent of the gross proceeds is known as

    a. issue costs.
    b. flotation costs.
    c. underwriter's spread.
    d. legal fees.

11. Which of the following is generally not an advantage of private placements?

    a. Speed
    b. Reduced flotation costs
    c. Financing flexibility
    d. Interest costs

12. Which of the following is not an example of a money market instrument?

    a. U.S. Treasury bills
    b. Common stock
    c. Federal agency securities
    d. Commercial paper

13. An agreement which obligates the investment banker to underwrite securities that are not accepted by privileged investors is known as a

    a. privileged subscription.
    b. standby agreement.
    c. negotiated purchase.
    d. best-efforts basis.

14. The demand for funds by the federal government puts upward pressure on interest rates, causing private investors to be pushed out of the financial markets. This is called

    a. the big squeeze.
    b. the efficient market hypothesis.
    c. the crowding-out effect.
    d. liquidity preference.
    e. government intervention.

15. Insurance companies invest in the "long-end" of the securities market. In which of the following instruments would an insurance company be least likely to invest most of its funds in?

    a. Mortgages
    b. Corporate bonds
    c. Commercial paper
    d. Corporate stocks

16. Which of the following is/are NYSE listing requirements?

    a. Profitability
    b. Market value
    c. Public ownership
    d. All of the above
    e. None of the above

17. The indirect method of transferring savings in which securities are not transformed, but passed through to other purchasers, most frequently involves

    a. an established relationship between buyer and issuer.
    b. a finance company.
    c. a commercial bank.
    d. an investment banker.
    e. all of the above.

18. Which of the following does not describe an organized security exchange?

    a. It occupies physical space as opposed to being strictly communication links among traders.
    b. It is strictly regional in scope.
    c. It is regulated by the Securities and Exchange Commission.
    d. Its trades are conducted strictly by exchange members.

31

19. Shelf registration refers to the process of

    a. registering single issues with the SEC through the use of SEC-prepared, standardized forms.
    b. selecting and seeking SEC approval for an investment banker from their approved or "shelf" list of investment bankers.
    c. registering a chosen underwriting syndicate with the SEC.
    d. receiving a blanket-order approval from the SEC to issue securities periodically over the next two years.

20. Primary markets are distinguished from secondary markets by the fact that

    a. primary markets sell securities for corporations with assets over $2 million, while secondary markets sell securities for corporations with assets less than $2 million.
    b. primary markets are more developed than the secondary markets.
    c. primary markets trade new securities issues while secondary markets trade existing securities.
    d. primary markets enjoy higher trading volume than the secondary markets.

21. How many registered stock exchanges are there in the United States?

    a. 4
    b. 5
    c. more than 5
    d. none

22. What is the correct <u>sequence</u> of steps for the negotiated purchase distribution method? The key steps follow each Roman numeral, below.

    I. File a registration statement and prospectus with SEC.
    II. Hold a due diligence meeting.
    III. Form an underwriting syndicate.
    IV. Form a contractual agreement among syndicate members to terminate the syndicate.
    V. Form a selling group to distribute new securities.

    a. I, II, III, IV, V
    b. II, III, I, V, IV
    c. III, I, V, II, IV
    d. IV, I, II, III, V

23. The primary market is governed by

    a.   the Banking Act of 1933.
    b.   the Glass-Steagall Act of 1933.
    c.   the Securities Act of 1933.
    d.   the Securities Exchange Act of 1934.

24. In terms of risk, it is correct to say:

    a.   Government securities are less risky than common stocks, but more risky than corporate bonds.
    b.   Corporate bonds are less risky than common stocks.
    c.   Long-term government securities are less risky than short-term government securities.
    d.   Common stocks of large companies are more risky than the common stocks of small firms.

25. The term structure of interest rates refers to

    a.   the different risk levels of interest rates.
    b.   the different interest rates of securities with the same maturity dates.
    c.   the different interest rates of securities with the same risk but with different maturity dates.
    d.   the terms of agreement associated with a bond's interest payments.

# CHAPTER 3

# Evaluating a Firm's Financial Performance and Measuring Cash-flow

Orientation:  Financial analysis can be defined as the process of assessing the financial condition of a firm. The principal analytical tool of the financial analyst is the financial ratio.  In this chapter, we provide a brief overview of a firm's basic financial statements followed by a survey of a set of key financial ratios and a discussion of their effective use.

I.    Basic financial statements

    A.    The income statement

        1.    The income statement reports the results from operating the business for a period of time, such as a year.

        2.    It is helpful to think of the income statement as comprising four types of activities:

            a.    Selling the product

            b.    The cost of producing or acquiring the goods or services sold

            c.    The expenses incurred in marketing and distributing the product or service to the customer, along with administrative operating expenses

            d.    The financing costs of doing business; for example, interest paid to creditors and dividend payments to the preferred stockholders

3.    An example of an income statement is provided in Table 3-1 for the McDonalds Corporation.

B.    The balance sheet

1.    The balance sheet provides a snapshot of the firm's financial position at a specific point in time, presenting its asset holdings, liabilities, and owner-supplied capital.

    a.    Assets represent the resources owned by the firm

        1.    Current assets--consisting primarily of cash, marketable securities, accounts receivable, inventories, and prepaid expenses

        2.    Fixed or long-term assets--comprising equipment, buildings, and land

        3.    Other assets--all assets not otherwise included in the firm's current assets or fixed assets, such as patents, long-term investments in securities, and goodwill

    b.    The liabilities and owners' equity indicate how those resources are financed.

        1.    The debt consists of such sources as credit extended from suppliers or a loan from a bank.

        2.    The equity includes the stockholders' investment in the firm and the cumulative profits retained in the business up to the date of the balance sheet.

2.    The balance sheet is not intended to represent the current market value of the company, but rather reports the historical transactions recorded at their cost.

3.    Balance sheets for the McDonalds Corporation are presented in Table 3-2.

C.    The cash flow statement

1.    The cash flow statement shows the actual cash flows generated by the firm for the year.

36

2.   Cash flow from operations

    a.   A firm's cash flow from operations consists of collections from customers and payments to suppliers for the purchase of materials.

    b.   Also included are other operating cash outflows, such as marketing and administrative expenses and interest payments, and cash tax payments.

3.   Cash flows--Investment activities

This section includes such transactions as the purchase (or sales) of fixed assets, land, and patents.

4.   Cash flows--Financing activities

This section deals with financing activities, including any cash inflows or outflows to or from the firm's investors, both lenders of debt and owners.  Examples include dividends paid, payments on debt, or issuing new shares of stock.

5.   Interpreting the cash flow statement

This section provides an analysis of different possible cash flow patterns that can occur.  Recognizing these patterns helps us understand more clearly the basic nature of a firm's cash flows.

II.   Financial ratio analysis

A.   Financial ratios help us identify some of the financial strengths and weaknesses of a company.

B.   The ratios give us a way of making meaningful comparisons of a firm's financial data at different points in time and with other firms.

C.   We could use ratios to answer some important questions about a firm's operations.

1.   Question 1:  How liquid is the firm?

    a.   The liquidity of a business is defined as its ability to meet maturing debt obligations.  That is, does or will the firm have the resources to pay the creditors when the debt comes due?

b.　There are two ways to approach the liquidity question.

   (1)　We can look at the firm's assets that are relatively liquid in nature and compare them to the amount of the debt coming due in the near term.

   (2)　We can look at how quickly the firm's liquid assets are being converted into cash.

2.　Question 2: Is management generating adequate operating profits on the firm's assets?

a.　We want to know if the profits are sufficient relative to the assets being invested.

b.　We have several choices as to how we measure profits: gross profits, operating profits, or net income. Gross profits is not acceptable because it overlooks important information such as marketing and distribution expenses. Net income includes the unwanted effects of the firm's financing policies. This leaves operating profits as our best choice in measuring the firm's operating profitability. Thus, the appropriate measure is the operating income return on investment (OIROI):

$$\text{OIROI} = \frac{\text{operating income}}{\text{total assets}}$$

3.　Question 3: How is the firm financing its assets?

Here, we are concerned with the mix of debt and equity capital the firm is using. Two primary ratios used to answer this question are the debt ratio and times interest earned. The debt ratio is the proportion of total debt to total assets. Times interest earned compares operating income to interest expense for a crude measure of the firm's capacity to service its debt.

4.　Question 4: Are the owners (stockholders) receiving an adequate return on their investment?

a.　We want to know if the earnings available to the firm's owners or common equity investors are attractive when compared to the returns of owners of similar companies in the same industry.

b.     Return on equity (ROE) $= \dfrac{\text{net income}}{\text{comon equity}}$

c.     The effect of using debt on net income: an example.

This example shows how, through the use of debt, firms can affect their return on equity.

d.     Return on equity is a function of:

(1)     the operating income return on investment less the interest rate paid, and

(2)     the amount of debt used in the capital structure relative to the equity

D.     An integrative approach to ratio analysis: the DuPont analysis

The DuPont analysis is another approach used to evaluate a firm's profitability and return on equity. Its graphic technique may be helpful in seeing how ratios relate to one another and the account balances.

E.     Limitations of ratio analysis

This list warns of the many pitfalls that may be encountered in computing and interpreting financial ratios. Ratio users should be aware of these concerns prior to making decisions based solely on ratio analysis.

## Study Problems

1.     Prepare a balance sheet for the A. R. Peterson Mfg. Co. from the scrambled list of items below. The owner's equity balance is not given but it can be determined as a balancing figure.

| | | | |
|---|---|---|---|
| Building | $49,100 | Office equipment | 4,100 |
| Accounts receivable | 21,600 | Land | 22,000 |
| Machinery | 2,950 | Notes payable | 14,000 |
| Cash | 9,200 | Owners' equity | |
| Accounts payable | 16,500 | | |

SOLUTION

## A. R. Peterson Mfg. Co.
## Balance Sheet

| Cash | $ 9,200 | Accounts payable | 16,500 |
|---|---|---|---|
| Accounts receivable | 21,600 | Notes payable | 14,000 |
| Land | 22,000 | Owners' equity | 78,450 |
| Building | 49,100 | | |
| Machinery | 2,950 | | |
| Office equipment | 4,100 | Total liabilities | |
| Total assets | $108,950 | & owner's equity | $108,950 |

2. By studying the successive balance sheets for AMP, Inc. found below, determine what transactions have occurred. Prepare a list of the transactions and the corresponding balance-sheet dates. For example, on March 31, 1993, the firm's owners invested $200,000 in AMP, Inc. and started the business.

(a)
## AMP, Inc.
## Balance Sheet
## March 31, 1993

| Assets | | Owner's Equity | |
|---|---|---|---|
| Cash | $200,000 | Owners' equity | $200,000 |

(b)
## AMP, Inc.
## Balance Sheet
## April 2, 1993

| Assets | | Owner's Equity | |
|---|---|---|---|
| Cash | $100,000 | Owners' equity | $200,000 |
| Land | 100,000 | | |
| | $200,000 | | $200,000 |

40

(c)

AMP, Inc.
Balance Sheet
April 15, 1993

| Assets | | Owner's Equity | |
|---|---|---|---|
| Cash | $ 50,000 | Owners' equity | $200,000 |
| Building | 50,000 | | |
| Land | 100,000 | | |
| | $200,000 | | $200,000 |

(d)

AMP, Inc.
Balance Sheet
May 2, 1993

| Assets | | Liabilities & Owners' Equity | |
|---|---|---|---|
| Cash | $50,000 | Accounts payable | $25,000 |
| Inventories | 25,000 | Owner's equity | 200,000 |
| Building | 50,000 | | |
| Land | 100,000 | | |
| | $225,000 | | $225,000 |

(e)

AMP, Inc.
Balance Sheet
May 15, 1993

| Assets | | Liabilities & Owners' Equity | |
|---|---|---|---|
| Cash | $60,000 | Accounts payable | $25,000 |
| Inventories | 25,000 | Notes payable | 25,000 |
| Equipment | 15,000 | Owner's equity | 200,000 |
| Building | 50,000 | | |
| Land | 100,000 | | |
| | $250,000 | | $250,000 |

SOLUTION

(a) On March 31, 1993, the firm's owners invested $200,000 in AMP, Inc. and started the business.

(b) On April 2, 1993, $100,000 of the original investment by the owners was used to acquire land.

(c) On April 15, 1993, $50,000 of the original cash was used to acquire a building.

(d) On May 2, 1993, $25,000 of inventory was purchased on account (credit).

(e) On May 15, 1993, a $25,000 loan was obtained and $15,000 of the proceeds used to purchase equipment.

3. Balance sheets for Marion Mfg. Co. and the Sterlington Corp. are found below. Both firms are involved in the manufacture of electrical components used in small electronic calculators and digital wristwatches. Since both firms are less than 3 years old, their book values are reasonably close to actual market value.

Marion Mfg. Co.
Balance Sheet
November 30, 1993

| Assets | | Liabilities & Equity | |
|---|---|---|---|
| Cash | $ 50,000 | Notes payable | $ 520,000 |
| Accounts receivable | 90,000 | (due in 30 days) | |
| Building | 225,000 | Accounts payable | 420,000 |
| Machinery | 350,000 | Owners' equity | 150,000 |
| Land | 375,000 | | |
| | $1,090,000 | | $1,090,000 |

## Sterlington Co.
## Balance Sheet
## November 30, 1993

| Assets | | Liabilities & Equity | |
|---|---|---|---|
| Cash | $ 50,000 | Notes payable | $120,000 |
| Accounts receivable | 200,000 | (due in 30 days) | |
| Land | 10,000 | Accounts payable | 150,000 |
| Machinery | 350,000 | Owners' equity | 640,000 |
| Building | 300,000 | | |
| | $910,000 | | $910,000 |

(a)  Assume the role of a commercial banker who has been approached by both of the previous firms with a request for a 90-day loan for $200,000. For which of the firms are you most likely to approve the loan? Why?

(b)  If you were considering the purchase of one of these firms and assuming the liabilities of each, for which one would you be willing to pay the higher price? (Obviously, you would want more information in order to make a complete analysis, but make your evaluation based on the balance sheets above.)

SOLUTION

(a)  Sterlington Corp. In reviewing requests for short-term loans, the commercial loan officer is most interested in the liquidity of the subject firm. The current ratio of Marion Mfg. Co. is a very weak 0.15 while Sterlington Corp.'s current ratio is .93. In addition, a quick glance at the balance sheet of Marion Mfg. shows that a very substantial note of $520,000 comes due in 30 days which the company may have difficulty paying.

(b)  Sterlington Corp. If it is assumed that book values are reasonably close to actual market values, the difference between Sterlington's total assets and assumed debt is $640,000, as opposed to Marion's net difference of $150,000.

4.  Burruss, Inc. had the following condensed balance sheet at the end of operation for 1993:

## Burruss, Inc.
## Balance Sheet
## December 31, 1993

| | | | |
|---|---|---|---|
| Cash | $ 24,000 | Current liabilities | $ 30,000 |
| Other current assets | 51,000 | Long-term notes | |
| Total current assets | $ 75,000 | payable | 33,000 |
| Investments | 40,000 | Bonds payable | 40,000 |
| Fixed assets (net) | 125,000 | Capital stock | 150,000 |
| Land | 62,000 | Retained earnings | 49,000 |
| | $302,000 | | $302,000 |

During 1994 the following occurred:

(a)  Burruss, Inc. sold some of its investments for $20,600 which resulted in a gain of $600.

(b)  Additional land for a plant expansion was purchased for $12,000.

(c)  Bonds payable were paid in the amount of $10,000.

(d)  An additional $20,000 in capital stock was issued.

(e)  Dividends of $15,000 were paid to stockholders.

(f)  Net income for 1994 was $42,000 after allowing for $18,000 in depreciation.

(g)  A second parcel of land was purchased through the issuance of $12,000 in bonds, $6,000 in long-term notes payable, and internally generated funds.

Required:

(a)  Using the indirect method, prepare a cash flow statement for 1993.

(b)  Prepare a condensed balance sheet for Burruss, Inc. at December 1993.

Assume that current liabilities (including accounts payable and accruals) remain unchanged and *other* current assets did not change during the year.

SOLUTION

(a)

Burruss, Inc.<br>
Statement of Cash Flow<br>
For the Year Ended December 31, 1993

**Cash flows from operating activities:**

| | |
|---|---:|
| Net income (from the statement of income) | $42,000 |
| Add (deduct) to reconcile net income to net cash flow | |
|     Depreciation expense | 18,000 |
| Gain from the sale of investments (included in sales price below) | (600) |
| Net cash inflow from operating activities | $59,400 |

**Cash flows from investing activities:**

| | |
|---|---:|
| Sale of investments | 20,600 |
| Purchase of land | (30,000) |

**Cash flows from financing activities:**

| | |
|---|---:|
| Issuance of capital stock | 20,000 |
| Issuance of bonds | 12,000 |
| Issuance of notes payable | 6,000 |
| Repayment of bonds payable | (10,000) |
| Dividends | (15,000) |
| | |
| Net increase (decrease) in cash during the period | $63,000 |

(b)

Burruss, Inc.<br>
Balance Sheet<br>
December 31, 1993

| | | | |
|---|---:|---|---:|
| Cash | $ 87,000 | Current liabilities | $ 30,000 |
| Other current assets | 51,000 | Long-term notes | 39,000 |
|   Total current assets | $138,000 |   payable | |
| Investments | 20,000 | Bonds payable | 42,000 |
| Fixed assets (net) | 107,000 | Capital stock | 170,000 |
| Land | 92,000 | Retained earnings | 76,000 |
| | $357,000 | | $357,000 |

5. The financial manager of Sudhop, Inc. has just hired you (a recent finance graduate). Now he wishes to test your familiarity with financial ratios and your overall ability to work with financial statements. He gives you the following incomplete year-end balance sheet:

Sudhop, Inc.
Balance Sheet
December 31, 1993

| | | | |
|---|---|---|---|
| Cash | $ | Accounts payable | $ |
| Accounts receivable | | Long-term debt | |
| Inventory | | Total debt | $ |
| Total current assets | $ | Common stock | 125,000 |
| Fixed assets | 400,000 | Retained earnings | 275,000 |
| | $ | | $ |

He then gives you the following additional information and asks you to complete the above balance sheet.

| | |
|---|---|
| Average collection period (assume a 360-day year) | 30 days |
| Interest paid on long-term debt (10% rate) | $5,000 |
| Debt-to-equity ratio | 75% |
| Sales to total assets | 2.0 times |
| Quick ratio | 1.1 |
| Current ratio | 1.2 |

SOLUTION

Sudhop, Inc.
Balance Sheet
December 31, 1993

| | | | |
|---|---|---|---|
| Cash | $225,000 | Accounts payable | $250,000 |
| Accounts receivable | 50,000 | Long-term debt | 50,000 |
| Inventory | 25,000 | Total debt | $300,000 |
| Total current assets | $300,000 | Common stock | 125,000 |
| Fixed assets | 400,000 | Retained earnings | 275,000 |
| Total assets | $ 700,000 | Total debt and equity | $700,000 |

Computations:

a.  Since debt to equity is 0.75, than debt must be $300,000 (0.75 x $400,000 equity).

b.  Debt plus equity equals total debt and equity and total assets, which comes to $700,000.

c.  Current assets equal total assets less fixed assets ($700,000 - $400,000).

d.  Since current assets ÷ current liabilities equals 1.20, then current liabilities equal $250,000 ($300,000 ÷ current liabilities = 1.2).

e.  Sales ÷ total assets = 2.0; so, sales ÷ $700 = 2.0; and sales = $1,400

f.  Accounts receivable may be determined to be $50,000 as follows:

$$\text{Average collection period} = \frac{\text{accounts receivable}}{\text{daily credit sales}}$$

From what we already know and assuming all sales are on credit,

$$30 = \frac{\text{accounts receivable}}{\$1,400 \div 360}$$

g.  Given a quick ratio of 1.1, then inventory must be $25,000:

$$\frac{\$300,000 - \text{inventories}}{\$250,000} = 1.1.$$

h.  Cash equals current assets minus accounts receivable and inventory.

6.  The balance sheet and income statement for Miller Company are given for the year 1993 in addition to various financial ratios for the industry in which Miller operates.

## Miller Company
### Balance Sheet
#### December 31, 1993
##### (000's)

| | | | |
|---|---|---|---|
| Cash | $ 230 | Notes payable | $ 1,015 |
| Accounts receivable | 9,380 | Accounts payable | 3,545 |
| Inventories | 7,515 | Accrued taxes | 225 |
| Current assets | 17,125 | Current liabilities | 4,785 |
| Fixed assets (net) | 34,125 | Long-term debt | 18,035 |
| Total assets | $51,250 | Deferred income taxes | 2,840 |
| | | Total debt | $20,875 |
| | | Common stock—par | 575 |
| | | Paid in capital | 7,945 |
| | | Retained earnings | 17,070 |
| | | Common equity | 25,590 |
| | | Total liabilities & net worth | $51,250 |

## Miller Company
### Income Statement
#### Year Ended December 31, 1993

| | |
|---|---|
| Net sales (credit) | $46,235 |
| Cost of sales | 33,167 |
| Gross profit | 13,068 |
| General and administrative expense | 9,590 |
| Operating income | 3,478 |
| Interest changes | 1,120 |
| Net income before taxes | 2,358 |
| Income taxes | 1,130 |
| Net income | $ 1,228 |

### Industry Ratios

| | Industry |
|---|---|
| Current ratio | 4.02 |
| Acid-test ratio | 3.00 |
| Inventory turnover | 7.50 |
| Average collection period | 63.1 |
| Operating profit margin | 6.0% |
| Total asset turnover | 2.0 |
| Fixed asset turnover | 3.0 |
| Debt ratio | 38.0% |
| Times interest earned | 3.90 |
| Return on equity | 4.0% |

Required:

Evaluate Miller's financial performance, using the "four-question approach" presented in Chapter 3 of the text.

SOLUTION

(a)

|  | Industry | Miller |
|---|---|---|
| Current ratio | 4.02 | 3.58 |
| Acid-test ratio | 3.00 | 2.01 |
| Inventory turnover | 7.50 | 4.41 |
| Average collection period | 63.1 | 74.1 |
| Operating profit margin | 6.0% | 7.5 |
| Total asset turnover | 2.0 | 0.9 |
| Fixed asset turnover | 3.0 | 1.4 |
| Debt ratio | 38.0% | 50.1% |
| Times interest earned | 3.90 | 3.11 |
| Return on equity | 4.0% | 4.8% |

(b) Miller's *liquidity* ratios are well below the industry averages. The most serious problem is with inventory turnover which is almost one-half the industry norm.

The operating income return on investment, OIROI, for Miller and the industry are determined as follows:

$$\text{OIROI} = \frac{\text{operating}}{\text{profit margin}} \times \frac{\text{total asset}}{\text{turnover}}$$

| Miller: | 7.5% | x | 0.9 | = | 6.8% |
|---|---|---|---|---|---|
| Industry: | 6.0% | x | 2.0 | = | 12% |

Thus, Miller's management is not generating satisfactory operating profits on the firm's assets, while Miller's operating profit margin exceeds the industry, which suggests that they are better than the average firm at some combination of:

1. Receive above-average prices for their products.

2. Sell more units of their products.

3. Lower cost of goods sold.

4. Lower operating expenses (general and administrative and marketing).

However, the firm is clearly not using its assets efficiently, as suggested by all the turnover ratios and collection period, to generate sales.

The net effect of the operating profit margin and the asset turnovers is a low OIROI.

The firm uses more debt to finance its assets, as reflected by the higher debt ratio and the lower times interest earned. The low times interest earned is also due to the lower OIROI, which affects the numerator of the ratio.

Miller's stockholders received an above-average return on their investment (return on equity), but it was accomplished by using more debt, which exposes the investors to greater financial risk.

## Self Tests

TRUE-FALSE

_____ 1. The balance sheet is a statement of the firm's financial position over a specified time interval.

_____ 2. Noncurrent assets are those which are not expected to be converted into cash within the firm's operating cycle.

_____ 3. The income statement represents an attempt to measure the net results of the firm's operations on a given date.

_____ 4. The owner's equity represents the book value of the owner's investment in the assets of the firm.

_____ 5. A firm attempts to match sales from the period's operations with the expenses incurred in generating those revenues by compiling the income statement on an accrual basis.

_____ 6. Reported sales and expenses must represent actual cash flows for the period when the income statement is prepared on an accrual basis.

_____ 7. Investments in securities are always considered to be current assets.

_____ 8. Payments to suppliers for the purchase of materials is a component of the financing activities section of a cash flow statement.

_____ 9. Because fixed assets are used in operations, any purchases of fixed assets belong in the cash flow operating activities section.

_____ 10. Financial ratios help us identify financial strengths and weaknesses of companies by way of being able to make meaningful comparisons of firm's financial data at different points in time and with other firms.

_____ 11. A firm's cash account is not considered in determining its liquidity.

_____ 12. The current ratio is more conservative than the acid-test ratio.

_____ 13. Inventory turnover and the average collection period may be used to measure the same thing--operating profitability.

_____ 14. Return on equity measures the dividends investors received in the current year.

_____ 15. The DuPont analysis is another approach frequently used to evaluate a firm's liquidity and financing decisions.

MULTIPLE CHOICE

1. Which of the following is generally considered to be the most important financial statement for judging the economic well-being of a firm?

   a. Income statement
   b. Balance sheet
   c. Cash flow statement
   d. All of the above
   e. None of the above

2. The most important section of the cash flow statement for a firm as far as its ability to continue as a going concern is the

   a. operations section.
   b. investment activities section.
   c. financing activities section.
   d. all the sections are equally important.

3.  Collections from customers and payments to suppliers should be included as part of the _____ section of a cash flow statement.

    a.  financing activities
    b.  investment activities
    c.  working capital
    d.  operating

4.  Interest expense is considered a(n) _____ on the income statement and a(n) _____ on the cash flow statement.

    a.  operating expense, operating activities item
    b.  financing expense, financing activities item
    c.  operating expense, financing activities item
    d.  financing expense, operating activities item

5.  The difference between the current ratio and the quick ratio is

    a.  inventories.
    b.  inventories is subtracted from the numerator.
    c.  inventories is subtracted from the denominator.
    d.  the current ratio is more conservative.

6.  The ratio of total debt over total assets is

    a.  the current ratio.
    b.  the debt ratio.
    c.  a measure of a firm's liquidity.
    d.  referred to as the quick ratio because it is so easily determined.

7.  Robert Morris Associates and other published industry averages are

    a.  offered for every industry.
    b.  scientifically determined averages.
    c.  only approximations.
    d.  good for many years.

8.  An industry average is best used as

    a.  a desirable target or norm for the firm.
    b.  a guide to the financial position of the average firm in the industry.
    c.  a scientifically determined average of the ratios of a representative sample of firms within an industry.
    d.  a point or rule with which to measure profitability.

9.  Operating income return on investment is affected by

    a.   depreciation expense.
    b.   interest expense.
    c.   income tax.
    d.   all of the above.

10. The direct method beginning with _____ and the indirect method beginning with _____ are two approaches for determining _____on the cash flow statement.

    a.   net sales, operating income, cash flows from operations
    b.   net income, cash collected form the firm's customers, cash flows from operations
    c.   net income, cash collected from the firm's customers, total cash flows
    d.   cash collected from the firm's customers, net income, cash flows from operations

# CHAPTER 4

# Financial Forecasting, Planning, and Budgeting

Orientation: In this chapter, we develop predictions of the firm's future financing needs based on a sales forecast. This entails construction of a pro forma income statement and balance sheet. We also discuss the concept of a firm's sustainable rate of growth. This is the maximum rate at which sales can grow and the firm's financial ratios remain unchanged and no new common stock being issued. The chapter also reviews the preparation and use of the cash budget as an essential tool of financial planning.

I.   Financial forecasting and planning

    A.   The need for forecasting in financial management arises whenever the future financing needs of the firm are being estimated. There are three basic steps involved in predicting financing requirements.

        1.   Project the firm's sales revenues and expenses over the planning period.

        2.   Estimate the levels of investment in current and fixed assets which are necessary to support the projected sales level.

        3.   Determine the financing needs of the firm throughout the planning period.

    B.   The key ingredient in the firm's planning process is the sales forecast. This forecast should reflect (1) any past trend in sales that is expected to continue and (2) the effects of any events which are expected to have a material effect on the firm's sales during the forecast period.

C. The traditional problem faced in financial forecasting begins with the sales forecast and involves making forecasts of the impact of predicted sales on the firm's various expenses, assets, and liabilities. There are a number of techniques that can be used to make these forecasts.

II. Financial planning and budgeting

A. In general, a business will use four types of budgets: physical, cost, profit, and cash.

1. *Physical budgets* include budgets for unit sales, personnel or manpower, unit production, inventories, and actual physical facilities. They are also used as a basis for generating cost and profit budgets.

2. *Cost budgets* are prepared for every major expense category of the firm, such as manufacturing or production cost, selling cost, and administrative cost.

3. The *profit budget* is prepared based upon information generated from the sales budget and cost budget.

4. The *cash budget* is generated by converting into a cash basis all budget information previously discussed.

B. The cash budget represents a detailed plan of future cash flows and can be broken down into four components: cash receipts, cash disbursements, net change in cash for the period, and new financing needed. Cash budgets can also be either fixed or variable.

1. In a *fixed cash budget*, cash flow estimates are made for a single set of sales estimates.

2. The *variable cash budget* involves the preparation of several budgets with each budget corresponding to a different set of sales estimates. This budget fulfills two basic needs:

a. The variable budget gives management more information on the range of possible financing needs of the firm.

      b.    Management is provided with a standard against which it can measure the performance of subordinates responsible for various cost and revenue items contained in the budget.

C.    Although no strict guidelines exist, as a general rule, the budget period shall be long enough to show the effect of management policies, yet short enough so that estimates can be made with reasonable accuracy. For instance, the capital expenditure budget may be properly developed for a 10-year period, while a cash budget may cover only 12 months.

D.    The development of pro forma financial statements represents the final stage of the budgeting process.

    1.    A *pro forma income statement* represents a statement of planned profit or loss for the future period and is based primarily on information generated in the cash budget.

    2.    The *pro forma balance sheet* for a future date is developed by adjusting present balance-sheet figures for projected information found primarily within the cash budget and pro forma income statement.

## Study Problems

1.    The most recent balance sheet for the Parino Manufacturing Co. is shown in the table below. The company is about to embark on an advertising campaign, which is expected to raise sales from the present level of $10 million to $14 million by the end of next year. The firm is presently operating at full capacity and will have to increase its investment in both current and fixed assets to support the projected level of new sales. In fact, the firm estimates that both categories of assets will rise in direct proportion to the projected increase in sales.

The firm's net profits were 4% of current year's sales but are expected to rise to 5% of next year's sales. To help support its anticipated growth in asset needs next year, the firm has suspended plans to pay cash dividends to its stockholders. In past years, a $1.50 per share dividend has been paid annually.

Parino Manufacturing Co., Inc. ($ millions)

| | Present Level | Percent of Sales | Projected Level |
|---|---|---|---|
| Current assets | $2.0 | | |
| Net fixed assets | 3.0 | | |
| Total | $5.0 | | |
| Accounts payable | $0.5 | | |
| Accrued expenses | 0.5 | | |
| Notes payable | - - | | |
| Current liabilities | $1.0 | | |
| Long-term debt | $2.0 | | |
| Common stock | 0.5 | | |
| Retained earnings | 1.5 | | |
| Common equity | $2.0 | | |
| Total | $5.0 | | |

Parino's payables and accrued expenses are expected to vary directly with sales. In addition, notes payable will be used to supply the funds needed to finance next year's operations and that are not forthcoming from other sources.

Fill in the table and project the firm's needs for discretionary financing. Use notes payable as the balancing entry for future discretionary financing needed.

SOLUTION ($ millions)

| | | |
|---|---|---|
| Current sales | $10 | |
| Predicted sales | 12 | |
| Net profit margin | 5% | |

| | Present Level | Percent of Sales | Projected Level |
|---|---|---|---|
| Current assets | $2.00 | 0.20 | $2.40 |
| Net fixed assets | 3.00 | 0.30 | 3.60 |
| Total | 5.00 | 0.50 | 6.00 |

| | | | |
|---|---|---|---|
| Accounts payable | 0.50 | 0.05 | 0.60 |
| Accrued expenses | 0.50 | 0.05 | 0.60 |
| Notes payable | | | |
| Current liabilities | 1.00 | 0.10 | 1.20 |
| Long-term debt | 2.00 | No Change | 2.00 |
| Common stock | 0.50 | No Change | 0.50 |
| Retained earnings | 1.50 | Ret. Earnings + NI | 2.10 |
| Common equity | 2.00 | | 2.60 |
| Total | $5.00 | | |
| | Total financing provided | | $5.80 |
| | Discretionary financing needed | | $ .20 |

2. The Horn Corporation's projected sales for the first 8 months of 1998 are as follows:

| | | | |
|---|---|---|---|
| January | $300,000 | May | $1,200,000 |
| February | 450,000 | June | 1,000,000 |
| March | 540,000 | July | 900,000 |
| April | 960,000 | August | 700,000 |

Twenty percent of Horn's sales are for cash, another 40% is collected in the month following sale, and 40% is collected in the second month following sale. November and December sales for 1997 were $800,000 and $650,000, respectively.

Horn purchases raw materials equal to 60% of sales, and it makes its purchases 2 months in advance of sales. The supplier is paid 1 month after the purchase. For example, purchases for April sales are made in February and are paid for in March.

Furthermore, Horn pays $42,000 per month for rent and $90,000 per month for other expenditures. Finally, tax deposits of $85,000 are made each quarter, beginning in March.

The company's cash balance at December 31, 1997, was $80,000, and a minimum balance of $50,000 must be maintained at all times. Assume that any short-term financing needed to maintain the minimum cash balance would be paid off in the month following the month of financing with interest paid at a 12% annual rate.

Prepare a cash budget for Horn covering the first 6 months of 1998.

# SOLUTION

|  | January | February | March | April | May | June |  |
|---|---|---|---|---|---|---|---|
| Sales | $300,000 | $450,000 | $540,000 | $960,000 | $1,200,000 | $1,000,000 | $ |
| Cash sales | 60,000 | 90,000 | 108,000 | 192,000 | 240,000 | 200,000 | |
| Collections 1 month later | 260,000 | 120,000 | 180,000 | 216,000 | 384,000 | 480,000 | |
| 2 months later | 320,000 | 260,000 | 120,000 | 180,000 | 216,000 | 384,000 | |
| Total collections from sales | 640,000 | 470,000 | 408,000 | 588,000 | 840,000 | 1,064,000 | |
| | | | | | | | |
| Purchases | 324,000 | 576,000 | 720,000 | 600,000 | 540,000 | 420,000 | |
| Payments on purchases | 270,000 | 324,000 | 576,000 | 720,000 | 600,000 | 540,000 | |

Cash Receipts:

| | January | February | March | April | May | June | |
|---|---|---|---|---|---|---|---|
| Collections from sales | 640,000 | 470,000 | 408,000 | 588,000 | 840,000 | 1,064,000 | 1, |

Cash disbursements:

| | January | February | March | April | May | June | |
|---|---|---|---|---|---|---|---|
| Payments on purchases | 270,000 | 324,000 | 576,000 | 720,000 | 600,000 | 540,000 | |
| Other expenditures | 90,000 | 90,000 | 90,000 | 90,000 | 90,000 | 90,000 | |
| Rent | 42,000 | 42,000 | 42,000 | 42,000 | 42,000 | 42,000 | |
| Tax deposits | | | 85,000 | | | 85,000 | |
| Total disbursements | 402,000 | 456,000 | 793,000 | 852,000 | 732,000 | 757,000 | |
| | | | | | | | |
| Net change for the month | 238,000 | 14,000 | (385,000) | (264,000) | 108,000 | 307,000 | |
| | | | | | | | |
| Beginning cash balance | 80,000 | 318,000 | 332,000 | 50,000 | 50,000 | 50,000 | |
| Plus: net change | 238,000 | 14,000 | (385,000) | (264,000) | 108,000 | 307,000 | |
| Borrowing | ----- | ----- | 103,000 | 265,000 | 104,320 | (263,710) | |
| Interest for prior month's borrowing | ----- | ----- | ----- | 1,030* | 3,680 | 2,637 | |
| Ending cash balance | $318,000 | $332,000 | $ 50,000 | $ 50,000 | $ 50,000 | $ 90,653 | |
| | | | | | | | |
| Cumulative borrowing | ----- | ----- | ----- | $368,030 | $263,710 | | |

*0.12 x 103,000 x ½ = $1,030

60

TRUE-FALSE

\_\_\_\_ 1. Budgets perform the basic functions of (1) providing the basis for taking corrective action and (2) providing the basis for performance evaluation.

\_\_\_\_ 2. Physical budgets are used as the basis for generating cost and profit budgets.

\_\_\_\_ 3. Depreciation expense is an essential element in the cash budget.

\_\_\_\_ 4. Performance evaluation is a principal function that can be performed through the use of budgets.

\_\_\_\_ 5. A budget of expected research and development costs for the coming year is an example of a physical budget.

\_\_\_\_ 6. The sustainable rate of growth represents the rate at which a firm's sales can grow if it wants to maintain its present capital structure and does not want to sell new equity.

\_\_\_\_ 7. As a general rule, all budgets of the firm should project no longer than one year in the future so that estimates can be made with reasonable accuracy.

\_\_\_\_ 8. The plowback ratio reflects the proportion of a firm's earnings that are paid in dividends.

\_\_\_\_ 9. The cash budget is only as useful as the accuracy of the forecasts that are used in its preparation.

\_\_\_\_ 10. Future net fixed assets are estimated for the pro forma balance sheet by adding planned expenditures to existing net fixed assets and adding to this sum, depreciation for the period.

MULTIPLE CHOICE

1.  The most important element in determining the accuracy of most cash budgets is the

    a.  forecast of cash disbursements.
    b.  forecast of collection schedule.
    c.  forecast of sales.
    d.  Cannot be determined.
    e.  None of the above.

2.  Pro forma statements embody:

    a.  forecasts of prospective future cash positions of the firm.
    b.  forecasts of all assets and liabilities.
    c.  forecasts of the firm's personnel requirements.
    d.  all of the above.
    e.  a and b only.

3.  Which of the following items would be included in the cash budget?

    a.  Depreciation charges
    b.  Goodwill
    c.  Patent amortization
    d.  All of the above
    e.  None of the above

4.  The cash budget provides the following information:

    a.  The exact amount of borrowing needed for the budget interval.
    b.  The type of loan which should be obtained to meet the cash needs for the time interval.
    c.  A point estimate of the borrowing needs for the budget interval.
    d.  An estimate of the cash needed for depreciation expense
    e.  None of the above.

5.  In general, a firm will use the following type(s) of budgets:

    a.  Profit budgets.
    b.  Cash budgets.
    c.  Cost budgets.
    d.  Physical budgets.
    e.  All of the above.

6. Which of the following would *not* fall under the physical budget classification?

    a. Unit sales budget
    b. Physical facilities budget
    c. Production cost budget
    d. Unit production budget
    e. None of the above

# CHAPTER 5

# The Time Value of Money

Orientation: In this chapter, the concept of a time value of money is introduced; that is, a dollar today is worth more than a dollar received a year from now. Thus, if we are to logically compare projects and financial strategies, we must move all dollar flows either back to the present or out to some common future date.

I.   Compound interest results when the interest paid on the investment during the first period is added to the principal and, during the second period, the interest is earned on the original principal plus the interest earned during the first period.

A.   Mathematically, the future value of an investment if compounded annually at a rate of i for n years will be:

$$FV_n = PV (1 + i)^n$$

where n   =   the number of years during which the compounding occurs,

i   =   the annual interest (or discount) rate,

PV   =   the present value or original amount invested at the beginning of the first year,

$FV_n$   =   the future value of the investment at the end of n years.

1.   The future value of an investment can be increased either by increasing the number of years we let it compound or by compounding it at a higher rate.

65

2. If the compounded period is less than 1 year, the future value of an investment can be determined as follows:

$$FV_n = PV \left( 1 + \frac{i}{m} \right)^{mn}$$

where m = the number of times compounding occurs during the year. monthly x12
quarterly x4

II. Determining the present value, that is, the value in today's dollars of a sum of money to be received in the future, involves nothing other than inverse compounding. The differences in these techniques come about merely from the investor's point of view.

A. Mathematically, the present value of a sum of money to be received in the future can be determined with the following equation:

$$PV = FV_n \left( \frac{1}{(1 + i)^n} \right)$$

where n = the number of years until payment will be received,

i = the annual interest (or discount) rate,

PV = the present value of the future sum of money,

$FV_n$ = the future value of the investment at the end of n years

1. The present value of a future sum of money is inversely related to both the number of years until the payment will be received and the opportunity rate.

III. An annuity is a series of equal dollar payments for a specified number of years. Because annuities occur frequently in finance, for example, bond interest payments, we treat them specially.

A. A compound annuity involves depositing or investing an equal sum of money at the end of each year for a certain number of years and allowing it to grow.

66

1. This can be done by using our compounding equation and compounding each one of the individual deposits to the future or by using the following compound annuity equation:

$$FV_n = PMT \left( \sum_{t=0}^{n-1} (1+i)^t \right)$$

where PMT = the annuity payment deposited or received at the end of each year,

   i = the annual interest (or discount) rate,

   n = the number of years for which the annuity will last,

   $FV_n$ = the future value of the annuity at the end of the nth year.

B. Pension funds, insurance obligation, and interest received from bonds all involve annuities. To compare these financial instruments, we would like to know the present value of each of these annuities.

1. This can be done by using our present value equation and discounting each one of the individual cash flows back to the present or by using the following present value of an annuity equation:

$$PV = PMT \left( \sum_{t=1}^{n} \frac{1}{(1+i)^t} \right)$$

where PMT = the annuity payment deposited or received at the end of each year,

   i = the annual interest (or discount) rate,

   PV = the present value of the future annuity,

   n = the number of years for which the annuity will last.

C.  This procedure of solving for PMT, the annuity value when i, n, and PV are known, is also the procedure used to determine what payments are associated with paying off a loan in equal installments. Loans paid off in this way, in periodic payments, are called amortized loans.

   1.  Here again, we know three of the four values in the annuity equation and are solving for a value of PMT, the annual annuity.

   2.  For example: Suppose a firm borrows $5,000 to be repaid in five equal payments at the end of each of the next 5 years to purchase some machinery and the interest rate that is paid to the lender is 15% on the outstanding portion of the loan. Using the annuity equation to solve, we get

$$\$5,000 \ = \ PMT \left( \sum_{t=1}^{5} \frac{1}{(1 + .15)^t} \right)$$

$$\$5,000 \ = \ PMT(3.352)$$

$$PMT \ = \$1,491.65$$

IV.  A perpetuity is an annuity that continues forever; that is, every year from now on this investment pays the same dollar amount.

A.  An example of a perpetuity is preferred stock which yields a constant dollar dividend infinitely.

B.  The following equation can be used to determine the present value of a perpetuity:

$$PV \ = \ \frac{PP}{i}$$

where   $PV$ =   the present value of the perpetuity,

$PP$ =   the constant dollar amount provided by the perpetuity,

$i$ =   the annual interest or discount rate.

68

V.   To aid in the calculations of present and future values, tables are provided at the back of *Foundations of Finance (FOF)*.

A.   To aid in determining the value of $FV_n$ in the compounding formula

$$FV_n = PV (1 + i)^n = PV (FVIF_{i,n})$$

tables have been compiled for values of $FVIF_{i,n}$ or $(i + 1)^n$ in Appendix B, "Compound Sum of \$1," in *FOF*.

B.   Thus, to determine the value of:

$$FV_{10} = \$1,000(1 + 0.08)^{10}$$

we need merely to look up the value of $FVIF_{8\%,10 \text{ yr.}}$ in Appendix B and substitute it in. The table value given in the $n = 10$ row and 8% column of Appendix B is 2.159. Substituting this in the equation, we get

$$FV_{10} = \$1,000(2.159)$$

$$FV_{10} = \$2,159$$

C.   To aid in the computation of present values

$$PV = FV_n \frac{1}{(1 + i)^n} = FV_n (PVIF_{i,n})$$

tables have been compiled for values of

$$\frac{1}{(1 + i)^n} \quad \text{or} \quad PVIF_{i,n}$$

and appear in Appendix C in the back of *FOF*.

D.   Because of the time-consuming nature of compounding an annuity,

$$FV_n = PMT \sum_{t=0}^{n-1} (1 + i)^t = PMT (FVIFA_{i,n})$$

Tables are provided in Appendix D of *FOF* for

$$\sum_{t=0}^{n-1} (1 + i)^t \quad \text{or} \quad FVIFA_{i,n}$$

for various combinations of n and i.

E.   To simplify the process of determining the present value of an annuity

$$PV = PMT \left( \sum_{t=1}^{n} \frac{1}{(1 + i)^t} \right) = PMT \, (PVIFA_{i,n})$$

tables are provided in Appendix E of *FOF* for various combinations of n and i for the value

$$\sum_{t=1}^{n} \frac{1}{(1 + i)^t} \quad \text{or} \quad PVIFA_{i,n}$$

## Study Problems

1.   What will $1,000 invested for 10 years at 10% compounded annually accumulate to?

SOLUTION

Substituting into the compound value formula, we get:

$$FV_n = PV(1 + i)^n$$

$$FV_{10} = \$1,000(1 + 0.10)^{10}$$

$$FV_{10} = \$1,000(2.594)$$

$$FV_{10} = \$2,594$$

2. How many years will it take $500 to grow to $1,586 if it is invested at 8% compounded annually?

SOLUTION

From the compound value formula we know:

$$FV_n = PV(1+i)^n$$

Substituting in the values that we know, we get:

$$\$1,586 = \$500(1+0.08)^n$$

or using table values, we get:

$$\$1,586 = \$500 \ (FVIF_{8\%,\ n\ yr.})$$

Dividing both sides by $500, we get:

$$3.172 = FVIF_{8\%,\ n\ yr.}$$

Looking in the 8% column, we find a value of 3.172 in the 15-year row. Thus, it will take 15 years.

3. At what annual rate would $1,000 have to be invested in order to grow to $4,046 in 10 years?

SOLUTION

From the compound value formula, we know:

$$FV_n = PV(1+i)^n = PV(FVIF_{i,n})$$

Substituting the table value given in Appendix B of *FOF* for $(1+i)^n$, we get:

$$FV_n = PV(FVIF_{i,n})$$

Substituting in the given values, we get:

$$\$4,046 = \$1,000 \ (FVIF_{i, \ 10 \ yr.})$$

$$4.046 = FVIF_{i, \ 10 \ yr.}$$

Thus, we are looking for a table value of 4.046 in the 10-year row of Appendix B. This appears in the 15% column; thus, 15% is the annual rate we are looking for.

4.   What is the present value of $1,000 to be received 8 years from now discounted back to present at 10%?

SOLUTION

Substituting in the present value formula, we get:

$$PV = FV_n \left( \frac{1}{(1 + i)^n} \right) = FV_n \ (PVIF_{i,n})$$

$$PV = \$1,000 \left( \frac{1}{(1 + 0.10)^8} \right)$$

$$PV = \$1,000[0.467]$$

$$PV = \$467$$

5.   What is the accumulated sum of the following streams of payments, $1,000 per year for 5 years compounded annually at 5%?

SOLUTION

Substituting into the compound annuity formula, we get:

$$FV_n = PMT \sum_{t=0}^{n-1} (1 + i)^t = PMT(FVIFA_{i,n})$$

$$FV_5 = \$1,000 \sum_{t=0}^{5-1} (1 + 0.05)^t$$

$$FV_5 = \$1,000(5.526)$$

$$FV_5 = \$5,526$$

72

6.  What is the present value of $100 a year for 15 years discounted back to the present at 15%?

    SOLUTION

    Substituting into the present value of an annuity formula:

    $$PV = PMT \left( \sum_{t=1}^{n} \frac{1}{(1 + i)^t} \right) = PMT \ (PVIFA_{i,n})$$

    $$PV = \$100 \left( \sum_{t=1}^{15} \frac{1}{(1 + 0.15)^t} \right)$$

    $$PV = \$100(5.847)$$

    $$PV = \$584.70$$

7.  If you receive a 9% $100,000 loan that has annual payments of $14,695.08, how many loan payments must you make in order to pay off the loan?

    SOLUTION

    Substituting into the present value of an annuity formula:

    $$PV = PMT \left( \sum_{t=1}^{n} \frac{1}{(1 + i)^t} \right)$$

    $$\$100,000 = \$14,695.08 \ PVIFA_{9\%, \ n \ yr.}$$

    $$6.805 = PVIFA_{9\%, \ n \ yr.}$$

    Looking down the 9% column of Appendix E, we find a value of 6.805 in the 11-year row. Thus, in 11 years, the loan will be paid off.

8.    At what annual rate would the following have to be invested?

    a.    $550 to grow to $1,898.60 in 13 years

    b.    $275 to grow to $406.18 in 8 years

    c.    $60 to grow to $279.66 in 20 years

    d.    $180 to grow to $486.00 in 6 years

SOLUTION

(a)  $FV_n$    $= PV (1+i)^n$

    $1,898.60 = \$550 (1+i)^{13}$

    $3.452$    $= FVIF_{i\%, 13 \text{ yr}.}$

Thus, i    = 10% (because the Appendix B value of 3.452 occurs in
              the 12-year row in the 10% column)

(b)  $FV_n$    $= PV (1+i)^n$

    $406.18$    $= \$275 (1+i)^8$

    $1.477$    $= FVIF_{i\%, 8 \text{ yr}.}$

    Thus, i  =  5%

(c)  $FV_n$    $= PV (1+i)^n$

    $279.66$  $= \$60 (1+i)^{20}$

    $4.661$    $= FVIF_{i\%, 20 \text{ yr}.}$

    Thus, i  =  8%

(d) $FV_n \quad = \quad PV(1+i)^n$

$\quad \$486.00 \quad = \quad \$180(1+i)^6$

$\quad 2.700 \quad = \quad FVIF_{i\%,\ 6\ yr.}$

$\quad$ Thus, $i \quad = \quad 18\%$

9. What is the accumulated sum of each of the following streams of payments?

a. $500 a year for 10 years compounded annually at 6%

b. $150 a year for 5 years compounded annually at 11%

c. $35 a year for 8 years compounded annually at 7%

d. $25 a year for 3 years compounded annually at 2%

SOLUTION

(a) $FV_n \quad = \quad PMT \left( \sum_{t=0}^{n-1} (1+i)^t \right)$

$\quad FV_{10} \quad = \quad \$500 \left( \sum_{t=0}^{10-1} (1+0.06)^t \right)$

$\quad FV_{10} \quad = \quad \$500\,(13.181)$

$\quad FV_{10} \quad = \quad \$6{,}590.50$

(b) $FV_n \quad = \quad PMT \left( \sum_{t=0}^{n-1} (1+i)^t \right)$

$\quad FV_5 \quad = \quad \$150 \left( \sum_{t=0}^{5-1} (1+0.11)^t \right)$

$\quad FV_5 \quad = \quad \$150\,(6.228)$

$\quad FV_5 \quad = \quad \$934.20$

(c) $\quad FV_n \quad = \quad PMT \left( \sum_{t=0}^{n-1} (1+i)^t \right)$

$\quad FV_7 \quad = \quad \$35 \left( \sum_{t=0}^{8-1} (1+0.07)^t \right)$

$\quad FV_7 \quad = \quad \$35 \ (10.260)$

$\quad FV_7 \quad = \quad \$359.10$

(d) $\quad FV_n \quad = \quad PMT \left( \sum_{t=0}^{n-1} (1+i)^t \right)$

$\quad FV_3 \quad = \quad \$25 \left( \sum_{t=0}^{3-1} (1+0.02)^t \right)$

$\quad FV_3 \quad = \quad \$25 \ (3.060)$

$\quad FV_3 \quad = \quad \$76.50$

10.  Stefani Moore purchased a new house for $150,000. She paid $30,000 down and agreed to pay the rest over the next 25 years in 25 equal annual payments that include principal payments plus 10% compound interest on the unpaid balance. What will these equal payments be?

SOLUTION

$PV \quad = \quad PMT \left( \sum_{t=1}^{n} \dfrac{1}{(1+i)^t} \right)$

$\$120,000 \quad = \quad PMT \left( \sum_{t=1}^{25} \dfrac{1}{(1+0.1)^t} \right)$

$\$120,000 \quad = \quad PMT(9.077)$

Thus, $PMT \quad = \quad \$13.220.23$ per year for 25 years

11. How much do you have to deposit today so that beginning 11 years from now you can withdraw $10,000 a year for the next 5 years (periods 11 through 15) plus an *additional* amount of $15,000 in that last year (period 15)? Assume an interest rate of 7%.

SOLUTION

The present value of the $10,000 annuity over years 11-15.

$$PV = PMT \left[ \left( \sum_{t=1}^{15} \cdot \frac{1}{(1 + .07)^t} \right) - \left( \sum_{t=1}^{10} \cdot \frac{1}{(1 + .07)^t} \right) \right]$$

$$= \$10,000(9.108 - 7.024)$$

$$= \$10,000(2.084)$$

$$= \$20,840$$

The present value of the $15,000 withdrawal at the end of year 15:

$$PV = FV_{15} \left( \frac{1}{(1 + .07)^{15}} \right)$$

$$= \$15,000(.362)$$

$$= \$5,430$$

Thus, you would have to deposit $20,840 + $5,430 or $26,270 today.

## TRUE-FALSE

___T___ 1. The fact that there is an opportunity cost to money brings on the concept of the time value of money.

___T___ 2. The higher the rate used to compound a given sum, the larger it will be at some future date.

___F___ 3. The future value of an investment can be increased by reducing the number of years we let it compound.

___T___ 4. There is an inverse relationship between the present value of a future cash flow and the discount rate.

___T___ 5. Daily, as opposed to annual, compounding takes on importance because it allows interest to be earned on interest more frequently.

___T___ 6. Determining present value is merely the inverse of compounding.

___T___ 7. A compound annuity involves depositing or investing an equal sum of money at the end of each year for a certain number of years and allowing it to grow.

___F___ 8. A perpetuity is an annuity that continues for 30 years or more.

___T___ 9. The present value of an annuity increases as the discount rate decreases.

___F___ 10. An example of perpetuity is the interest received on long-term bonds.

MULTIPLE CHOICE

1. To determine the present value of a future sum, we need only multiply it by,

   ✓ a. $\dfrac{1}{(1+i)^n}$

   b. $\dfrac{1}{(1+n)^1}$

   c. $(1+n)^i$

   d. $(1+i)^n$

2. The present value of a $100 perpetuity discounted back to present at 6% is

   a. $6,000.00.
   b. $6,666.66.
   ✓ c. $1,666.67.
   d. $1,200.00.

3. If we place $100 in a savings account that yields 6% compounded semiannually, what will our investment grow to at the end of 5 years?

   a. $133.80
   b. $130.00
   c. $125.00
   ✓ d. $134.40

4. A bond maturing in 10 years pays $80 each year and $1,000 upon maturity. Assuming 10% to be the appropriate discount rate, the present value of the bond is

   a. $1,010.84.
   b. $925.74.
   ✓ c. $877.60.
   d. $1,000.00.

5.  The Fuller Company has received a $50,000 loan. The annual payments are $6,202.70. If the Fuller Company is paying 9% interest per year, how many loan payments must the company make?

    a.  15
    b.  13
    c.  12
    d.  19

# CHAPTER 6

# Valuation and Characteristics
# of Bonds

Orientation: This chapter introduces the concepts that underlie asset valuation. We are specifically concerned with bonds. We also look at the concept of the bondholder's expected rate of return on an investment.

I.   Definitions of value

    A.   Book value is the value of an asset shown on a firm's balance sheet which is determined by its historical cost rather than its current worth.

    B.   Liquidation value is the amount that could be realized if an asset is sold individually and not as part of a going concern.

    C.   Market value is the observed value of an asset in the marketplace where buyers and sellers negotiate an acceptable price for the asset.

    D.   Intrinsic value is the value based upon the expected cash flows from the investment, the riskiness of the asset, and the investor's required rate of return. It is the value in the eyes of the investor and is the same as the present value of expected future cash flows to be received from the investment.

II.  Valuation:  an overview

    A.   Value is a function of three elements:

        1.   The amount and timing of the asset's expected cash flow

2. The riskiness of these cash flows

3. The investors' required rate of return for undertaking the investment

B. Expected cash flows are used in measuring the returns from an investment.

C. Riskiness of the cash flows

1. Risk can be defined as the possible variation in cash flow about an expected cash flow.

2. Statistically, risk may be measured by the standard deviation about the expected cash flow.

III. Bond valuation

A. Terminology and characteristics of bonds

1. A bond is a long-term promissory note that promises to pay the bondholder a predetermined, fixed amount of interest each year until maturity. At maturity, the principal will be paid to the bondholder.

2. In the case of a firm's insolvency, a bondholder has a priority of claim to the firm's assets before the preferred and common stockholders. Also, bondholders must be paid interest due them before dividends can be distributed to the stockholders.

3. A bond's par value is the amount that will be repaid by the firm when the bond matures, usually $1,000.

4. The contractual agreement of the bond specifies a *coupon interest rate* that is expressed either as a percent of the par value or as a flat amount of interest which the borrowing firm promises to pay the bondholder each year. For example: A $1,000 par value bond specifying a coupon interest rate of 9% is equivalent to an annual interest payment of $90.

5. The bond has a *maturity date*, at which time the borrowing firm is committed to repay the loan principal.

6.  An indenture (or trust deed) is the legal agreement between the firm issuing the bonds and the bond trustee who represents the bondholders.  It provides the specific terms of the bond agreement such as the rights and responsibilities of both parties.

7.  The current yield on a bond refers to the ratio of annual interest payment to the bond's market price.

8.  Bond ratings

    a.  Bond ratings are simply judgments about the future risk potential of the bond in question.  Bond ratings are extremely important in that a firm's bond rating tells much about the cost of funds and the firm's access to the debt market.

    b.  Three primary rating agencies exist--Moody's, Standard and Poor's, and Fitch Investor Services.

    c.  The different ratings and their implications are described.

B.  Types of bonds

    1.  *Debentures*:  unsecured long-term debt.

    2.  *Subordinated debentures*:  bonds that have a lower claim on assets in the event of liquidation than do other senior debtholders.

    3.  *Mortgage bonds*:  bonds secured by a lien on specific assets of the firm, such as real estate.

    4.  *Eurobonds*:  bonds issued in a country different from the one in whose currency the bond is denominated; for instance, a bond issued in Europe or Asia that pays interest and principal in U.S. dollars.

    5.  *Zero* and *low coupon bonds* allow the issuing firm to issue bonds at a substantial discount from their $1,000 face value with a zero or very low coupon.

        a.  The disadvantages are, when the bond matures, the issuing firm will face an extremely large nondeductible cash outflow much greater than the cash inflow they experienced when the bonds were first issued.

b. Discount bonds are not callable and can be retired only at maturity.

c. On the other hand, annual cash outflows associated with interest payments do not occur with zero coupon bonds.

6. *Junk bonds*: bonds rated BB or below.

C. Procedure for valuing a bond

1. The value of a bond is simply the present value of the future interest payments and maturity value discounted at the bondholder's required rate of return. This may be expressed as:

$$V_b = \sum_{t=1}^{N} \frac{\$I_t}{(1+k_b)^t} + \frac{\$M}{(1+k_b)^N}$$

where $I_t$ = the dollar interest to be received in each payment
$M$ = the par value of the bond at maturity
$k_b$ = the required rate of return for the bondholder
$N$ = the number of periods to maturity

In other words, we are discounting the expected future cash flows to the present at the appropriate discount rate (required rate of return).

2. If interest payments are received semiannually (as with most bonds), the valuation equation becomes:

$$V_b = \sum_{t=1}^{2N} \frac{\frac{\$I_t}{2}}{\left(1+\frac{k_b}{2}\right)^t} + \frac{\$M}{\left(1+\frac{k_b}{2}\right)^{2N}}$$

IV. Bondholder's Expected Rate of Return

A. The bondholder's expected rate of return is the rate the investor will earn if the bond is held to maturity, provided, of course, that the company issuing the bond does not default on the payments.

B. We compute the bondholder's expected rate of return by finding the discount rate that gets the present value of the future interest payments and principal payment just equal to the bond's current market price.

V. Bond value: three important relationships

A. First relationship

A decrease in interest rates (required rates of return) will cause the value of a bond to increase; an interest rate increase will cause a decrease in value. The change in value caused by changing interest rates is called *interest rate risk.*

B. Second relationship

1. If the bondholder's required rate of return (current interest rate) equals the coupon interest rate, the bond will sell at par, or maturity value.

2. If the current interest rate exceeds the bond's coupon rate, the bond will sell below par value, or at a "discount."

3. If the current interest rate is less than the bond's coupon rate, the bond will sell above par value, or at a "premium."

C. Third relationship

A bondholder owning a long-term bond is exposed to greater interest rate risk than when owning a short-term bonds.

Study Problems

1. Gents Clothiers, Inc. has bonds maturing in 6 years and pays 6% interest semiannually on a $1000 face value.

   a. If your required rate of return is 10%, what is the value of the bond?

   b. How would your answer change if the interest were paid annually?

SOLUTION

a. Value of bond if interest is paid semiannually:

    (1)   Present value of interest payments:

$$= \$30 \ (PVIFA_{12,5\%}) = \$30 \ (8.863)$$

$$= \$265.89$$

    (2)  Present value of principal:

$$= \$1,000 \ (PVIFA_{12,5\%}) = \$1,000(0.557)$$

$$= \$557$$

    (3)   Present value of the interest and principal

| | |
|---|---|
| Present value of the interest | $265.89 |
| Present value of the principal | 557.00 |
| Value of the bond | $822.89 |

b. Value of bond if interest is paid annually:

    (1)   Present value of the interest payments:

$$= \$60 \ (PVIFA_{6,10\%}) = \$60(4.355)$$

$$= \$261.30$$

    (2)   Present value of the principal:

$$= \$1,000 \ (PVIFA_{6,10\%}) = \$1,000(0.564)$$

$$= \$564$$

    (3)   Present value of the interest and principal

| | |
|---|---|
| Present value of the interest | $261.30 |
| Present value of the principal | 564.00 |
| Value of the bond | $825.30 |

2. Edge Manufacturing Corporation's bonds are selling in the market for $1,193.96. These 15-year bonds pay 8% interest (annually) on a $1,000 par value. If they are purchased at the market price, what is the expected rate of return?

SOLUTION

Expected Rate of Return:

$$\$1,193.96 = \$80\,(PVIFA_{15,k_b}) + \$1,000\,(PVIF_{15,k_b})$$

where $k_b$ is the expected rate of return to be solved for by trial and error. Try a 6% rate of return. At 6% the present value of the interest and principal is equal to

$$\$80(9.712) + \$1,000(0.417) = \$1,193.96$$

The expected rate of return is 6%.

(Note: With a financial calculator, there is no need to guess as to the rate. The rate may be determined by the calculator.)

3. The market price is $865.60 for a 5-year, 12% bond ($1,000 face value) that pays interest semiannually. What is the expected rate of return?

SOLUTION

$$\$865.60 = \$60\,(PVIFA_{10,k_b}) + \$1,000\,(PVIF_{10,k_b})$$

where $k_b$ is the expected rate of return (to be solved by trial and error).

Try 8%:

$$\$60(6.710) + \$1,000(0.463) = \$865.60$$

The required rate of return is 8% (on a semiannual basis) or 16% (on an annual basis).

Self Tests

TRUE-FALSE

_T_ 1. The par value of a bond is essentially independent of the market value of a bond.

_T_ 2. The only variable that can cause the value of a bond to increase or decrease is a change in the bondholder's required rate of return.

_T_ 3. In an efficient marketplace, the intrinsic value of a security will equal its market value.

_T_ 4. If the market price of a security is larger than the value assigned to the security by an investor, then the expected rate is greater than the required rate of return.

_F_ 5. Bond ratings indicate the chance that the bondholder will experience interest rate risk with a given bond.

_T_ 6. The intrinsic value of an asset can be defined as the present value of the asset's expected future cash flows.

_F_ 7. The yield to maturity of a bond is the current value of the bond.

_T_ 8. The three items that directly affect the cash flows from owning a bond are the bond's par value, maturity date, and the coupon rate of interest.

_T_ 9. The expected rate of return is equal to the required rate of return of bondholders who are willing to pay the present market price for the bonds.

_F_ 10. An increase in interest rates will cause the value of a bond to increase.

_F_ 11. An increase in interest automatically drives bonds' stated rates up.

_F_ 12. Changes in interest rates have a greater impact on the value of short-term bonds as opposed to the value of long-term bonds.

_F_ 13. The stated coupon rate of interest has no effect on the market price of a bond.

_F_ 14. Investors are attracted to zero coupon bonds by their high periodic interest payments.

_T_ 15. In the case of insolvency, bondholders are honored before common stock but after preferred stock.

_T_ 16. A bond denominated by yen, issued in Japan, and not registered with the SEC could not be classified as a Eurobond.

_F_ 17. Junk bonds differ from high-yield bonds in that junk bonds will almost always carry a lower rating than high-yield bonds.

_T_ 18. In an efficient marketplace, the intrinsic value of a security will equal its market value.


MULTIPLE CHOICE

1. For a $1,000 par-value bond carrying an 8% coupon (interest paid quarterly) and having a 10% yield to maturity, the quarterly interest payments would be

    ✓a. $20.
    b. $30.
    c. $25.
    d. $50.
    e. $10.

2. The value of a security may be expressed as a function of

    a. expected cash flows.
    b. riskiness of cash flows.
    ✓c. the investor's required rate of return.
    d. a and b only.
    e. a, b, and c.

3. If the market is in equilibrium, the expected rate of return and the required rate of return

    ✓a. will be the same.
    b. will be different.
    c. have no relationship to each other.

4.  If everything else is assumed to be constant, as the investor's required rate of return decreases, the value of a security

    a.  stays the same.
    b.  increases.
    c.  decreases.
    d.  has no relationship to the investor's required rate of return.

5.  In the basic security valuation model

    $$V = \sum_{t=1}^{n} \frac{C_t}{(1+R)^t}$$

    $C_t$ stands for

    a.  the investor's required rate of return.
    b.  cash flow to be received in year t.
    c.  the intrinsic value of an asset producing expected future cash flows.
    d.  none of the above.

6.  The _____ of an asset is the observed value for the asset in the marketplace.

    a.  intrinsic value
    b.  liquidation value
    c.  market value
    d.  none of the above

7.  The _____ is the legal agreement that provides the specific terms of the loan agreement.

    a.  mortgage
    b.  debenture
    c.  indenture
    d.  prospectus

8. A(n) ____ is a bond secured by a lien on real property.

   a. mortgage bond
   b. subordinated debenture
   c. Eurobond
   d. coupon bond

9. Junk bonds have all the following characteristics except

   a. rated BB or lower.
   b. low rates of return.
   c. highly speculative.
   d. no security.

10. Bond valuation depends on all but

   a. the amount of cash flows to be received.
   b. the maturity date of the loan.
   c. the investor's required rate of return.
   d. when the loan was issued.

11. When a bond is worth more than its face value, it is said to sell

   a. at a discount.
   b. at a premium.
   c. at its maturity value.
   d. above its market return.

12. When the market interest rate rises above the stated interest rate of a bond, the bond

   a. will sell at a discount.
   b. will sell at a premium.
   c. will sell at its par or stated value.
   d. will not sell because investors can receive a better return from the market.

13. The risk of changing bond values due to the variability of future interest rates is

    a.     time value of money.
    b.     interest-rate risk.
    c.     timing risk.
    d.     investment risk.

14. The current yield on a bond refers to

    a.     the interest payments due within the next year.
    b.     the ratio of the annual interest payment to the bond's market price.
    c.     the interest earned in the current period.
    d.     the coupon rate of interest.

15. Bond ratings are favorably affected by all except

    a.     profitable operations.
    b.     large firm size.
    c.     low variability in past earnings.
    d.     taking more advantage of financial leverage.

16. When bond prices are quoted, they are generally expressed at

    a.     par value.
    b.     face value.
    c.     a percentage of par value.
    d.     current yield.

17. The current interest rate can also be called
    a.     the yield to maturity.
    b.     the coupon interest rate.
    c.     the expected rate of return.
    d.     the risk premium.
    e.     a and c

# CHAPTER 7

# Valuation and Characteristics
# of Stock

Orientation: This chapter continues the introduction of concepts underlying asset valuation begun in Chapter 6. We are specifically concerned with valuing preferred stock and common stock. We also look at the concept of a stockholder's expected rate of return on an investment.

I.   Preferred stock

    A.   Features of preferred stock

        1.   Owners of preferred stock receive dividends instead of interest.

        2.   Most preferred stocks are perpetuities (non-maturing).

        3.   Multiple classes, each having different characteristics, can be issued.

        4.   Preferred stock has priority over common stock with regard to claims on assets in the care of bankruptcy.

        5.   Most preferred stock carries a cumulative feature that requires all past unpaid preferred stock dividends to be paid before any common stock dividends are declared.

        6.   Preferred stock may contain other protective provisions.

        7.   Preferred stock contain provisions to convert to a predetermined number of shares of common stock.

8. Retirement features for preferred stock are frequently included.

    a. Callable preferred refers to a feature which allows preferred stock to be called or retired, like a bond.

    b. A sinking fund provision requires the firm periodically to set aside an amount of money for the retirement of its preferred stock.

B. Valuation of preferred stock ($V_{ps}$):

The value of a preferred stock equals the present value of all future dividends. If the stock is non-maturing, where dividends are expected in equal amount each year in perpetuity, the value may be calculated as follows:

$$V_{ps} = \frac{\text{annual dividend}}{\text{required rate of return}} = \frac{D}{k_{ps}}$$

## II. Common stock

A. Features of common stock

1. As owners of the corporation, common shareholders have the right to the residual income and assets after bondholders and preferred stockholders have been paid.

2. Common stock shareholders are generally the only security holders with the right to elect the board of directors.

3. Preemptive rights entitles the common shareholder to maintain a proportionate share of ownership in the firm.

4. Common stock shareholders' liability as owners of the corporation is limited to the amount of their investment.

5. Common stock's value is equal to the present value of all future cash flows expected to be received by the stockholder.

B. Valuing common stock

1. Company growth occurs either by:

    a. The infusion of new capital.

b.	The retention of earnings, which we call internal growth. The internal growth rate of a firm equals:

$$\text{Return on equity} \times \left( \begin{array}{l} \text{Percentage of earnings} \\ \text{retained within the firm} \end{array} \right)$$

2.	Although the bondholder and preferred stockholder are promised a specific amount each year, the dividend for common stock is based on the profitability of the firm and the management's decision either to pay dividends or retain profits for reinvestment.

3.	The common dividend typically increases along with the growth in corporate earnings.

4.	The earnings growth of a firm should be reflected in a higher price for the firm's stock.

5.	In finding the value of a common stock ($V_{cs}$), we should discount all future expected dividends ($D_1$, $D_2$, $D_3$, ..., $D_\bullet$) to the present at the required rate of return for the stockholder ($k_c$). That is:

$$V_{cs} = \frac{D_1}{(1+k_{cs})^1} + \frac{D_2}{(1+k_{cs})^2} + ... + \frac{D_\infty}{(1+k_{cs})^\infty}$$

6.	If we assume that the amount of dividend is increasing by a constant growth rate each year,

$$D_t = D_0 (1+g)^t$$

where $g$  = the growth rate

$D_0$  = the most recent dividend payment

If the growth rate, $g$, is the same each year and is less than the required rate of return, $K_c$, the valuation equation for common stock can be reduced to

$$V_{cs} = \frac{D_1}{k_{cs} - g} = \frac{D_0 (1+g)}{k_{cs} - g}$$

95

III. Shareholder's Expected Rate of Return

    A.    The shareholder's expected rate of return is of great interest to financial mangers because it tells about the investor's expectations.

    B.    Preferred stockholder's expected rate of return.

        If we know the market price of a preferred stock and the amount of the dividends to be received, the expected rate of return from the investment can be determined as follows:

$$\text{expected rate of return} = \frac{\text{annual dividend}}{\text{market price of the stock}}$$

or

$$\overline{k}_{ps} = \frac{D}{P_{ps}}$$

    C.    Common stockholder's expected rate of return

        1.    The expected rate of return for common stock can be calculated from the valuation equations discussed earlier.

        2.    Assuming that dividends are increasing at a constant annual growth rate (g), we can show that the expected rate of return for common stock, $K_c$ is

$$\overline{k}_{cs} = \left(\frac{\text{dividend in year 1}}{\text{market price}}\right) + \left(\begin{array}{c}\text{growth}\\\text{rate}\end{array}\right)$$

$$= \frac{D_1}{P_{ps}} + g$$

Since dividend ÷ price is the "dividend yield," the

$$\text{Expected rate of return} = \left(\begin{array}{c}\text{dividend}\\\text{yield}\end{array}\right) + \left(\begin{array}{c}\text{growth}\\\text{rate}\end{array}\right)$$

96

# Study Problems

1. The preferred stock of Craft Company pays a $3 dividend. What is the value of the stock if your required rate of return is 8%?

   SOLUTION

$$\text{Value of preferred stock} = \frac{\text{dividend}}{\text{required rate of return}}$$

$$P_{ps} = \frac{\$3}{0.08} = \$37.50$$

2. Universal Machines' common stock paid $1.50 in dividends *last year*, and dividends are expected to grow indefinitely at an annual 6% rate. What is the value of the stock if you require a 12% return?

   SOLUTION

$$\text{Value } (P_{cs}) = \frac{\text{dividend in year 1}}{\text{required rate - growth rate}} = \frac{D_1}{k_{cs} - g}$$

   where $D_1 = D_0(1+g)$    $= \$1.50(1 + 0.06)$    $= \$1.59$

   Then,

$$P_{cs} = \frac{\$1.59}{0.12 - 0.06} = \$26.50$$

3. Texas Mining Company's common stock is selling for $35. The stock paid dividends of $2.50 last year and has a projected growth rate of 10%. If you buy the stock at the market price, what is the expected rate of return?

   SOLUTION

   Expected rate of return $(k_{cs})$:

$$\bar{k}_{cs} = \frac{\text{dividend in year 1}}{\text{price}} + \frac{\text{growth}}{\text{rate}} = \frac{D_1}{P_{cs}} + g$$

97

where $D_1 = D_0 (1+g) = \$2.50 (1 + 0.10) = \$2.75$

$$P_0 = \$35$$

$$\bar{k}_{cs} = \frac{\$2.75}{\$35.00} + 0.10 = 0.1785$$

$$= 17.85\%$$

4. Idalou Power Company's preferred stock is selling for $25 in the market and pays $2.50 in dividends.

   a. What is the expected rate of return on the stock?

   b. If your required rate of return is 12%, what is the fair value of the stock for you?

   c. Should you acquire the stock?

   SOLUTION

   a. Expected rate of return $= \dfrac{\$2.50}{\$25.00} = 10\%$

   b. Value of the stock to you $= \dfrac{\$2.50}{0.12} = \$20.83$

   c. Since your required rate of return is higher than the expected rate of return, you should not acquire it.

5. The market price of International Electric Corporation is $40. The price at the end of one year is expected to be $45. Dividends for next year should be $2.50. What is the expected rate of return for a single holding period of one year?

SOLUTION

current price $(P_{cs})$ =

$$\frac{\text{dividend in year 1}}{1 + \text{expected rate of return}} + \frac{\text{price in year 1}}{1 + \text{expected rate of return}}$$

$$\frac{\text{expected}}{\text{return}} = \frac{\text{dividend in year 1} + \text{price in year 1}}{\text{current price}} - 1$$

$$\frac{\text{expected}}{\text{return}} = \frac{\$2.50 + \$45.00}{\$40.00} - 1 = 18.75\%$$

Self Tests

TRUE-FALSE

_____ 1.    An assumption necessary in the model for common stock valuation

$$P_{cs} = \frac{D_1}{k_{cs} - g}$$

is that the amount of the dividend increases by a constant percent each year.

_____ 2.    Protective provisions can allow preferred stockholders a voting right in the event of nonpayment of dividends.

_____ 3.    If the market price of a security is larger than the value assigned to the security by an investor, then the expected rate is greater than the required rate of return.

_____ 4.    The term "growth" when used in the context of a valuation model includes growth from reinvesting profits and from issuing stock.

_____ 5.    The value of a preferred stock is the future value of the stock at maturity.

_____ 6. The constant growth common stock valuation model is defined as:

$$\text{common stock value} = \frac{\text{required rate of return}}{\text{dividend in year 1}}$$

assuming the dividends grow each year at a constant rate.

_____ 7. Valuation does not support the financial officer's objective of maximizing the value of the firm's common stock.

_____ 8. The option involved in convertible preferred stock belongs to the corporations issuing the shares.

_____ 9. A sinking-fund provision requires the firm to pay all unpaid preferred stock dividends before any common stock dividends are declared.

_____ 10. A cumulative feature requires the firm to set aside an amount of money for the retirement of its preferred stock.

_____ 11. The preemptive right entitles current shareholders to get the first opportunity to purchase new stock issues.

_____ 12. Preferred stockholders have a stronger voice in company operations than common stockholders.

_____ 13. An advantage of preferred stock over common stock is the regular interest payments that must be paid before dividends can be paid to common stockholders.

_____ 14. A majority voting feature pertains to the margin by which elections must be won.

_____ 15. A proxy allows a designated party to temporarily vote for someone else.

MULTIPLE CHOICE

1.      The most recent dividend paid by Xeron on its common stock was $1.50 (annual). The required rate of return for the security is 6%. Growth is anticipated to be at 4% annually. The market price of the stock should be

        a.      $78.
        b.      $100.
        c.      $50.
        d.      $150.
        e.      $75.

2.      The income received by the holder of a preferred stock is similar to the income received from which other financial asset in terms of it being a constant amount each year?

                a. Common stocks
                b. Bonds
                c. Both a and b
                d. None of the above

3.      What is the expected rate of return for a stock with a current market price of $44, if the expected dividend at the conclusion of this year is $2.20, and earnings are growing at a 10% annual rate?  (Assume that the dividends are anticipated to grow at the same rate.)

        a.      25%
        b.      10%
        c.      5%
        d.      15%

4.      Which of the following is not a common trait of preferred stock?

        a.      Convertibility
        b.      Cumulative dividends
        c.      Voting rights
        d.      Preferred claim on assets and income over common stock

5. _____ allows the preferred stockholder to be paid beyond the payment of the stated dividend.

   a. A carry-back feature
   b. A cumulative feature
   c. A stock premium
   d. A preemptive right

6. _____ allows the issuing corporation to retire the stock.

   a. A preemptive right
   b. Convertibility
   c. Callable preferred
   d. PIK preferred

7. Common stock involves _____ the corporation.

   a. ownership in
   b. personally managing
   c. being a creditor of
   d. the maturity of

8. _____ allows a designated party the temporary power of attorney to vote for the signee at the corporation's annual meeting.

   a. Majority voting
   b. A proxy
   c. Absentee voting
   d. Protective provisions

9. _____ gives the shareholder one vote for each share of stock, and each board position is voted on separately.

   a. Cumulative voting
   b. A proxy
   c. Majority voting
   d. Preemptive right

10. Which of the following does not affect the value of a stock?

   a. Expected cash inflow
   b. Riskiness of the stock
   c. The investor's required rate of return
   d. The stock's par or stated value

11. Common stock dividends must be _____ before issued.

    a. approved by common stockholders
    b. registered with the SEC
    c. approved by preferred stockholders
    d. declared by the firm's board of directors

12. Common stock dividends are

    a. limited to twice the amount received by preferred stockholders
    b. unlimited
    c. always paid on a monthly basis
    d. recognized before preferred stock dividends

# CHAPTER 8

# The Meaning and Measurement
# of Risk and Return

<u>Orientation</u>: In this chapter, we examine the factors that determine rates of return (discount rates) in the capital markets. We are particularly interested in the relationship between risk and rates of return. We look at risk both in terms of the riskiness of an individual security and that of a portfolio of securities.

I.   Expected return defined and measured

     A.   The expected benefits or returns to be received from an investment come in the form of the cash flows the investment generates.

     B.   Conventionally, we measure the expected cash flow, $\overline{X}$, as follows:

$$\overline{X} = \sum_{i=1}^{n} X_i P(X_i)$$

       where    $n$   =   the number of possible states of the economy.

                         $X_i$   =   the cash flow in the ith state of the economy.

                     $P(X_i)$ =   the probability of the ith cash flow.

II.   Risk defined and measured

     A.   Risk can be defined as the possible variation in cash flow about an expected cash flow.

     B.   Statistically, risk may be measured by the standard deviation about the expected cash flow.

III. Rates of return: the investors' experience

    A.    Data have been compiled by Ibbotson and Sinquefield on the actual returns for various portfolios of securities from 1926-1995.

    B.    The following portfolios were studied:

        1.    Common stocks of large firms
        2.    Common stocks for small firms
        3.    Corporate bonds
        4.    Long-term U.S. government bonds
        5.    Intermediate U.S. government bonds
        6.    U.S. Treasury bills

    C.    Investors historically have received greater returns for greater risk-taking with the exception of the long-term U.S. government bonds.

    D.    The only portfolio with returns consistently exceeding the inflation rate has been common stocks.

IV. Risk and diversification

    A.    The market rewards diversification. We can lower risk without sacrificing expected return, and/or we can increase expected return without having to assume more risk.

    B.    Diversifying among different kinds of assets is called asset allocation. Compared to diversification within the different asset classes, the benefits received are far greater through effective asset allocation.

    C.    Total variability can be divided into:

        1.    The variability of returns unique to the security (diversifiable or unsystematic risk)

        2.    The risk related to market movements (nondiversifiable or systematic risk)

    D.    By diversifying, the investor can eliminate the "unique" security risk. The systematic risk, however, cannot be diversified away.

E.    Measuring market risk

    1.    The *characteristic line* tells us the average movement in a firm's stock price in response to a movement in the general market, such as the S&P 500 Index. The slope of the characteristic line, which has come to be called *beta*, is a measure of a stock's systematic or market risk. The slope of the line is merely the ratio of the "rise" of the line relative to the "run" of the line.

    2.    If a security's beta equals one, a 10% increase (decrease) in market returns will produce on average a 10% increase (decrease) in security returns.

    3.    A security having a higher beta is more volatile and, thus, more risky than a security having a lower beta value.

F.    A portfolio's beta is equal to the average of the betas of the stocks in the portfolio.

G.    Risk and diversification can be demonstrated by a comparison of three portfolios consisting of short-term government securities, long-term government bonds, and large-company stocks.

V.    The investor's required rate of return

A.    The required rate of return is the minimum rate necessary to compensate an investor for accepting the risk he or she associates with the purchase and ownership of an asset.

B.    Two factors determine the required rate of return for the investor:

    1.    The risk-free rate of interest which recognizes the time value of money.

    2.    The risk premium which considers the riskiness (variability of returns) of the asset and the investor's attitude toward risk.

107

C.   Capital asset pricing model--CAPM

   1.   The required rate of return for a given security can be expressed as

   $$\text{Required rate} = \text{risk-free rate} + \text{beta} \times \left(\text{market return} - \text{risk-free rate}\right)$$

   or

   $$k_j = k_{rf} + \beta_j (k_m - k_{rf})$$

   2.   Security market line

      a.   Graphically illustrates the CAPM.

      b.   Designates the risk-return tradeoff existing in the market, where risk is defined in terms of beta, according to the CAPM equation.

D.   The Fama and French attack on the CAPM

   1.   Criticism of CAPM

      a.   Differences in betas do not explain the differences in stock returns.

      b.   Total market value of a firm's equity and the ratio of a firm's equity book value to its market equity value explain more of the variation in returns than do betas.

   2.   Supporters of the CAPM argue that:

      a.   Fama and French's research methodology was flawed, or

      b.   Their contentions are theoretically incomplete.

   3.   Weighing the evidence has caused the academic community to come to grips with the fundamental shortcomings of the CAPM.

108

## Study Problems

1.    Phillips, Inc. is considering an investment in one of two common stocks. Given the information below, which investment is better, based on risk and return?

| Common Stock A | | Common Stock B | |
|---|---|---|---|
| *Probability* | *Return* | *Probability* | *Return* |
| 0.10 | -10% | 0.30 | 5% |
| 0.20 | 6 | 0.20 | 12 |
| 0.40 | 15 | 0.40 | 10 |
| 0.30 | 9 | 0.10 | 20 |

## SOLUTION

*Common Stock A*

### Expected Return

$$= 0.1(-10\%) + 0.2(6\%) + 0.4(15\%) + 0.3(9\%)$$
$$= -1\% + 1.2\% + 6\% + 2.7\% = 8.9\%$$

### Standard Deviation

$$= [(-10\% - 8.9\%)^2(0.10) + (6\% - 8.9\%)^2(0.2)$$
$$+ (15\% - 8.9\%)^2 (0.4) + (9\% - 8.9\%)^2(0.30)]^{1/2}$$
$$= (35.721\% + 1.682\% + 14.884\% + 0.003\%)^{1/2} = .23\%$$

*Common Stock B*

### Expected Return

$$= 0.3(5\%) + 0.2(12\%) + 0.4(10\%) + 0.10(20\%)$$
$$= 1.5\% + 2.4\% + 4\% + 2\% = 9.9\%$$

### Standard Deviation

$$= [(5\% - 9.9\%)^2(0.3) + (12\% - 9.9\%)^2(0.2)$$
$$+ (10\% - 9.9\%)^2(0.4) + (20\% - 9.9\%)^2(0.1)]^{1/2}$$
$$= (7.203\% + 0.882\% + 0.004\% + 10.201\%)^{1/2} = 4.28\%$$

Common stock B has both a higher expected return and a smaller standard deviation (less risk). Hence, B is better.

2.  Compute the annual holding-period return for the following stock.

| Year | Stock Price |
|------|-------------|
| 1988 | $98 |
| 1989 | 105 |
| 1990 | 115 |
| 1991 | 100 |
| 1992 | 120 |

SOLUTION

| Year | Return |
|------|--------|
| 1988 | |
| 1989 | 7.1% |
| 1990 | 9.5% |
| 1991 | -13.0% |
| 1992 | 20.0% |

3.  From the graph below, estimate Archie's beta.

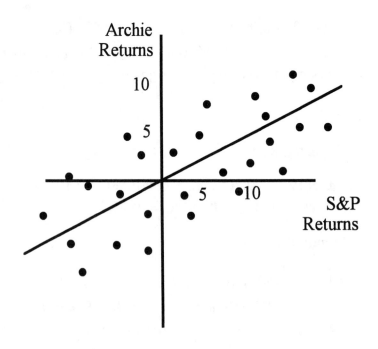

## SOLUTION

Archie's beta is about 0.50, since Archie's returns change about 5% while the market's returns change 10%. Thus, $5 \div 10 = 0.50$.

4.  BC Incorporated, has a beta of 0.65. If the expected market return is 10% and the risk-free rate is 5%, what is the appropriate expected return of BC Incorporated?

## SOLUTION

Expected return of BC Incorporated

$$= \text{risk-free rate} + \text{Beta} \begin{pmatrix} \text{expected} & & \text{risk} \\ \text{market} & - & \text{free} \\ \text{return} & & \text{rate} \end{pmatrix}$$

$$= 5\% + 0.65(10\% - 5\%)$$

$$= 5\% + 3.25\% = 8.25\%$$

## Self Tests

## TRUE-FALSE

_____ 1.  The investor's required rate of return is the minimum rate necessary to attract an investor to purchase or hold a security.

_____ 2.  Risk, as defined in this chapter, is the variation in returns about an expected value.

_____ 3.  Time value of money can be represented by a risk-free rate of return only for risk-free securities.

_____ 4.  A proxy for the risk-free rate is the Corporate AA Bond rate.

_____ 5.  An investor's required rate of return is always greater than the expected rate of return.

_____ 6.  By proper diversification, an investor can eliminate the market-related (systematic) risk.

_____ 7. A security having a beta of 1 will move up (or down) on average with the market by the same percentage.

_____ 8. The addition of a security with a beta of 0 provides no additional risk to a well-diversified portfolio.

_____ 9. The annual return on common stock historically has been greater than that of U.S. Treasury bills.

_____ 10. A security with an expected return of 15.9% and a standard deviation of 9.8% is obviously better than a Treasury bill earning 8%.

_____ 11. The real average annual rate of return is the nominal return minus the risk-free rate of return.

_____ 12. Corporate bonds are always more risky than Treasury bills and long-term government bonds.

MULTIPLE CHOICE

1. Under the capital-asset pricing model, the relevant risk is

   a. diversifiable risk.
   b. systematic risk.
   c. financial risk.
   d. standard deviation.

2. If the required return for a security is 15% and the risk-free rate is 6%, the risk premium is

   a. 0%.
   b. 6%.
   c. 10%.
   d. 9%.
   e. 15%.

112

3. In terms of the security market line, a security with a beta of 1.5 should provide a risk premium _____ times the risk premium existing for the market as a whole.

   a. 0
   b. 1
   c. 1.5
   d. 2.5
   e. 0.5

4. The beta for a portfolio is determined by

   a. calculating the standard deviation of the betas of the individual stocks in the portfolio.
   b. computing the unweighted average of the individual betas.
   c. calculating a weighted average of the individual stock betas, where the weights equal the individual stocks' expected returns.
   d. calculating a weighted average of the individual stock betas, where the weights equal the percentage invested in each stock.

5. A stock's holding period return represents

   a. the dividend received each period.
   b. the rate of return that would be earned on a stock if bought at the beginning of the period and sold at the end of the period.
   c. the return received from diversifying one's portfolio.
   d. the return from a stock relative to the return of the portfolio.

6. An investor's required rate of return should be a function of

   a. the riskiness of the investment being made without regard for the riskiness of other investments.
   b. the risk-free rate of return less the inflation rate.
   c. the risk-free rate of return plus the inflation rate.
   d. the risk-free rate of return plus a risk premium for the stock's systematic risk.

7. You should expect a higher rate of return from

   a. long-term corporate bonds than from common stocks.
   b. small company stocks than from common stocks of large firms.
   c. U.S. Treasury bills than from long-term government securities.
   d. none of the above.

8.    Market risk can also be called

      a.  unsystematic risk
      b.  non-diversifiable risk
      c.  diversifiable risk
      d.  firm-specific risk
      e.  company-unique risk

9.    _____ is the only risk that matters to investors with broadly
      diversified portfolios.

      a.  Systematic risk
      b.  Unsystematic risk
      c.  Firm-specific risk
      d.  Diversifiable risk

# CHAPTER 9

# Capital-Budgeting Techniques And Practice

Orientation: Capital budgeting involves the decision-making process with respect to investment in fixed assets; specifically, it involves measuring the incremental cash flows associated with investment proposals and evaluating the attractiveness of these cash flows relative to the project's costs. This chapter focuses on the various decision criteria. It also examines how to deal with complications in the capital-budgeting process including mutually exclusive projects and capital rationing.

I.    Methods for evaluating projects

    A.  The payback period method

        1.  The payback period of an investment tells the number of years required to recover the initial investment. The payback period is calculated by adding the cash flows up until they are equal to the initial fixed investment.

        2.  Although this measure does, in fact, deal with cash flows and is easy to calculate and understand, it ignores any cash flows that occur after the payback period and does not consider the time value of money within the payback period.

B. Present-value methods

1. The net present value of an investment project is the present value of the cash inflows less the present value of the cash outflows. By assigning negative values to cash outflows, it becomes

$$NPV = \sum_{t=1}^{n} \frac{ACF_t}{(1+k)^t} - IO$$

where $ACF_t$ = the annual after-tax cash flow in time period t (this can take on either positive or negative values)

$k$ = the required rate of return or appropriate discount rate or cost of capital

$IO$ = the initial cash outlay

$n$ = the project's expected life

a. The acceptance criteria are

accept if $NPV \geq 0$

reject if $NPV < 0$

b. The advantage of this approach is that it takes the time value of money into consideration in addition to dealing with cash flows.

2. The profitability index is the ratio of the present value of the expected future net cash flows to the initial cash outlay, or

$$\text{profitability index} = \frac{\sum_{t-1}^{n} \frac{ACF_t}{(1+k)^t}}{IO}$$

a. The acceptance criteria are

accept if $PI \geq 1.0$

reject if $PI < 1.0$

b. The advantages of this method are the same as those for the net present value.

c. Either of these present-value methods will give the same accept/reject decisions to a project.

C. The internal rate of return is the discount rate that equates the present value of the project's future net cash flows with the project's initial outlay. Thus the internal rate of return is represented by IRR in the equation below:

$$IO = \sum_{t=1}^{n} \frac{ACF_t}{(1 + IRR)^t}$$

1. The acceptance-rejection criteria are:

   accept if IRR $^3$ required rate of return
   reject if IRR $<$ required rate of return

   The required rate of return is often taken to be the firm's cost of capital.

2. The advantages of this method are that it deals with cash flows and recognizes the time value of money; however, the procedure is rather complicated and time-consuming.

II. Mutually exclusive projects: Although the IRR and the present-value methods will, in general, give consistent accept-reject decisions, they may not rank projects identically. This becomes important in the case of mutually exclusive projects.

A. A project is mutually exclusive if acceptance of it precludes the acceptance of one or more projects. Then, in this case, the project's relative ranking becomes important.

B. Ranking conflicts come as a result of the different assumptions on the reinvestment rate on funds released from the proposals.

C. Thus, when conflicting ranking of mutually exclusive projects results from the different reinvestment assumptions, the decision boils down to which assumption is best.

117

D. In general, the net present value method is considered to be theoretically superior.

III. Capital rationing is the situation in which a budget ceiling or constraint is placed upon the amount of funds that can be invested during a time period.

A. Theoretically, a firm should never reject a project that yields more than the required rate of return. Although there are circumstances that may create complicated situations in general, an investment policy limited by capital rationing is less than optimal.

## Study Problems

1. The cost of new machinery for a given investment project will be $100,000. Incremental cash flows after taxes will be $40,000 in years 1 and 2 and will be $60,000 in year 3. What is the payback period for this project, and if acceptable projects must recover the initial investment in 2.5 years, should this project be accepted or rejected?

SOLUTION

After 2 years they will have recovered $80,000 of the $100,000 outlay and they expect to recover an additional $60,000 in the third year. Thus, the payback period becomes

$$2 \text{ years} + \frac{\$20,000}{\$60,000} = 2.33 \text{ years}$$

2.33 years < 2.5 years. Therefore, accept the project.

2. A given investment project will cost $50,000. Incremental annual cash flows after taxes are expected to be $10,000 per year for the life of the investment, which is 5 years. There will be no salvage value at the end of the 5 years. The required rate of return is 14%. On the basis of the profitability index method, should the investment be accepted?

SOLUTION

PV of cash flow = $10,000(3.433) = $34,330

PV of cash outlay = $50,000

$$PI = \frac{\$34,330}{\$50,000} = 0.6866 < 1$$

Therefore, the project should be rejected.

3. Determine the internal rate of return on the following projects:

   a. An initial outlay of $10,000 resulting in a cash flow of $2,146 at the end of each year for the next 10 years

   b. An initial outlay of $10,000 resulting in a cash flow of $1,960 at the end of each year for the next 20 years

   c. An initial outlay of $10,000 resulting in a cash flow of $1,396 at the end of each year for the next 12 years

   d. An initial outlay of $10,000 resulting in a cash flow of $3,197 at the end of each year for the next 5 years

   SOLUTION

   a. $IO = ACF_t [PVIFA_{IRR\%,t \ yrs}]$

      $\$10,000 = \$2,146 [PVIFA_{IRR\%,10 \ yrs}]$

      $4.659 = PVIFA_{IRR\%,10 \ yrs}$

      Thus, IRR = 17%

   b. $\$10,000 = \$1,960 [PVIFA_{IRR\%,20 \ yrs}]$

      $5.102 = PVIFA_{IRR\%,20 \ yrs}$

      Thus, IRR = 19%

   c. $\$10,000 = \$1,396 [PVIFA_{IRR\%,12 \ yrs}]$

      $7.163 = PVIFA_{IRR\%,12 \ yrs}$

      Thus, IRR = 9%

d.     $\$10,000 = \$3,197 \, [PVIFA_{IRR\%,5 \, yrs}]$

     $3.128 = PVIFA_{IRR\%,5 \, yrs}$

     Thus, IRR $= 18\%$

4.   The Battling Bishops Corporation is considering two mutually exclusive pieces of machinery that perform the same task. The two alternatives available provide the following set of after-tax net cash flows:

| Year | Equipment A | Equipment B |
|------|-------------|-------------|
| 0 | -$20,000 | -$20,000 |
| 1 | 13,000 | 6,500 |
| 2 | 13,000 | 6,500 |
| 3 | 13,000 | 6,500 |
| 4 | | 6,500 |
| 5 | | 6,500 |
| 6 | | 6,500 |
| 7 | | 6,500 |
| 8 | | 6,500 |
| 9 | | 6,500 |

Equipment A has an expected life of 3 years, whereas equipment B has an expected life of 9 years. Assume a required rate of return of 14%.

a.   Calculate each project's payback period.

b.   Calculate each project's net present value.

c.   Calculate each project's internal rate of return.

d.   Are these projects comparable?

e.   Compare these projects using replacement chains and EAAs. Which project should be selected? Support your recommendation.

SOLUTION

   a.   Payback A $= 1.5385$ years
         Payback B $= 3.0769$ years

b. $\text{NPV}_A = \sum_{t=1}^{3} \dfrac{\$13,000}{(1 + 0.14)^t} - \$20,000$

$= \$13,000\,(2.322) - \$20,000$

$= \$30,186 - \$20,000$

$= \$10,186$

$\text{NPV}_B = \sum_{t=1}^{9} \dfrac{\$6,500}{(1 + 0.14)^t} - \$20,000$

$= \$6,500\,(4.946) - \$20,000$

$= \$32,149 - \$20,000$

$= \$12,149$

c. $\$20,000 = \$13,000\;[\text{PVIFA}_{\text{IRR}_A\%,3\text{ yrs}}]$

Thus, $\text{IRR}_A =$ over 40% (42.75%)

$\$20,000 = \$6,500\;[\text{PVIFA}_{\text{IRR}_B\%,9\text{ yrs}}]$

Thus, $\text{IRR}_B =$ 29%

d. These projects are not comparable because future profitable investment proposals are affected by the decision currently being made. If project A is taken, at its termination the firm could replace the machine and receive additional benefits, while acceptance of project B would exclude this possibility.

e.    Using 3 replacement chains, project A's cash flows would become:

| Year | Cash flow |
|------|-----------|
| 0 | -$20,000 |
| 1 | 13,000 |
| 2 | 13,000 |
| 3 | - 7,000 |
| 4 | 13,000 |
| 5 | 13,000 |
| 6 | - 7,000 |
| 7 | 13,000 |
| 8 | 13,000 |
| 9 | 13,000 |

$$NPV_A = \sum_{t=1}^{9} \frac{\$13,000}{(1+0.14)^t} - \$20,000 - \frac{\$20,000}{(1+0.14)^3} - \frac{\$20,000}{(1+0.14)^6}$$

$$= \$13,000(4.946) - \$20,000 - \$20,000\,(0.675)$$
$$- \$20,000\,(0.456)$$

$$= \$64,298 - \$20,000 - \$13,500 - \$9,120$$

$$= \$21,678$$

The replacement chain analysis indicated that project A should be selected, as the replacement chain associated with it has a larger NPV than project B.

Project A's EAA:

Step 1:  Calculate the project's NPV (from part b):

$$NPV_A = \$10,186$$

Step 2:  Calculate the EAA:

$$EAA_A = NPV\,/\,PVIFA_{14\%,\ 3\ yr.}$$

$$= \$10,186\,/\,2.322$$

$$= \$4,387$$

Project B's EAA:

Step 1: Calculate the project's NPV (from part b):

$NPV_B = \$12,149$

Step 2: Calculate the EAA:

$EAA_B = NPV / PVIFA_{14\%, 9 \text{ yr.}}$

$= \$12,149 / 4.946$

$= \$2,256$

Project B should be selected because it has a higher EAA.


## Self Tests

TRUE-FALSE

\_\_\_\_ 1. Capital rationing occurs because profitable projects must be rejected because of a lack of capital.

\_\_\_\_ 2. The net present value of a project decreases as the required rate of return increases.

\_\_\_\_ 3. The higher the discount rate, the more valued is the proposal with the early cash flows, all else being equal.

\_\_\_\_ 4. The net present value of a project will equal zero whenever the profitability index equals 1.0.

\_\_\_\_ 5. The net present value of a project will equal zero whenever the payback period of a project equals the firm's required payback period.

\_\_\_\_ 6. Capital rationing is not an optimal capital-budgeting strategy.

\_\_\_\_ 7. The profitability index provides the same accept/reject decision result as the net present value method.

_____ 8.  If two projects are mutually exclusive, the one with the highest expected value should always be chosen, even if it is riskier.

_____ 9.  One difference between the NPV and IRR approaches is the reinvestment rate assumption.

_____ 10. The NPV approach is preferred over the profitability index for mutually exclusive projects because it measures worth in absolute terms while the PI measures worth in relative terms.

## MULTIPLE CHOICE

1. Which of the following considers the time value of money?

    a.  Payback method
    b.  Return on investment
    c.  Profitability index
    d.  None of the above

2. Which of the following is a non-discounted cash flow approach?

    a.  Payback period
    b.  Profitability index
    c.  Internal rate of return
    d.  Net present value

3. If the internal rate of return is greater than the required rate of return,

    a.  the present value of all the cash flows will be less than the initial outlay.
    b.  the payback will be less than the life of the investment.
    c.  the project should be accepted.
    d.  a and c.

4. If the cash flow pattern for a project has two sign reversals, then there can be as many as _____ positive IRRs.

    a.  1
    b.  2
    c.  3
    d.  4

# APPENDIX 9A

# Self-Teaching Supplement: Capital-Budgeting Techniques

## I. Net Present Value and Profitability Index Methods

In making investment decisions regarding fixed assets, the analyst compares the benefits of projects with their associated costs. Unfortunately, this comparison is complicated by the fact that the benefits and costs accruing from a given project usually do not occur in the same time period and, thus, are not directly comparable. This incomparability is a result of the time value of money (i.e., a dollar received today is worth more than a dollar received in the future). This comes about because a dollar today can be put into the bank and earn interest, resulting in a larger sum in the future. In economic terms, we refer to the time value of money as its opportunity cost.

### A. Using the net present value and profitability index

In this section, we compare the present value of a project's benefits with the present value of its cost. The difference in these present values is referred to as the net present value, and the ratio of benefits to cost is called the profitability index. Definitionally, then

$$\text{net present value} = \binom{\text{present value of}}{\text{future net cash flows}} - \binom{\text{initial}}{\text{cash outlay}}$$

$$\text{profitability index} = \frac{\binom{\text{present value of}}{\text{future net cash flows}}}{\binom{\text{initial}}{\text{cash outlay}}}$$

125

Although both capital-budgeting techniques provide us with the same accept/reject decision, they may rank two or more projects differently. This difference results because the net-present-value criterion measures the total dollar value of a project, while the profitability index measures its value relative to project cost. The decision criteria used in applying these decision tools are:

|  | NPV | PI |
|---|---|---|
| Accept | $\geq 0$ | $\geq 1$ |
| Reject | $< 0$ | $< 1$ |

SOLVED PROBLEMS

EXERCISE 1

The initial cash outlay of a project is $100; the present value of the cash flows is $75. Compute the project's net present value and its profitability index. Should it be accepted?

SOLUTION

$$\text{net present value} = \left(\begin{array}{c}\text{present value of}\\\text{future net cash flows}\end{array}\right) - \left(\begin{array}{c}\text{initial}\\\text{cash outlay}\end{array}\right)$$

$$= \$75 - \$100 = -\$25$$

$$\text{profitability index} = \frac{\left(\begin{array}{c}\text{present value of}\\\text{future net cash flows}\end{array}\right)}{\left(\begin{array}{c}\text{initial}\\\text{cash outlay}\end{array}\right)}$$

$$= \frac{\$75}{\$100} = 0.75$$

Thus, the project should be rejected because its net present value is negative and its profitability index is less than 1.

EXERCISE 2

The present value of a project's future net cash flow is $580, and the initial cash outlay is $500. What is the project's net present value, and what is its profitability index? Should the project be accepted?

SOLUTION

NPV = $580 - $500 = $80

$$PI = = = \frac{\$580}{\$500} = 1.16$$

This project should be accepted because the project's net present value is positive and its profitability index is greater than 1.0.


EXERCISE 3

A project's net present value is $300; the initial outlay is $500. What is the present value of the project's net cash flows?

SOLUTION

NPV = PV of project's net cash flows - initial outlay

$300 = PV of project's net cash flows - $500

$800 = PV of project's net cash flows


EXERCISE 4

A project's profitability index is 1.5, and the present value of its net cash flows is $450. What is the project's initial cash outlay?

SOLUTION

$$PI = \frac{\left(\begin{array}{c}\text{present value of}\\\text{future net cash flows}\end{array}\right)}{\left(\begin{array}{c}\text{initial}\\\text{cash outlay}\end{array}\right)}$$

$$1.5 = \frac{\$450}{X}$$

$$X = \$300$$

EXERCISE 5

If either the net-present-value criterion or the profitability index gives an accept signal, will the other criteria give a similar signal?

SOLUTION

Yes. The net-present-value and profitability index will always give similar accept/reject signals. Any time the present value of future net cash flows is greater than the initial outlay, the net-present-value criterion will be positive, signaling accept, and the profitability index will be greater than 1.0, signaling accept. However, because of size differences in projects, a small project, which is relatively more profitable than a project requiring a larger initial outlay, may have a smaller net present value. In this case, unless there is a limit on the amount of funds that is allocated, the net-present-value criterion should be used.

**B.   Compounding and Discounting:  Single Cash Flows**

To determine the present value of future cash flows, it is necessary to discount those cash flows back to the present. As demonstrated in Chapter 3 of the text, discounting cash flows back to the present is merely the reverse of compounding. For example, if we put $100 (P) in the bank, earning a rate of 10% (i) annually, at the end of 1 year (n) we would have $110 ($FV_1$):

128

$$FV_1 = PV(1 + i)$$

$$\$110 = \$100(1 + 0.10)$$

Correspondingly, at the end of 3 years we would have $133.10:

$$\$133.10 = \$100(1 + 0.10)^3$$

On the other hand, with an opportunity rate of 10%, the present value (PV) of $110 to be received in 1 year can be found as follows:

$$\$110 = \$100(1 + 0.10)$$

$$PV = \$110 \left( \frac{1}{(1 + 0.10)} \right)$$

$$= \$100$$

The present value of $133.10 to be received in 3 years is found similarly:

$$\$100 = \$133.10 \left( \frac{1}{(1 + 0.10)^3} \right)$$

SOLVED PROBLEMS

EXERCISE 1

What is the present value of $300 to be received in 3 years discounted at:

(a)   10% per annum?
(b)   5% per annum?
(c)   100% per annum?

SOLUTION

(a) $PV = FV_n \left( \dfrac{1}{(1+i)^n} \right)$

$\qquad = \$300 \left( \dfrac{1}{(1+0.10)^3} \right)$

$\qquad = \dfrac{\$300}{1.331} = \$225.39$

(b) $PV = \$300 \left( \dfrac{1}{(1+0.05)^3} \right)$

$\qquad = \dfrac{\$300}{1.157625} = \$259.15$

(c) $PV = \$300 \left( \dfrac{1}{(1+01.0)^3} \right)$

$\qquad = \dfrac{\$300}{8} = \$37.50$

EXERCISE 2

If the appropriate discount rate is 8%, what is the present value of $300 to be received in:

(a) 5 years?
(b) 10 years?
(c) 25 years?

SOLUTION

(a) $PV = FV_n \left( \dfrac{1}{(1 + i)^n} \right)$

$\quad\quad = \$300 \left( \dfrac{1}{(1 + 0.08)^5} \right)$

$\quad\quad = \dfrac{\$300}{1.4693} = \$204.18$

(b) $PV = \$300 \left( \dfrac{1}{(1 + 0.08)^{10}} \right)$

$\quad\quad = \dfrac{\$300}{2.15189} = \$138.96$

(c) $PV = \$300 \left( \dfrac{1}{(1 + 0.08)^{25}} \right)$

$\quad\quad = \dfrac{\$300}{6.8485} = \$43.81$

Fortunately, it is not necessary to do the individual calculation for $1/(1 + i)^n$ because, in the table in Appendix C (hereafter referred to as Table C with the table values being referred to as $PVIF_{i,n}$) of the text, the results of these calculations are presented for a large number of combinations of i and n. Thus, in order to determine the value of $1/(1 + 0.08)^5$, we need only look in the row of Table C corresponding to the fifth period and the 8% column to find an appropriate value of 0.681. Similarly, in Appendix B, a table is provided (hereafter referred to as Table B with the table values being referred to as $FVIF_{i,n}$) which gives the value of $(1 + i)^n$ for various combinations of i and n. This table can be used in compounding.

SELF TEST 1

1.  What is the present value of $250 to be received in 10 years if the appropriate discount rate is 8%?

2.  How much must I put in the bank compounded annually at 6% to have $5,000 at the end of 10 years?

3.  If a new machine costs $5,000 and will return $3,000 the first year, $4,000 the second year, $2,000 the third year, and my opportunity rate on money is 8%, what is the project's profitability index?

4.  What is the NPV for the project in question 3? Should it be accepted?

5.  If a new tractor costs $10,000 and will return $3,000 the first year, $5,000 the second year, and $4,000 the third year, calculate the net present value and profitability index using a 10% discount rate. Should the project be accepted?

6.  Calculate the net present value and profitability index for the following. Assume a 12% discount rate:

| Year | Benefit (+) or Cost (-) |
|------|-------------------------|
| 0    | $-8,000                 |
| 1    | +3,000                  |
| 2    | +6,000                  |
| 3    | +2,000                  |
| 4    | +1,000                  |
| 5    | -1,000                  |

7.  What is the net present value of a bond that pays $100 per year in interest at the end of each year for 10 years, and additionally at the end of 10 years will pay the $1,000 par value if the appropriate discount rate is 8% and the bond costs $1,093?

132

## C.  Compounding and Discounting:  Annuities

Problem 7 of Self Test 1 was actually an annuity problem. An annuity is simply a series of fixed payments for a specified number of years. This situation comes up frequently in finance, and in order to make the calculation of the present value of an annuity easier, you are provided with the present value of an annuity table (hereafter referred to as Table E with the table values being referred to as $PVIFA_{i,n}$) in Appendix E of the text, which gives present-value factors for an annuity. In addition, a compound annuity or sum of an annuity of $1 for n periods table (hereafter referred to as Table D with the table values referred to as $FVIFA_{i,n}$) is provided in Appendix D of the text. Now, in order to determine the present value of $1,000 received at the end of each year for 5 years, discounted back to present at 7%, you have two alternatives. You could use Table C and discount each one of the five $1,000 flows individually as follows:

$$FV_n \left( \frac{1}{(1 + 0.07)^1} \right) \quad = \quad \$1,000 \ (0.935) \quad = \quad \$935.00$$

$$FV_n \left( \frac{1}{(1 + 0.07)^2} \right) \quad = \quad \$1,000 \ (0.873) \quad = \quad \$873.00$$

$$FV_n \left( \frac{1}{(1 + 0.07)^3} \right) \quad = \quad \$1,000 \ (0.816) \quad = \quad \$816.00$$

$$FV_n \left( \frac{1}{(1 + 0.07)^4} \right) \quad = \quad \$1,000 \ (0.763) \quad = \quad \$763.00$$

$$FV_n \left( \frac{1}{(1 + 0.07)^5} \right) \quad = \quad \$1,000 \ (0.713) \quad = \quad \underline{\$713.00}$$

$$\underline{\$4,100.00}$$

Alternatively, you could look up the annuity discount factor in Table E. The annuity factor for 5 years at 7% is 4.100; multiplying this times $1,000 gives $4,100—the same answer you obtained using Table C.

This is because you really have only one table, Table C, the values of which have been summed to form Table E. Thus, the annuity discount factor for 5 years at 7% in Table E is equal to the sum of the discount factors for years 1 through 5 at 7% as found in Table C. Therefore, the annuity table value for n years at i% is equal to:

$$PVIFA_{i,n} = \left( \sum_{t=1}^{n} \frac{1}{(1 + i)^t} \right) = \sum_{t=1}^{n} (PVIF_{i,n})$$

SOLVED PROBLEMS

EXERCISE 1

Pick any number in Table E; note the number of years (call it n) and the discount rate (call it i). Now look in Table C and add up the table values in the i discount rate column for the first n years. What do you find?

SOLUTION

The value found in Table E is equal (except perhaps for minor rounding errors) to the value found from summing the values in Table C.

EXERCISE 2

What is the present value of $50 to be received each year for 5 years if the appropriate discount rate is 8%? Solve this problem by using Table C.

SOLUTION

Present value

= $50 (PVIF$_{8\%, \, 1 \, yr.}$) + $50 (PVIF$_{8\%, \, 2 \, yr.}$)
+ $50 (PVIF$_{8\%, \, 3 \, yr.}$) + $50 (PVIF$_{8\%, \, 4 \, yr.}$)
+ $50 (PVIF$_{8\%, \, 5 \, yr.}$)

134

$$= \$50(0.926) + \$50(0.857) + \$50(0.794) + \$50(0.735)$$
$$+ \$50(0.681)$$

$$= \$46.30 + \$42.85 + \$39.70 + \$36.75 + \$34.05$$

$$= \$199.65$$

EXERCISE 3

Solve Exercise 2 using Table E.

SOLUTION

Present value = $\$50(PVIFA_{8\%, \, 5 \, yr.}) = \$50 \, (3.993)$

$$= \$199.65$$

EXERCISE 4

What is the NPV of a bond that yields $80 per year in interest at the end of each year for the next 15 years and matures in 15 years, at which time it pays an additional $1,000; it is currently selling for $800 and your discount rate is 10%?

SOLUTION

$$
\begin{aligned}
NPV &= \$\text{-}800 + \$80(PVIFA_{10\%, \, 15 \, yr.}) \\
&\quad + \$1,000(PVIF_{10\%, \, 15 \, yr.}) \\
&= \$\text{-}800 + \$80(7.606) + \$1,000(0.239) \\
&= \$\text{-}800 + \$608.48 + \$239.00 \\
&= \$47.48
\end{aligned}
$$

EXERCISE 5

What is the profitability index for the bond described in Exercise 4?

SOLUTION

$$PI = \frac{\$847.48}{\$800} = 1.059$$

EXERCISE 6

Given the following cash flows:

| Year | Cash Flow |
|------|-----------|
| 0 | $-10,000 |
| 1 | + 5,000 |
| 2 | + 5,000 |
| 3 | + 5,000 |
| 4 | + 5,000 |
| 5 | + 5,000 |
| 6 | + 5,000 |
| 7 | +10,000 |

What is the NPV of this project given an appropriate discount rate of

(a)    5%?
(b)   10%?
(c)   30%?

SOLUTION

(a) NPV   = $-10,000 + $5,000(PVIFA$_{5\%, \, 6 \text{ yr.}}$)
            + $10,000(PVIF$_{5\%, \, 7 \text{ yr.}}$)

= $-10,000 + $5,000(5.076) + $10,000(0.711)
= $-10,000 + $25,380 + $7,110
= $22,490

(b) NPV $= \$-10{,}000 + \$5{,}000(\text{PVIFA}_{10\%,\ 6\ \text{yr.}})$
$+ \$10{,}000(\text{PVIF}_{10\%,\ 7\ \text{yr.}})$

$= \$-10{,}000 + \$5{,}000(4.355) + \$10{,}000(0.513)$
$= \$-10{,}000 + \$21{,}775 + \$5{,}130$
$= \$16{,}905$

(c) NPV $= \$-10{,}000 + \$5{,}000(\text{PVIFA}_{30\%,\ 6\ \text{yr.}})$
$+\$10{,}000(\text{PVIF}_{30\%,\ 7\ \text{yr.}})$

$= \$-10{,}000 + \$5{,}000(2.643) + \$10{,}000(0.159)$
$= \$-10{,}000 + \$13{,}215 + \$1{,}590$
$= \$4{,}805$

## SELF TEST 2

1.  What is the NPV of the following cash flows if the appropriate discount rate is 20%?

| Year | Cash Flow |
|------|-----------|
| 0 | $-15,000 |
| 1 | + 2,000 |
| 2 | + 2,000 |
| 3 | + 4,000 |
| 4 | + 5,000 |
| 5 | + 6,000 |

What is the profitability index?  Should the project be accepted?

2.  For how many years must $1,000 compound at 8% to accumulate to $2,000?

3.  At what rate must $1,000 compound to accumulate to $3,000 in 7 years?

4.  How much must you put in the bank compounded annually at 8% to accumulate to $3,000 at the end of 10 years?

5. What is the present value of $100 to be received at the end of each of the next 10 years discounted back to the present at

    (a)   5%?
    (b)  10%?
    (c)  20%?
    (d)  30%?

6. How much is $50 worth if it is to be received at the end of 4 years if the appropriate discount rate is

    (a)  10%?
    (b)  20%?
    (c)   0%?
    (d) 100%?

7. What is the future value of $100 if it is placed in the bank for 5 years and compounded at 16%?

    (a)  Annually?
    (b)  Semiannually?
    (c)  Quarterly?

8. A company is examining a new machine to replace an existing machine that currently has a book value of $5,000 and can be sold for $2,000. The old machine has 5 years of expected life left, is being depreciated on a simplified straight-line basis, and will have a salvage value of zero in 5 years. The new machine will perform the same task but more efficiently, resulting in cash benefits before depreciation and taxes of $10,000. The expected life of the new machine is 5 years; it costs $20,000 and has no salvage value at the end of the fifth year. Assuming simplified straight-line depreciation, a 40% tax rate, and an appropriate discount rate of 14%, find the NPV and profitability index of the project.

## II. The Internal-Rate-of-Return Method

In the previous section, we made capital-budgeting decisions through the use of the profitability index and net present-value criteria, by comparing the present value of the benefits of the project with the present value of its costs either through division (determining the profitability index) or subtraction (determining a net present value). In each case, you were supplied with an appropriate discount rate or cost of capital with which to determine the present value of future flows. You will now examine a method of evaluating projects that does not rely on an input discount rate but determines the discount rate that would make the project's NPV = 0, or, alternatively, makes its profitability index = 1.0. With the PI and NPV criteria, we have a measure of the relative profitability and absolute profitability of the project, with all flows adjusted for the time value of money. The next criterion we examine, the internal rate of return, can be thought of as a rate of return or yield on the project. The decision rules on this criterion can be stated as follows: If the IRR is greater than or equal to the required rate of return or hurdle rate, the project should be accepted; otherwise, the project should be rejected. Although this seems quite straightforward and easy to understand, one finds that the solution process is often complex and time-consuming.

## A. The Internal Rate of Return: The Case of a Single Cash Inflow

The internal rate of return is defined as that rate, IRR, which equates the present value of a project's anticipated cash inflows with the present value of the relevant cash outflows. Where $ACF_t$ is the cash flow for period t, whether it be positive (an inflow) or negative (an outflow), and n is the last period in which any cash flow is expected, the internal rate of return is represented by IRR in equation (A.l):

$$\sum_{t=0}^{n} \frac{ACF_t}{(1 + IRR)^t} = 0 \qquad (A.l)$$

A solution to this problem becomes quite simple in the case in which the only outlay occurs in time period 0 (the initial outlay, IO) and *only one* cash inflow occurs, say in time period t:

$$IO = \frac{ACF_t}{(1 + IRR)^t}$$

Since you can determine a numerical value for $IO/ACF_t$ and you know that Table C in the text gives you values for $1/(1 + IRR)$, we can easily solve for IRR. All we have to do is look in Table C in the nth row (corresponding to the number of years until the cash inflow) until we find the value $IO/ACF_t$; the column that gives this value indicates the appropriate value of IRR.

## SOLVED PROBLEMS

## EXERCISE 1

What is the internal rate of return on a project with an initial outlay of $6,000 which in the ninth year will produce one cash inflow of $18,000?

SOLUTION

$$\$6,000 = \frac{\$18,000}{(1 + IRR)^9}$$

$$\frac{\$6,000}{\$18,000} = \frac{1}{(1 + IRR)^9}$$

$$0.333 = \frac{1}{(1 + IRR)^9}$$

The value of 0.333 is found in the 9-year row of Table C in the 13% column; thus, 13% is the project's internal rate of return.

## EXERCISE 2

Given the following cash flows, what is the project's internal rate of return?

| Year | Cash Flow |
|------|-----------|
| 0 | $-10,000 |
| 5 | +40,000 |

SOLUTION

$$\frac{\$10,000}{\$40,000} = \frac{1}{(1 + IRR)^5}$$

$$0.25 = \frac{1}{(1 + IRR)^5}$$

Looking in Table C, IRR = 32%

EXERCISE 3

If a project requires an initial outlay of $6,000 and will return $10,000 in year 13, what is its internal rate of return?

SOLUTION

$$\frac{\$6,000}{\$10,000} = \frac{1}{(1 + IRR)^{13}}$$

$$0.6 = \frac{1}{(1 + IRR)^{13}}$$

Looking in Table C, IRR = 4%

The accept/reject criteria for the internal-rate-of-return method states that if the project's internal rate of return is greater than the required rate of return or hurdle rate, the project should be accepted; otherwise, the project should be rejected. In other words,

IRR $\geq$ required rate of return,    Accept

IRR $<$ required rate of return,    Reject

Thus, if the required rate of return in Exercises 1 through 3 were 10%, the projects examined in Exercises 1 and 2 would be accepted, and the project in Exercise 3 would be rejected.

## B. The Internal Rate of Return: Multiple and Equal Cash Inflows

In the case in which there is more than one cash inflow resulting from a project's acceptance, and the cash inflows form an annuity, a similar approach to that just outlined but using Table E instead of Table C will result in a correct solution. In this case, the simplification proceeds as follows:

$$IO = \sum_{t=0}^{T} \frac{ACF_t}{(1 + IRR)^t}$$

If all the ACF values are equal and occur periodically (e.g., annually),we have an annuity. The value of the annuity discount factor,

$$\sum_{t=0}^{T} 1/(1 + IRR)^t,$$ can be found in Table E. Since we know the term of the annuity, n years, when solving for IRR we need merely look in the T-year row until we find the value $IO/ACF_t$; then looking to the column heading yields the internal rate of return.

SOLVED PROBLEMS

EXERCISE 1

What is the internal rate of return on a project with an initial outlay of $24,000 which will produce cash inflows of $6,000 for each of the next 15 years?

SOLUTION

$$\$24,000 = \sum_{t=0}^{15} \frac{\$6,000}{(1 + IRR)^t}$$

$$4.0 = \sum_{t=0}^{15} \frac{1}{(1 + IRR)^t}$$

Looking in Table E, IRR = 24%.

EXERCISE 2

What is the internal rate of return on a project with an initial outlay of $18,000 which will produce cash inflows of $3,000 for each year for the next 9 years?

SOLUTION

$$\$18,000 = \sum_{t=0}^{9} \frac{\$3,000}{(1 + IRR)^t}$$

$$6.0 = \sum_{t=0}^{9} \frac{1}{(1 + IRR)^t}$$

Looking in Table E, IRR = 9%.

EXERCISE 3

Given the following cash flows, what is this project's internal rate of return?

| Year | Cash Flow |
|------|-----------|
| 0 | $20,000 |
| 1 | 5,000 |
| 2 | 5,000 |
| 3 | 5,000 |
| 4 | 5,000 |
| 5 | 5,000 |

SOLUTION

$$\$20,000 = \sum_{t=0}^{5} \frac{\$5,000}{(1 + IRR)^t}$$

$$4.0 = \sum_{t=0}^{5} \frac{1}{(1 + IRR)^t}$$

Looking in Table E, IRR = 8%.

For Exercises 1 through 3, if the required rate of return were 10%, the project in Exercise 1 would be accepted and the projects in Exercises 2 and 3 would be rejected.

C. The Internal Rate of Return: Multiple and Unequal Cash Flows

The solution using the internal-rate-of-return criterion becomes more complex when there are unequal cash inflows resulting from a project's acceptance. In this case, the solution can be found only by trial and error, or with the use of a good financial calculator, or even a not-so-good calculator. Without the calculator, we first arbitrarily pick a return and solve the problem; then, depending on the result, raise or lower that rate until the present value of the inflows equals the present value of the outflows.

143

SOLVED PROBLEMS

EXERCISE 1

What is the internal rate of return on a project that costs $20,000 and returns $3,000 per year for the first 4 years and $5,000 per year in years 5 through 8?

SOLUTION

$$\$20,000 = \sum_{t=1}^{4} \frac{\$3,000}{(1+.IRR)^t} + \sum_{t=5}^{8} \frac{\$5,000}{(1+IRR)^t}$$

First, solve the problem using a discount rate picked arbitrarily. Try 20%. In this case, this equation reduces to

$$\$20,000 = \$3,000(2.589) + \$7,000(3.837 - 2.589)$$

$$= \$7,767 + \$8,736$$

$$\_\$16,503$$

Thus, 20% is not this project's internal rate of return. If it were the internal rate of return, the present value of the inflows would equal the present value of the outflows; but the present value of the inflows is much less than the present value of the outflows. Since all the inflows occur in the future, the present value of these flows will increase as the discount rate is lowered, so here you should try a lower discount rate. If you try 13%, this equation becomes

$$\$20,000 = \$3,000(2.974) + \$7,000(4.799 - 2.974)$$

$$= \$8,922 + \$21,775$$

$$\_\$21,697$$

This time, the present value of the inflows is less than the present value of the outflows. In order to raise the present value of the inflows, the discount rate must be lowered. This time, try 15%.

$$\$20,000 = \$3,000(2.855) + \$7,000(4.487 - 2.855)$$

$$= \$8,565 + \$11,424$$

$$\approx \$19,989$$

Now, the present value of the inflows is approximately equal to the present value of the outflows using a discount rate of 15%; the project's internal rate of return is very close to 15%.


EXERCISE 2

Given the following cash flows, what is the project's IRR?

| Year | Cash Flow |
|------|-----------|
| 0 | $-12,000 |
| 1 | + 4,000 |
| 2 | + 4,000 |
| 3 | + 4,000 |
| 4 | + 4,000 |
| 5 | + 4,000 |
| 6 | + 2,000 |

SOLUTION

First, try 30%:

$$\$12,000 = \$4,000(2.436) + \$2,000(0.207)$$
$$= \$9,744 + \$414$$
$$\_ \ \$10,158$$

Since the present value of the cash inflows is too low, you must lower the discount rate and try again. This time, try 23%:

$$\$12,000 = \$4,000(2.689) + \$2,000(0.262)$$
$$= \$10,756 + \$524$$
$$\_\ \$11,280$$

Again, the present value of the cash inflows is too low. Therefore, the discount rate is lowered and the problem is tried again. Next, try 20%:

$$\$12,000 = \$4,000(2.991) + \$2,000(0.335)$$
$$= \$11,964 + \$670$$
$$\_\ \$12,634$$

Since the present value of the cash inflows is too high, the discount rate must be raised. We arbitrarily raise it to 23%:

$$\$12,000 = \$4,000(2.803) + \$2,000(0.289)$$
$$= \$11,212 + \$578$$
$$\_\ \$11,790$$

This time, the present value of the inflows is too low; thus, the discount rate is lowered. We now try 22%:

$$\$12,000 = \$4,000(2.864) + \$2,000(0.303)$$
$$= \$11,456 + \$606$$
$$\approx \$12,062$$

Thus, the IRR for this problem is between 22% and 23%, and closer to 22%.

146

EXERCISE 3

What is the IRR associated with this project?

| Year | Cash Flow |
|------|-----------|
| 0 | $-10,000 |
| 1 | + 3,000 |
| 2 | + 6,000 |
| 3 | + 9,000 |

SOLUTION

Try 20%:

$$\$10,000 = \$3,000(0.833) + \$6,000(0.694)$$
$$+ \$9,000 (0.579)$$

$$= \$2,499 + \$4,164 + \$5,211$$

$$\_ \$11,874$$

The present value of the cash inflows is too large; therefore, the discount rate must be raised. Try 30%:

$$\$10,000 = \$3,000(0.769) + \$6,000(0.592)$$
$$+ \$9,000(0.455)$$

$$= \$2,307 + \$3,552 + \$4,095$$

$$\_ \$9,954$$

Now, it is too small; so try 29%:

$$\$10,000 = \$3,000(0.775) + \$6,000(0.601)$$
$$+ \$9,000(0.466)$$

$$= \$2,325 + \$3,606 + \$4,194$$

$$\_ \$10,125$$

Thus, this project's IRR is just under 30%.

As you can see by now, calculating the IRR can become quite time-consuming when a trial-and-error search is necessitated. If it is necessary, remember the following guidelines:

1.  Always try a larger discount rate (or trial IRR) when the present value of the cash inflows is larger than the initial outlay.

2.  Always try a smaller discount rate (or trial IRR) when the present value of the cash inflows is smaller than the initial cash outlay.

SELF TEST 3

1.  What is the internal rate of return on a project that requires an initial outlay of $10,000 and returns $14,000 at the end of the fifth year?

2.  What is the internal rate of return on a project that requires an initial outlay of $700 and returns $1,857 at the end of the twentieth year?

3.  What is the internal rate of return on a project that requires a $30,000 outlay and returns $6,000 at the end of each of the next 10 years?

4.  What is the internal rate of return on a project that requires an initial outlay of $20,000 and returns $3,928 at the end of each year for the next 15 years?

5.  Given the following cash flows, determine an internal rate of return.

| Year | Cash Flow |
| --- | --- |
| 0 | $-40,000 |
| 1 | +10,000 |
| 2 | +10,000 |
| 3 | +10,000 |
| 4 | +10,000 |
| 5 | +10,000 |
| 6 | +15,000 |

6.  Given the following cash flows, determine an internal rate of return.

| Year | Cash Flow |
|------|-----------|
| 0 | $-61,630 |
| 1 | +10,000 |
| 2 | +10,000 |
| 3 | +10,000 |
| 4 | +10,000 |
| 5 | +10,000 |
| 6 | +10,000 |
| 7 | +70,000 |

7.  Given the following cash flows, determine an internal rate of return.

| Year | Cash Flow |
|------|-----------|
| 0 | $-2,992 |
| 1 | +700 |
| 2 | +1,400 |
| 3 | +3,000 |

8.  Given the following cash flows, determine an internal rate of return.

| Year | Cash Flow |
|------|-----------|
| 0 | $5,492 |
| 1 | 2,000 |
| 2 | 2,000 |
| 3 | 4,000 |
| 4 | 3,000 |

9.  What is the internal rate of return on a project that requires an initial outlay of $1,000 and returns $4,000 at the end of the second year?

149

## APPENDIX A

### SELF TEST 1

1.  $\$250(\text{PVIF}_{8\%,\ 10\ \text{yr.}})$

    $\$250(0.463) = \$115.75$

2.  $P = \text{FV}_{10}(\text{PVIF}_{6\%,\ 10\ \text{yr.}})$
    $= \$5,000(.558)$
    $= \$2,790$

3.  $\text{Profitability index} = \dfrac{\left(\begin{array}{c}\text{present value of}\\ \text{future net cash flows}\end{array}\right)}{\left(\begin{array}{c}\text{initial}\\ \text{cash outlay}\end{array}\right)}$

    Present value of future net cash flows

    $= \$3,000\ (\text{PVIF}_{8\%,\ 1\ \text{yr.}}) + \$4,000(\text{PVIF}_{8\%,\ 2\ \text{yr.}})$
    $\quad + \$2,000(\text{PVIF}_{8\%,\ 3\ \text{yr.}})$

    $= \$3,000(0.926) + \$4,000(0.857) + \$2,000(0.794)$

    $= \$2,778 + \$3,428 + \$1,588$

    $= \$7,794$

    Profitability index

    $= \dfrac{\$7,794}{\$5,000} = 1.5588$

4.  $\text{NPV} = \text{PV inflows - PV outflows}$

    $= \$7,794 - \$5,000$

    $= \$2,794$

Accept the project, because its NPV is positive and its PI is greater than 1.0.

5.  NPV $= \$-10{,}000 + \$3{,}000(\text{PVIF}_{10\%,\ 1\ \text{yr.}})$
$$+ \$5{,}000(\text{PVIF}_{10\%,\ 2\ \text{yr.}})$$
$$+ \$4{,}000(\text{PVIF}_{10\%,\ 3\ \text{yr.}})$$

$$= \$-10{,}000 + \$3{,}000(0.909) + \$5{,}000(0.826)$$
$$+ \$4{,}000(0.751)$$

$$= \$-10{,}000 + \$2{,}727 + \$4{,}130 + \$3{,}004$$

$$= \$-139$$

$$\text{PI} = \frac{\$9{,}861}{\$10{,}000} = 0.9861$$

Reject the project, because the NPV is negative and the PI is less than 1.0.

6.  NPV $= \$-8{,}000 + \$3{,}000\ (\text{PVIF}_{12\%,\ 1\ \text{yr.}})$
$$+ \$6{,}000\ (\text{PVIF}_{12\%,\ 2\ \text{yr.}})$$
$$+ \$2{,}000\ (\text{PVIF}_{12\%,\ 3\ \text{yr.}})$$
$$+ \$1{,}000\ (\text{PVIF}_{12\%,\ 4\ \text{yr.}})$$
$$- \$1{,}000\ (\text{PVIF}_{12\%,\ 5\ \text{yr.}})$$

$$= \$-8{,}000 + \$3{,}000(0.893) + \$6{,}000(0.797)$$
$$+ \$2{,}000(0.712) + \$1{,}000(0.636) - \$1{,}000(0.567)$$

$$= \$-8{,}000 + \$2{,}679 + \$4{,}782 + \$1{,}424 + \$636 - \$567$$

$$= \$954$$

$$\text{PI} = \frac{\$8{,}954}{\$8{,}000} = 1.1192$$

7.  NPV $= \$-1{,}093.00 + \$100(\text{PVIF}_{8\%,\ 1\ \text{yr.}}) + \$100(\text{PVIF}_{8\%,\ 2\ \text{yr.}}) +$
$$\$100(\text{PVIF}_{8\%,\ 3\ \text{yr.}}) + \$100(\text{PVIF}_{8\%,\ 4\ \text{yr.}}) + \$100(\text{PVIF}_{8\%,}$$
$$5\ \text{yr.}) + \$100(\text{PVIF}_{8\%,\ 6\ \text{yr.}}) + \$100(\text{PVIF}_{8\%,\ 7\ \text{yr.}}) +$$
$$\$100(\text{PVIF}_{8\%,\ 8\ \text{yr.}}) + \$100(\text{PVIF}_{8\%,\ 9\ \text{yr.}}) +$$
$$\$1{,}100(\text{PVIF}_{8\%,\ 10\ \text{yr.}})$$

$$NPV = \$-1,093.00 + \$100(0.926) + \$100(0.857) + \$100(0.794)$$
$$+ \$100(0.735) + \$100(0.681) + \$100(0.630)$$
$$+ \$100(0.583) + \$100(0.540) + \$100(0.500)$$
$$+ \$1,100(0.463)$$

$$= \$-1,093.00 + \$92.60 + \$85.70 + \$79.48 + \$73.50$$
$$+ \$68.10 + \$63.00 + \$58.30 + \$54.00 + \$50.00$$
$$+ \$509.30$$

$$= \$40.90$$

## SELF TEST 2

1.  $NPV = \$-15,000 + \$2,000(PVIFA_{20\%,\ 2\ yr.}) +$

    $\$4,000(PVIF_{20\%,\ 3\ yr.}) + \$5,000\ (PVIF_{20\%,\ 4\ yr.}) +$

    $\$6,000\ (PVIF_{20\%,\ 5\ yr.})$

    $= \$-15,000 + \$2,000(1.528) + \$4,000(0.579) + \$5,000(0.482)$
    $+ \$6,000(0.402)$

    $= \$-15,000 + \$3,056 + \$2,316 + \$2,410 + \$2,412$

    $= \$-4,806$

    $$PI = \frac{\$10,194}{\$15,000} = 0.6796$$

    The project should be rejected, because its NPV is negative and the PI is less than 1.0.

2.  $\$1,000 = \$2,000(PVIF_{8\%,\ ?\ yr.})$

    $0.500 = (PVIF_{8\%,\ ?\ yr.})$

    The table value in the 8% column comes closest to 0.500 in the 9-year row. Thus, it will take 9 years for $1,000 to accumulate to $2,000 if it is compounded at 8%.

3.  $\$1,000 = \$3,000 \ (\text{PVIF}_{?\%, \ 7 \ yr.})$

    $0.333 = (\text{PVIF}_{?\%, \ 7 \ yr.})$

    The table value in the 7-year row comes closest to 0.333 in the 17% column. Thus, it is necessary to compound $1,000 at 17% for 7 years in order to accumulate $3,000.

4.  $P = \$3,000 \ (\text{PVIF}_{8\%, \ 10 \ yr.})$

    $= \$3,000 \ (0.463)$

    $= \$1,389$

5.
    a.  $P = \$100 \ (\text{PVIFA}_{8\%, \ 10 \ yr.})$

        $= \$100 \ (7.722)$

        $= \$772.20$

    b.  $P = \$100 \ (\text{PVIFA}_{10\%, \ 10 \ yr.})$

        $= \$100(6.145)$
        $= \$614.50$

    c.  $P = \$100 \ (\text{PVIFA}_{20\%, \ 10 \ yr.})$

        $= \$100(4.192)$
        $= \$419.20$

    d.  $P = \$100 \ (\text{PVIFA}_{20\%, \ 10 \ yr.})$

        $= \$100(3.092)$

        $= \$309.20$

6.

a. $P = \$50 \, (\text{PVIF}_{10\%, \, 4 \text{ yr.}})$

   $= \$50 \, (0.683)$

   $= \$34.15$

b. $P = \$50 \, (\text{PVIF}_{20\%, \, 4 \text{ yr.}})$

   $= \$50(0.482)$

   $= \$24.10$

c. $P = \$50 \, \dfrac{1}{(1 + 0)^4}$

   $= \$50 \left(\dfrac{1}{1}\right)$

   $= \$50$

d. $P = \$50 \, \dfrac{1}{(1 + 1.0)^4}$

   $= \$50 \left(\dfrac{1}{16}\right)$

   $= \$3.125$

7.

a. $FV_5 = \$100 \, (\text{FVIF}_{16\%, \, 5 \text{ yr.}})$

   $= \$100 \, (2.100)$
   $= \$210.00$

b. $FV_{10} = \$100 \, (\text{FVIF}_{8\%, \, 10 \text{ yr.}})$

   $= \$100 \, (2.159)$
   $= \$215.90$

c.  $FV_{20} = \$100 \, (FVIF_{4\%, \, 20 \text{ yr.}})$

$= \$100 \, (2.191)$

$= \$219.10$

8.  a.  Initial Outlay

| | |
|---|---:|
| New machine | $-20,000 |
| Sale of old machine | + 2,000 |
| Tax gain | |
| ($5,000 - $2,000) 0.4 | + 1,200 |
| | $-16,800 |

b.  Annual cash flows

| | Book Method | Cash Method |
|---|:---:|:---:|
| Savings | $10,000 | $ 10,000 |
| Change in | | |
|   depreciation | (4,000 - 1,000) | |
| Taxable increase | 7,000 | |
| Taxes | 2,800 | 2,800 |
| | | |
| Annual net cash flow | | $ 7,200 |

c.  Terminal flow:

| | |
|---|---:|
| Annual cash flow | 7,200 |

d.  Cash flow diagram

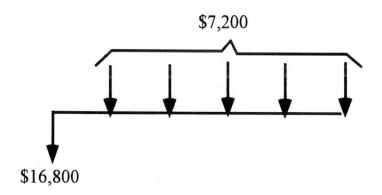

$7,200

$16,800

155

e.  NPV  =   -$16, 800 + $7,200 (PVIFA$_{14\%,\ 5\ yr.}$)

         =   -$16,800 + $7,200 (3.433)

         =   -$16,800 + $24,717.60

         =   $7,917.60

$$PI = \frac{\$24,717.60}{\$16,800} = \ = 1.47$$

## SELF TEST 3

1.  $$\$10,000 = \frac{\$14,000}{(1 + IRR)^5}$$

    $$0.714 = \frac{1}{(1 + IRR)^5}$$

Therefore, IRR = 7% because the Table C value for 5 years closest to 0.714 occurs in the 7% column (0. 713).

2.  $$\$700 = \frac{\$1,857}{(1 + IRR)^{20}}$$

    $$0.377 = \frac{1}{(1 + IRR)^{20}}$$

In Table C, we see that IRR = 5%

3.  $$\$30,000 = \$6,000 \sum_{t=0}^{10} \frac{1}{(1 + IRR)^t}$$

    $$5.0 = \sum_{t=0}^{10} \frac{1}{(1 + IRR)^t}$$

From Table E, IRR = approximately 15%.

4. $$\$20{,}000 = \$3{,}928 \sum_{t=0}^{15} \frac{1}{(1 + \text{IRR})^t}$$

$$5.092 = \sum_{t=0}^{15} \frac{1}{(1 + \text{IRR})^t}$$

From Table E, IRR = 18%.

5. $$\$40{,}000 = \$10{,}000 \sum_{t=1}^{5} \frac{\$1}{(1 + .\text{IRR})^t} + \$15{,}000 \frac{1}{(1 + \text{IRR})^6}$$

Try 20%

$\$40{,}000 = \$10{,}000(2.991) + \$15{,}000(0.335)$
$\qquad\quad = \$29{,}910 + \$5{,}025$
$\qquad\quad \neq \$34{,}935$

Try 15%:

$\$40{,}000 = \$10{,}000(3.352) + \$15{,}000(0.432)$
$\qquad\quad = \$33{,}520 + \$6{,}480$
$\qquad\quad = \$40{,}000$

Thus, 15% is the approximate IRR.

6. $$\$61{,}630 = \$10{,}000 \sum_{t=1}^{6} \frac{\$1}{(1 + .\text{IRR})^t} + \$70{,}000 \frac{1}{(1 + \text{IRR})^7}$$

Try 20%:

$\$61{,}630 = \$10{,}000(3.326) + \$70{,}000(0.279)$

$\qquad\quad = \$33{,}260 + \$19{,}530$

$\qquad\quad \neq \$52{,}790$

Try 15%:

$$\$61,630 = \$10,000(3.784) + \$70,000(0.376)$$

$$= \$37,840 + \$26,320$$

$$\neq \$64,160$$

Try 16%:

$$\$61,630 = \$100,000(3.685) + \$70,000(0.354)$$

$$= \$36,850 + \$24,780$$

$$= \$61,630$$

Therefore, IRR = 16%.

7.  $$\$2,992 = \$700\frac{\$1}{(1 + .IRR)} + \$1,400\frac{1}{(1 + IRR)^2}$$

$$+ \$3,000\frac{1}{(1 + IRR)^3}$$

Try 20%:

$$\$2,992 = \$700(0.833) + \$1,400(0.694) + \$3,000(0.579)$$

$$= \$583.10 + \$971.60 + \$1,737.00$$

$$\neq \$3,291.70$$

Try 25%:

$$\$2,992 = \$700(0.800) + \$1,400(0.640) + \$3,000(0.512)$$

$$= \$560 + \$896 + \$1,536$$

$$= \$2,992$$

Thus, the IRR = 25%.

8.  $$\$5,492 = \$2,000 \sum_{t=1}^{2} \frac{\$1}{(1+.IRR)} + \$4,000 \frac{1}{(1+IRR)^3}$$

$$+ \ \$3,000 \ \frac{1}{(1+IRR)^4}$$

Try 20%:

$$\$5,492 = \$2,000(1.528) + \$4,000(0.579) + \$3,000(0.482)$$

$$= \$3,056 + \$2,316 + \$1,446$$

$$\neq \$6,818$$

Try 30%

$$\$5,492 = \$2,000(1.361) + \$4,000(0.455) + \$3,000(0.350)$$

$$= \$2,722 + \$1,820 + \$1,050$$

$$\neq \$5,592$$

Try 31%

$$\$5,492 = \$2,000(1.346) + \$4,000(0.445) + \$3,000(0.340)$$

$$= \$2,692 + \$1,780 + \$1,020$$

$$= \$5,492$$

Thus, 31% is this project's IRR.

9.  $$\$1,000 = \$4,000 \ \frac{1}{(1+IRR)^2}$$

$$(1+IRR)^2 = 4.0$$

$$1+IRR = \sqrt{4.0}$$

$$1+IRR = 2.0$$

$$IRR = 1.0, \text{ or } IRR = 100\%$$

159

# APPENDIX 9B

# The Internal Rate of Return: An Intuitive Explanation

Contributed by

John T. Rose
Harriette L. and Walter G. Lacy, Jr.
Professors of Banking
Baylor University

This note elaborates on the internal rate of return (IRR) concept in order to make clear the intuition of this concept. To begin, consider a project requiring a net investment outlay of $30,000, with expected net operating cash flows of $10,000 per year for 5 years and an estimated after-tax salvage value of $5,000 at the end of year 5. What then is the annual rate of return, or IRR, on this project?

Initially, you might think the annual return is 33.3% ($10,000/$30,000) for 5 years. However, for that to be true, the firm would have to recover its original $30,000 investment in salvage value at the end of year 5 (analogous to the repayment of principal on a $30,000, 5-year loan at maturity). In the present case, however, the firm expects a salvage value of only $5,000. Thus, in calculating the true annual return, one must recognize not only the stream of annual net operating cash flows from the project but also the fact that the $5,000 salvage value is less than the initial investment of $30,000.

The concept of IRR recognizes all the cash flows associated with a project, including any recovery of invested capital in the form of salvage value at the end of the project's economic life. Technically, the IRR is defined as the discount rate that equates the net investment outlay on a project with the present value of the stream of expected net cash flows (net operating cash flows plus any after-tax salvage value) from the project. In the preceding example, that discount rate is 22.72%. This means the investing firm can expect an annual compound rate of return of 22.72% on its investment for 5 years.

This example is analogous to depositing $30,000 in an investment fund earning an annual rate of 22.72% and then withdrawing $10,000 at the end of each year through year 5 from the remaining principal and accumulated interest. As shown in Table 1, over the 5-year period, such a fund provides the investor a yearly cash flow of $10,000 as part of the annual return of 22.72% on the beginning-of-year fund balance. However, because the annual $10,000 cash withdrawal exceeds the interest earned each year, the fund balance declines each year due to principal draw-downs, to a balance of $5,000 at the end of year 5.

Table 1: Investment Fund Analogy ($30,000 Deposit at Year 0; 22.72% Annual Return; $10,000 Annual Cash Withdrawal through Year 5)

| End of Year t | (A) Earned Interest $[D_{t-1}(0.2272)]$ | (B) Fund Balance Before Cash Withdrawal $(D_{t-1} + A_t)$ | (C) Cash Withdrawal | (D) Fund Balance After Cash Withdrawal $(B_t - C_t)$ | (E) Principal Draw-down $(D_{t-1} - D_t)$ |
|---|---|---|---|---|---|
| 0 | | | | $30,000 | |
| 1 | $6,816 | $36,816 | $10,000 | $26,816 | $3,184 |
| 2 | $6,093 | $32,909 | $10,000 | $22,909 | $3,907 |
| 3 | $5,205 | $28,114 | $10,000 | $18,114 | $4,795 |
| 4 | $4,116 | $22,230 | $10,000 | $12,230 | $5,884 |
| 5 | $2,779 | $15,009 | $10,000 | $ 5,000[1] | $7,221 |

[1]Due to rounding the calculated final balance is not exactly $5,000.

In the case of the investment fund, therefore, the return each year consists of a cash withdrawal less a draw-down of principal. For example, the first-year total return of 22.72% consists of a cash return of $10,000/$30,000 = 33.33% less a principal reduction of $3,184/$30,000 = 10.61%, that is, 33.33% - 10.61% = 22.72%.

Similarly, in the case of the analogous capital budgeting project in which only a portion of the capital investment will be recovered in salvage value, the IRR can be viewed as an annual cash return less a yearly recapture of invested capital. Thus, for the first year, the project total return of 22.72% equals a cash return of $10,000 (33.33%) less a capital recapture of $3,184 (10.61%). Likewise, the second-year return consists of a cash return of $10,000/$26,816 = 37.29% less a capital recapture of $3,907/$26,816 = 14.57%, again totaling 22.72%. The recapture of invested capital as an offset to the annual cash returns on the project is made necessary to the extent that the investing firm does not expect to recover the full investment outlay in salvage value. In that case, the annual returns must be viewed in part as a recapture of the investment (rather than totally as earned income on the investment) over the project's economic life.[1]

Note that by the end of the project's life the initial investment outlay (less any expected salvage value) has been fully recaptured. In this example, the expected salvage value is greater than zero, resulting in a less-than-complete recapture of capital in annual returns over the 5-year life of the project. In the case of a zero salvage value, the calculated IRR would be less than 22.72%. However, the mix of cash return and annual capital recapture would still sum to the IRR each

---

[1]Alternatively, one may characterize the decrease in invested capital each year as an allocation of the investment outlay, that is, an annual expense, offsetting in part the annual cash return on the project. Such allocations are made necessary by the fact that the investing firm does not expect to recover the full investment outlay in salvage value and, thus, must "cost out" the unrecoverable portion of the investment over the project's economic life. This view is consistent with the financial accounting convention of depreciating the asset-cost portion (depreciable basis) of the investment to its anticipated salvage value.

year, with the entire investment outlay recaptured in annual returns by the end of the 5-year project life. Contrariwise, if the salvage value were $30,000, the IRR would be exactly 33.3% since none of the annual cash returns would represent a recapture of the investment. And if the salvage value exceeded $30,000, the IRR would be in excess of 33.3%.

# CHAPTER 10

# Cash Flows and Other Topics
# in Capital Budgeting

Orientation:  Capital budgeting involves the decision-making process with respect to investment in fixed assets; specifically, it involves measuring the incremental cash flows associated with investment proposals and evaluating the attractiveness of these cash flows relative to the project's costs. This chapter focuses on the estimation of those cash flows based on various decision criteria, and how to adjust for the riskiness of a given project or combination of projects.

I.      What criteria should we use in the evaluation of alternative investment proposals?

      A.      Use cash flows rather than accounting profits because cash flows allow us to correctly analyze the time element of the flows.

      B.      Examine cash flows on an after-tax basis because they are the flows available to shareholders.

      C.      Include only the incremental cash flows resulting from the investment decision. Ignore all other flows.

II.     Measure cash flows. We are interested in measuring the incremental after-tax cash flows resulting from the investment proposal. In general, there will be three major sources of cash flows: initial outlays, differential cash flows over the project's life, and terminal cash flows.

      A.      Initial outlays include whatever cash flows are necessary to get the project in running order, for example:

            1.      The installed cost of the asset

2. In the case of a replacement proposal, the selling price of the old machine plus (or minus) any tax gain (or loss) offsetting the initial outlay

3. Any expense items (for example, training) necessary for the operation of the proposal

4. Any other non-expense cash outlays required, such as increased working-capital needs

B. Differential cash flows over the project's life include the incremental after-tax flows over the life of the project, for example:

1. Added revenue (less added selling expenses) for the proposal

2. Any labor and/or material savings incurred

3. Increases in overhead incurred

4. These values are measured on an after-tax basis, thus allowing for the tax savings (or loss) from incremental increase (or decrease) in depreciation to be included.

5. A word of warning not to include financing charges (such as interest or preferred stock dividends), for they are implicitly taken care of in the discounting process.

C. Terminal cash flows include any incremental cash flows that result at the termination of the project; for example:

1. The project's salvage value plus (or minus) any taxable gains or losses associated with the project

2. Any terminal cash flow needed, perhaps disposal of obsolete equipment

3. Recovery of any non-expense cash outlays associated with the project, such as recovery of increased working-capital needs associated with the proposal

III. Risk and the investment decision

    A.    Up to this point, we have treated the expected cash flows resulting from an investment proposal as being known with perfect certainty. We will now introduce risk.

    B.    The riskiness of an investment project is defined as the variability of its cash flows from the expected cash flow.

IV. Incorporating risk into capital budgeting

    A.    The use of the risk-adjusted discount rate is based on the concept that investors demand higher returns for more risky projects.

        1.    If the risk associated with the investment is greater than the risk involved in a typical endeavor, then the discount rate is adjusted upward to compensate for this risk.

        2.    The expected cash flows are then discounted back to present at the risk-adjusted discount rate. Then, the normal capital budgeting criteria are applied, except in the case of the internal rate of return, in which case the hurdle rate to which the project's internal rate of return is compared now becomes the risk-adjusted discount rate.

        3.    Expressed mathematically, the net present value using the risk-adjusted discount rate becomes

$$NPV = \sum_{t=1}^{n} \frac{ACF_t}{(1+k^*)^t} - IO$$

where
$ACF_t$ = the annual after-tax cash flow in time period t
$IO$ = the initial outlay
$k^*$ = the risk-adjusted discount rate
$n$ = the project's expected life

V. Methods for measuring a project's systematic risk

    A. Theoretically, we know that systematic risk is the "priced" risk, and, thus, the risk that affects the stock's market price and, thus, the appropriate risk with which to be concerned. However, if there are bankruptcy costs (which are assumed away by the CAPM), if there are undiversified shareholders who are concerned with more than just systematic risk, if there are factors that affect a security's price beyond what the CAPM suggests, or if we are unable to confidently measure the project's systematic risk, then the project's individual risk carries relevance. Moreover, in general, a project's individual risk, is highly correlated with the project's systematic risk making it a reasonable proxy to use.

    B. In spite of problems in confidently measuring an individual firm's level of systematic risk, if the project appears to be a typical one for the firm, then using the CAPM to determine the appropriate risk-+return tradeoffs and then judging the project against them may be a warranted approach.

    C. If the project is not a typical project, we are without historical data and must either estimate the beta using accounting data or use the pure-play method for estimating beta.

        1. Using historical accounting data to substitute for historical price data in estimating systematic risk: To estimate a project's beta using accounting data, we need run only a time series regression of the division's return on assets on the market index. The regression coefficient from this equation would be the project's accounting beta and serves as an approximation for the project's true beta.

        2. The pure-play method for estimating a project's beta: The pure-play method attempts to find a publicly-traded firm in the same industry as the capital-budgeting project. Once the proxy or pure-play firm is identified, its systematic risk is determined and then used as a proxy for the project's systematic risk.

VI. Examining a project's risk through simulation

   A.   A simulation imitates the performance of the project being evaluated by randomly selecting observations from each of the distributions that affect the outcome of the project, combining those observations to determine the final output of the final project, and continuing with this process until a representative record of the project's probable outcome is assembled.

        1.   The firm's management then examines the resultant probability distribution, and, if management considers enough of the distribution lies above the normal cutoff criterion, it will accept the project.

        2.   The use of a simulation approach to analyze investment proposals offers two major advantages:

             a.   The financial managers are able to examine and base their decisions on the whole range of possible outcomes rather than just point estimates.

             b.   They can undertake subsequent sensitivity analysis of the project.

## Study Problems

1.   The R. T. Kleinman Corporation is considering selling one of its old assembly machines. The machine, purchased for $40,000 five years ago, had an expected life of 10 years and an expected salvage value of 0. Assume Kleinman uses simplified straight-line depreciation, creating depreciation of $4,000 per year, and could sell this old machine for $45,000. Also assume a 34% marginal tax rate.

     a.   What would be the taxes associated with this sale?

     b.   If the old machine were sold for $40,000, what would be the taxes associated with this sale?

     c.   If the old machine were sold for $20,000, what would be the taxes associated with this sale?

     d.   If the old machine were sold for $17,000, what would be the taxes associated with this sale?

SOLUTION

a.   Tax payments associated with the sale for $45,000:
     Recapture of depreciation
         = ($45,000-$20,000) (0.34) = $8,500

b.   Tax payments associated with sale for $40,000:
     Recapture of depreciation
         = ($40,000-$20,000) (0.34) = $6,800

c.   No taxes, because the machine would have been sold for its book value.

d.   Tax savings from sale below book value:
     Tax savings = ($20,000-$17,000) (0.34) = $1,020

2.   The G. Wolfe Corporation is considering replacing one of its bottling machines with a new, more efficient one. The old machine presently has a book value of $75,000 and could be sold for $60,000. The old machine is being depreciated using a simplified straight-line method down to 0 over the next 5 years generating depreciation of $15,000 per year. The replacement machine would cost $250,000, and have an expected life of 5 years after which it could be sold for $20,000. Because of reductions in defects and materials savings, the new machine would produce cash benefits of $100,000 per year before depreciation and taxes. Assume simplified straight-line depreciation, a 40% marginal tax rate, and a required rate of return of 18%, find:

a.   the payback period.
b.   the net present value.
c.   the profitability index.

SOLUTION

Initial Outlay

| | |
|---|---|
| Outflows: | |
|    Purchase price | $250,000 |
| Inflows: | |
|    Tax savings from sale of old | |
|    machine below book value | |
|    ($75,000 - $60,000) x .40 | - 6,000 |
|    Salvage value on old machine | -60,000 |
|             Net initial outlay | $184,000 |

Differential Annual Cash Flows  (Years 1-4)

| Savings: | *Book Profit* | *Cash* |
|---|---|---|
| *Flow* | | |
| Cash savings | $100,000 | $100,000 |
| Costs: | | |
| Increased depreciation | -35,000 | |
| ($50,000 - $15,000)* | | |
| Net savings before taxes | $ 65,000 | $100,000 |
| Taxes  (40%) | -26,000 ⟶ | -26,000 |
| | | $  74,000 |

*Note:  Annual depreciation on the new machine was calculated by taking the purchase price ($250,000) and dividing by the expected life (5 years).

Terminal Cash Flow (Year 5)

| Inflows: | |
|---|---|
| Differential cash flow | |
| Year 5 | $ 74,000 |
| Salvage value | 20,000 |
| Outflows: | |
| Taxes due on sale of new machine | |
| ($20,000 - 0)  x  .40 | -8,000 |
| | $ 86,000 |

a.   Payback period $= \dfrac{\$184,000}{\$74,000} = $ 2.49 years

b.   Net present value $= \displaystyle\sum_{t=1}^{4} \dfrac{\$74,000}{(1+.18)^t} + \dfrac{\$86,000}{(1+.18)^5} - \$184,000$

   $= \$74,000(2.690) + \$86,000(.437) - \$184,000$

   $= \$201,750 + \$37,582 - \$184,000 = \$55,332$

c.   The profitability index $= 1.3$

3.   El Gato's Motors is considering the purchase of a new production machine for $1,000,000. Although the purchase of this machine will not produce any increase in sales revenues, it will result in a before-tax reduction of labor costs by $400,000 per year. To operate this machine properly, workers would have to go through a brief training session that would cost $100,000.

In addition, it would cost $50,000 to install this machine properly. Also, because this machine is extremely efficient, its purchase would necessitate an increase in inventory of $150,000. This machine has an expected life of 10 years, after which it will have no salvage value. Assume simplified straight-line depreciation and that this machine is being depreciated down to zero, a 34% marginal tax rate, and a required rate of return of 12%:

a.      What is the initial outlay associated with this project?

b.      What are the annual after-tax cash flows associated with this project, for years 1 through 9?

c.      What is the terminal cash flow in year 10 (i.e., what is the annual after-tax cash flow in year 10 plus any additional cash flows associated with termination of the project)?

d.      Should this machine be purchased?


SOLUTION

a.    Initial Outlay

    Outflows:

| | |
|---|---:|
| Purchase price | $ 1,000,000 |
| Installation fee | 50,000 |
| Training session fee | 100,000 |
| Increased inventory | 150,000 |
| Net Initial outlay | $1,360,000 |

b.    Differential annual cash flows (years 1-9)

| | *Book Profit* | *Cash Flow* |
|---|---:|---:|
| Savings: | | |
| Reduction in labor costs | $400,000 | $400,000 |
| | | |
| Costs: | | |
| Increased Depreciation* | 105,000 | |
| Net savings before taxes | $295,000 | $400,000 |
| Taxes (.34) | 103,000 ⟶ | 103,000 |
| Annual net cash flow after taxes | | $297,000 |

*Annual Depreciation on the new machine is calculated by taking the purchase price ($1,000,000) and adding in costs necessary to get the new machine in operating order (the installation fee of $50,000) and dividing by the expected life.

c.   Terminal Cash flow (year 10)

    Inflows:

| | |
|---|---:|
| Differential flow in year 10 | $297,000 |
| Recapture of working capital (inventory) | 150,000 |
|     Total terminal cash flow | $447,000 |

d.   NPV  = $\$297,000 \, (PVIFA_{12\%,9 \, yr.}) + \$447,000 \, (PVIF_{12\%, 10 \, yr.})$
             - \$1,360,000

          =  $297,000 (5.328) + $447,000 (.322) - $1,360,000

          =  $1,582,416 + $143,934 - $1,360,000

          =  $336,350

4.   The Taiheiyo Chemical Corporation is considering replacing a 5-year-old machine that originally cost $50,000, presently has a book value of $25,000, and could be sold for $60,000. This machine is currently being depreciated using the simplified straight-line method down to a terminal value of zero over the next 5 years, generating depreciation of $5,000 per year. The replacement machine would cost $100,000 and have a 5-year expected life over which it would be depreciated down using the simplified straight-line method and have no salvage value at the end of 5 years. The new machine would produce savings before depreciation and taxes of $35,000 per year. Assuming a 34% marginal tax rate and a required rate of return of 10%, calculate:

a.   The payback period

b.   The net present value

c.   The profitability index

d.   The internal rate of return

    SOLUTION

    Initial outlay:

    Outflows:

| | |
|---|---:|
| Purchase price | $100,000 |
| Recapture of depreciation | |
| ($60,000 - $25,000) (0.34) | 11,900 |
| Total outflows | $111,900 |

Inflows:

|  |  |  |
|---|---|---|
| Salvage value of old machine | | - 60,000 |
| Net initial outlay | | $ 51,900 |

| Differential annual cash flows (years 1-4) | Book profit | Cash flow |
|---|---|---|
| Cash savings | $ 35,000 | $ 35,000 |
| Increased depreciation ($25,000-$5,000) | - 15,000 | |
| Net savings before taxes | $ 20,000 | $ 35,000 |
| Taxes (34%) | - 6,800 ➔ | - 6,800 |
| Annual net cash flow after taxes | | $ 28,200 |

| Terminal cash flow (year 5) | |
|---|---|
| Differential cash flow year 5 | $ 28,200 |
| Salvage value | 0 |
| Total terminal cash flow | $ 28,200 |

a.  Payback period = 1.84 years

b.  $$\text{NPV} = \sum_{t=1}^{5} \frac{\$28,200}{(1 + 0.10)^t} - \$51,900$$

$$= \$28,200 \,(3.791) - \$51,900$$

$$= \$106,906 - \$51,900$$

$$= \$55,006$$

c.  $$\text{PI} = \frac{\$106,906}{\$51,900}$$

$$= 2.06$$

d.  $$\$51,900 = \$28,200\,[\text{PVIFA}_{\text{IRR}\%,5\text{ yrs}}]$$

$$1.8404 = \text{PVIFA}_{\text{IRR}\%,5\text{ yrs}}$$

Thus, IRR is over 40% (actually, it is 46.20%).

5.  A firm is considering introducing a new product that has an expected life of 5 years. Since this product is much riskier than a typical project for this firm, the management feels that the normal required rate of return of 12% is not sufficient; instead, the minimally acceptable rate of return on this project should be 20%. The initial outlay would be $100,000 and the expected cash flows from this project are as given below:

| Year | Expected Cash Flow |
|:---:|:---:|
| 1 | $40,000 |
| 2 | 40,000 |
| 3 | 40,000 |
| 4 | 40,000 |
| 5 | 40,000 |

Should this project be accepted?

SOLUTION

Discounting this annuity back to present at 20% yields a present value of the future cash flows of $119,640. Since the initial outlay on this project is $100,000, the net present value becomes $19,640. The project should be accepted.

## Self Tests

## TRUE-FALSE

____  1.  Cash flow, not income, is what is important in capital budgeting.

____  2.  One way of evaluating risky projects is by discounting the expected cash flows at a risk-adjusted discount rate.

____  3.  The interest payments should be subtracted from the cash flows in evaluating projects financed with debt.

____  4.  While depreciation is not a cash flow item, it affects taxes which are a cash flow item.

____  5.  Any changes in inventory or working capital need not be considered in capital budgeting because these cash flows never leave the firm.

____  6.  Other things held constant, the use of accelerated depreciation causes profits to be less in the earlier years; therefore, taxes are lower in the earlier years, and, thus, cash flows are higher in the earlier years.

____  7.  The use of risk-adjusted discount rates is based on the concept that investors require a higher rate of return for more risky projects.

_____ 8. As the salvage value of the equipment being replaced increases, all else held constant, the net present value of the project will increase.

MULTIPLE CHOICE

1. Which of the following is not a method for adjusting for or measuring risk in capital budgeting?

   a. Simulation
   b. Risk-adjusted discount rate
   c. Inverse profitability index

2. An investment project will be more desirable

   a. the smaller the standard deviation.
   b. the less positive its correlations with existing average cash flows.
   c. the larger the coefficient of variation of its cash flow.
   d. a and b.

3. Which of the following is important to capital budgeting decisions?

   a. Depreciation method
   b. Salvage value
   c. Timing of cash flows
   d. Taxes
   e. All of the above

4. If the federal income tax rate were increased, the result would be to

   a. decrease the net present value.
   b. increase the net present value.
   c. increase the payback period.
   d. a and c.

# CHAPTER 11

# Cost of Capital

Orientation: In Chapters 6 and 7, we considered the valuation of debt and equity instruments. The concepts advanced there serve as a foundation for determining the required rate of return for the firm and for specific investment projects. The objective in this chapter is to determine the required rate of return to be used in evaluating investment projects.

I.      The concept of the cost of capital

      A.      Defining the cost of capital:

            1.      The rate that must be earned in order to satisfy the required rate of return of the firm's investors.

            2.      The rate of return on investments at which the price of a firm's common stock will remain unchanged.

      B.      Type of investors and the cost of capital

            1.      Each type of capital used by the firm (debt, preferred stock, and common stock) should be incorporated into the cost of capital, with the relative importance of a particular source being based on the percentage of the financing provided by each source of capital.

            2.      Using the cost of a single source of capital as the hurdle rate is tempting to management, particularly when an investment is financed entirely by debt. However, doing so is a mistake in logic and will result in the use of a hurdle rate that is too low.

II.    Factors determining the cost of capital

    A.    General economic conditions. These include the demand for and supply of capital within the economy, and the level of expected inflation. These are reflected in the riskless rate of return.

    B.    Market conditions. The security may not be readily marketable when the investor wants to sell; or even if a continuous demand for the security does exist, the price may vary significantly.

    C.    A firm's operating and financing decisions. Risk also results from the decisions made within the company. This risk is generally divided into two classes:

        1.    Business risk refers to the variability in returns on assets and is a direct consequence of the company's investment decisions.

        2.    Financial risk refers to the increased variability in returns to the common stockholders as a result of using debt and preferred stock financing.

    D.    In summary, as the level of risk rises, a larger risk premium must be earned to satisfy a firm's investors.

III.    Computing the weighted cost of capital. A firm's weighted cost of capital is a function of (1) the individual costs of capital and (2) the capital structure mix.

    A.    Determining individual costs of capital

        1.    The *before-tax cost of debt* is found by solving for $k_d$ in

$$NP_0 = \sum_{t=1}^{n} \frac{\$I_t}{(1+k_d)^t} + \frac{\$M}{(1+k_d)^N}$$

where $NP_0$ = the market price of the debt, less flotation costs,

$\$I_t$ = the annual dollar interest paid to the investor each year,

$\$M$ = the maturity value of the debt

$k_d$ = before-tax cost of the debt (before-tax required rate of return on debt)

$N$ = the number of years to maturity.

The *after-tax cost of debt* is then calculated using

$$k_d(1 - t)$$

where $T_c$ = the corporation's *marginal* tax rate

2. Cost of preferred stock (required rate of return on preferred stock), $K_p$, equals the dividend yield based upon the net price (market price less flotation costs) or

$$K_p = \frac{\text{dividend}}{\text{net price}} = \frac{D}{NP_0}$$

3. Cost of common stock. There are three measurement techniques to obtain the required rate of return on common stock.

   a. dividend-growth model
   b. capital asset pricing model
   c. risk-premium approach

4. Dividend-growth model

   a. Cost of internally generated common equity, $K_c$

$$K_c = \frac{\text{dividend in year 1}}{\text{market price}} + \left(\begin{array}{c}\text{annual growth}\\\text{in dividends}\end{array}\right)$$

$$K_c = \frac{D_1}{P_0} + g$$

b. Cost of new common stock, $K_{ns}$

$$K_{ns} = \frac{D_1}{NP_0} + g$$

where $NP_0$ = the market price of the common stock less flotation costs incurred in issuing new shares.

5. Capital asset pricing model

$$K_c = R_f + b(K_m - K_{rf})$$

where $K_c$ = the cost of common stock
$K_{rf}$ = the risk-free rate
$b$ = beta, measure of the stock's systematic risk
$K_m$ = the expected rate of return on the market

6. It is important to notice that the major difference between the equations presented here and the equations from Chapter 7 is that the _firm_ must recognize the flotation costs incurred in issuing the security.

B. Selection of weights. The individual costs of capital will be different for each source of capital in the firm's capital structure. To use the cost of capital in investment analyses, we must compute a weighted or overall cost of capital.

1. It will be assumed that the company's current financial mix resulting from the financing of previous investments is relatively stable and that these weights will closely approximate future financing patterns.

2. In computing weights, we can use either the current market values of the firm's securities or the book values as shown in the balance sheet. Since we will be issuing new securities at their _current_ market value and not at book (historical) values, we should use the market value of the securities in calculating our weights.

IV.    PepsiCo approach to weighted average cost of capital

    A.    PepsiCo calculates the divisional cost of capital for its snack, beverage, and restaurant organizations by first finding peer-group firms for each division and using their average betas, after adjusting for differences in financial leverage, to compute the division's cost of equity. They also use accounting betas in estimating the cost of equity. They then compute the cost of debt for each division. Finally, they calculate a weighted cost of capital for each division.

    B.    PepsiCo's WACC basic computation

$$k_{wacc} = k_c \left(\frac{E}{D+E}\right) + k_d[1\text{-}T_c]\left(\frac{D}{D+E}\right)$$

where:

| | | |
|---|---|---|
| $k_{wacc}$ | = | the weighted average cost of capital |
| $k_c$ | = | the cost of equity capital |
| $k_d$ | = | the before-tax cost of debt capital |
| $T_c$ | = | the marginal tax rate |
| E/(D+E) | = | percentage of financing from equity |
| D/(D+E) | = | percentage of financing from debt |

    C.    Calculating the cost of equity

Based on capital assets pricing model:

$$k_c = k_{rf} + b(k_m - k_{rf})$$

where $k_c$ = the cost of common stock
$k_{rf}$ = the risk-free rate
b = beta, measure of the stock's systematic risk
$k_m$ = the expected rate of return on the market

Betas for each division are estimated by calculating an average un-levered beta from a group of divisional peers.

The average beta for each division's peer group is unlevered and then re-levered using that division's target debt-to-equity ratio.

D.    Calculating the cost of debt

The after-tax cost of debt is equal to:

$k_d (1 - T_c)$

where:

$k_d$        =        before-tax cost of debt

$T_c$        =        marginal tax rate

## Study Problems

1.  A $1,000 par-value bond will sell in the market for $1,072 and carries a coupon interest rate of 9%. Issuance costs will be 7.5%. The number of years to maturity is 15, and the firm's tax rate is 46%. What is the after-tax cost for this security ($K_d$)?

SOLUTION

$$\$1,072(1 - 0.075) \text{ or } \$991.60 = \sum_{t=1}^{15} \frac{\$90}{(1 + k_d)^t} + \frac{\$1,000}{(1 + k_d)^t}$$

Try 10%: $923.54  =  $90(7.606) + $1,000(0.239).
Try  9%: $1,000   =  $90(8.061) + $1,000(0.275).

| 9% | $1,000.00 | | |
| | $991.60 | $8.40 | $76.46   ($1,000.00 - $923.54) |
| 10% | $923.54 | | |

$$k_d = 0.09 + \frac{\$8.40}{\$76.46} (0.01) = .0911 = 9.11\%$$

$$k_d = 9.11\%(1 - 0.46) = 4.92\%$$

2.  The current market price of ABC Company's common stock is $32.50. The firm expects to pay a dividend of $1.90, and the growth rate is projected to be 7% annually. The company is in a 40% tax bracket. Flotation costs would be 6% if new stock were issued. What is the cost of (a) internal and (b) external common equity?

SOLUTION

Let $K_c$ = cost of internal common
$K_{ns}$ = cost of external (new) common
$D_1$ = next dividend to be paid
$P_o$ = market price
$g$ = growth rate
$NP_o$ = market price less flotation costs

a.  $K_c = \dfrac{D_1}{P_o} + g$

$K_c = \dfrac{\$1.90}{\$32.50} + 0.07 = 12.85\%$

b.  $K_{ns} = \dfrac{D_1}{NP_o} + g$

$K_{ns} = \dfrac{\$1.90}{\$32.50(1 - 0.06)} + 0.07 = 13.22\%$

3.  Pharr, Inc.'s preferred stock pays a 16% dividend. The stock is selling for $62.75, and its par value is $40. Issuance costs are 5% and the firm's tax rate is 46%. What is the cost of this source of financing?

SOLUTION

$K_p = \dfrac{D}{NP_o}$

$K_p = \dfrac{\$40(0.16)}{\$62.75(1 - 0.05)} = \dfrac{\$6.40}{\$59.61} = 10.74\%$

4. The current capital structure of Smithhart, Inc. is as follows:

| | | |
|---|---|---|
| Bonds (7%, $1,000 par, 15 years) | | $ 750,000 |
| Preferred stock ($100 par, 7.25% dividend) | | 1,000,000 |

Common stock:
| | | |
|---|---|---|
| Par value ($2.50 par) | $500,000 | |
| Retained earnings | 350,000 | 850,000 |
| Total | | $2,600,000 |

The market price is $975 for the bonds, $60 for the preferred stock, and $21 for common stocks. Flotation costs are 9% for bonds and 5 percent for preferred stock. The firm's tax rate is 46%. Common stock will pay a $2.80 dividend which is not expected to grow. What is the weighted cost of capital using only internal common equity?

SOLUTION

| Source of Financing | Market Value | Weight |
|---|---|---|
| Bonds | $731,250[1] | 13.22% |
| Preferred stock | 600,000[2] | 10.85% |
| Common stock | 4,200,000[3] | 75.93% |
| | $5,531,250 | 100.00% |

[1] 750 bonds at $975 value each

[2] 10, 000 shares at $60 value each

[3] 200, 000 shares at $21 value each

Cost of debt

$$\$975(1 - 0.09) \text{ or } \$887.25 = \sum_{t=1}^{15} \frac{\$70}{(1 + k_d)}t + \frac{\$1,000}{(1 + k_d)}15$$

Using a financial calculator, $k_d$ equals 8.35%

$$K_d = 8.35\% \ (1 - 0.46)$$

$$K_d = 4.51\%$$

## Cost of preferred stock

$$K_p = \frac{\$7.25}{\$60\,(1 - 0.05)} = 12.72\%$$

## Cost of internal common equity

$$K_c = \frac{\$2.80}{\$21} + 0 = 13.33\%$$

## Weighted Cost of Capital

| Source of Financing | Cost | Weight | Weighted Costs |
|---|---|---|---|
| Bonds | 4.51% | .1322 | 0.596% |
| Preferred stock | 12.72 | .1085 | 1.381 |
| Common stock | 13.33 | .7593 | 10.124 |
| | | | 12.101% |

## Self Tests

### TRUE-FALSE

_____ 1. The cost of capital is defined as the rate of return on investments which increases the price of the firm's common stock.

_____ 2. The level of expected inflation is reflected in the risk premium.

_____ 3. The cost of capital is an appropriate investment criterion only for investments of similar risk level to the existing assets.

_____ 4. Financial risk is the risk that the price of the security may vary significantly.

_____ 5. Only those projects exceeding the cost of capital on a cost-of-capital curve should be accepted.

_____ 6. The cost of preferred stock must be adjusted for taxes.

_____ 7. In computing a weighted cost of capital, we generally assume that the company's current capital structure will not change.

_____ 8. New common stock would be issued only if internal common equity does not provide sufficient equity capital for the amount of investments under consideration.

_____ 9. The capital asset pricing model (CAPM) is based on estimates of three values: The risk-free rate, the firm's beta coefficient, and the market risk premium.

_____ 10. Beta measures the volatility of the project returns relative to the investor's widely diversified portfolio.


MULTIPLE CHOICE

1. What is/are the reason(s) for computing a firm's cost of capital?

    a. To determine the firm's future financing needs
    b. To assure the investors that their required rate of return is being met
    c. To use the cost of capital as an investment criterion
    d. b and c
    e. a and c
    f. a, b, and c

2. The cost of capital can be defined as

    a. the rate that must be earned in order to satisfy the required rate of return of the firm's investors.
    b. the rate of return on investments at which the price of the firm's common stock remains unchanged.
    c. the rate of return on investments which will increase the price of the firm's common stock.
    d. a and b.
    e. a and c.

3. All of the following variables are needed in the computation of the cost of debt *except*

    a. market price of debt.
    b. issuance cost.
    c. tax rate for the firm.
    d. growth rate.
    e. maturity value.

4. Adjustment for taxes is required for which cost?

   a. Cost of preferred stock
   b. Cost of debt
   c. Cost of common equity
   d. None of the above

5. Which of the following is a limitation of the return-risk equation?

   a. The assumption of no bankruptcy risk
   b. The requirement that the existing financial mix remains constant
   c. The standardization of the risk premium relative to the riskiness of the firm's average project
   d. None of the above

6. An investment with a beta of 0.80 means that the returns of the investment

   a. are more volatile than the market returns.
   b. are less volatile than the market returns.
   c. have no correlation with the market returns.
   d. are perfectly correlated with the market returns.

# CHAPTER 12

# Determining
# the Financing Mix

Orientation: This chapter focuses on useful aids to the financial manager in his or her determination of the firm's proper financial structure. It includes the definitions of the different kinds of risk, a review of break-even analysis, the concepts of operating leverage, financial leverage, the combination of both leverages, and their effect on EPS (earnings per share). Then the chapter concentrates on the way the firm arranges its sources of funds. The cost of capital-capital structure argument is highlighted in a straightforward manner without dwelling excessively on pure theory. A moderate view of the effect of financial leverage on the firm's overall cost of capital is highlighted and explained. Later, techniques useful to the financial officer faced with the determination of an appropriate financing mix are described. Agency theory and the concept of free cash flow as they relate to capital structure determination are also discussed. An overview of actual practice is also included.

I.     Business risk and financial risk

     A.     Risk has been defined as the likely variability associated with expected revenue streams.

          1.     Focusing on the financial decision, the variations in the income stream can be attributed to:

               a.     The firm's exposure to business risk.

               b.     The firm's decision to incur financial risk.

B.   Business risk can be defined as the variability of the firm's expected earnings before interest and taxes (EBIT).

      1.   Business risk is measured by the firm's corresponding expected coefficient of variation (i.e., the larger the ratio, the more risk a firm is exposed to).

      2.   Dispersion in operating income does not cause business risk. It is the result of several influences, for example, the company's cost structure, product demand characteristics, and intra-industry competition. These influences are a direct result of the firm's investment decision.

C.   Financial risk is a direct result of the firm's financing decision. When the firm is selecting different financial alternatives, financial risk refers to the additional variability in earnings available to the firm's common shareholders and the additional chance of insolvency borne by the common shareholder caused by the use of financial leverage.

      1.   Financial leverage is the financing of a portion of the firm's assets with securities bearing a fixed (limited) rate of return in hopes of increasing the ultimate return to the common shareholders.

      2.   Financial risk, is to a large extent, passed on to the common shareholders who must bear almost all of the potential inconsistencies of returns to the firm after the deduction of fixed payments.

II.   Break-even analysis

A.   The objective of break-even analysis is to determine the break-even quantity of output by studying the relationships among the firm's cost structure, volume of output, and operating profit.

      1.   The break-even quantity of output is the quantity of output (in units) that results in an EBIT level equal to zero.

B.   Use of the model enables the financial officer to:

      1.   Determine the quantity of output that must be sold to cover all operating costs.

2. Calculate the EBIT that will be achieved at various output levels.

C. Some actual and potential applications of break-even analysis include:

1. Capital expenditure analysis as a complementary technique to discounted cash flow evaluation models.

2. Pricing policy.

3. Labor contract negotiations.

4. Evaluation of cost structure.

5. The making of financial decisions.

D. Essential elements of the break-even model are:

1. Fixed costs are costs that do not vary in total amount as the sales volume or the quantity of output changes over some relevant range of output. For example, administrative salaries are considered fixed because these salaries are generally the same month after month. Other examples are:

a. Depreciation.

b. Insurance premiums.

c. Property taxes.

d. Rent.

The total fixed cost is unchanged regardless of the quantity of product output or sales, although, over some relevant range, these costs may be higher or lower (i.e., in the long run).

2. Variable costs are costs that tend to vary in total as output changes. Variable costs are fixed per unit of output. For example, direct materials are considered a variable cost because they vary with the amount of products produced. Other variable costs are:

   a. Direct labor.

   b. Energy cost associated with the production area.

   c. Packaging.

   d. Freight-out.

   e. Sales commissions.

3. To implement the behavior of the break-even model, it is necessary for the financial manager to:

   a. Identify the most relevant output range for his or her planning purposes.

   b. Approximate all costs in the semifixed, semivariable range and allocate them to the fixed and variable cost categories.

4. Total revenue and volume of output

   a. Total revenue from sales is equal to the price per unit multiplied by the quantity sold.

   b. The volume of output is the firm's level from operations and is expressed as sales dollars or a unit quantity.

E.   Finding the break-even point

1.   The break-even model is just a simple adaptation of the firm's income statement expressed in the following format:

sales - (total variable costs + total fixed costs) = profit

   a.   Trial and error

      (1)   Select an arbitrary output level.

      (2)   Calculate the corresponding EBIT amount.

      (3)   When EBIT equals zero, the break-even point has been found.

   b.   Contribution margin analysis

      (1)   The difference between the unit selling price and the unit variable cost equals the contribution margin.

      (2)   Then, the fixed cost divided by the contribution margin equals the break-even quantity in units.

   c.   Algebraic analysis

      (1)   $Q_B$ = the break-even level of units sold,
            P   = the unit sales price,
            F   = the total fixed cost for the period,
            V   = unit variable cost.

      (2)   Then,

$$Q_B = \frac{F}{P - V}$$

F. The break-even point in sales dollars:

    1.    Computing a break-even point in terms of sales dollars rather than units of output is convenient, especially if the firm deals with more than one product. Also, if the analyst cannot get unit cost data, he or she can compute a general break-even point in sales dollars by using the firm's annual report.

    2.    Since variable cost per unit and the selling price per unit are assumed constant, the ratio of total sales to total variable costs (VC/S) is a constant for any level of sales. So, if the break-even level of sales is denoted S*, the corresponding equation is:

$$S^* = \frac{F}{1 - \frac{VC}{S}}$$

G. Limitations of break-even analysis:

    1.    The cost-volume-profit relationship is assumed to be linear.

    2.    The total revenue curve is presumed to increase linearly with the volume of output.

    3.    A constant production and sales mix is assumed.

    4.    The break-even computation is a static form of analysis.

III. Operating Leverage

A. Operating leverage is the responsiveness of a firm's EBIT to fluctuations in sales. Operating leverage results when fixed operating costs are present in the firm's cost structure. It should be noted here that fixed operating costs do *not* include interest charges incurred from the firm's use of debt financing.

B.   The responsiveness of a firm's EBIT to fluctuating sales levels can be measured as follows:

$$\left(\begin{array}{c} \text{degree of operating} \\ \text{leverage from the} \\ \text{base sales level} \end{array}\right) = DOL_S = \frac{\% \text{ change in EBIT}}{\% \text{ change in sales}}$$

for example, if $DOL_S$ equals five times, a 10% rise in sales over the coming period will result in a 50% rise in EBIT. (This means of measure also holds true for the negative direction.)

C.   If unit costs are available, the $DOL_S$ can be measured by the following formula:

$$DOL_S = \frac{Q(P - V)}{Q(P - V) - F}$$

D.   If an analytical income statement is the only thing available, the following formula can be used to produce the same results:

$$DOL_S = \frac{\text{revenue before fixed costs}}{EBIT} = \frac{S - VC}{S - VC - F}$$

E.   It should be noted here that the three formulas stated above all produce the same results. But, more important is the understanding that, in this example, a 1% change in sales will result in a 5% change in EBIT.

F.   Implications of operating leverage:

1.   At each point above the break-even, level the degree of operating leverage decreases (i.e., the greater the sales level, the lower the $DOL_S$) .

2.   At the break-even level of sales, the degree of operating leverage is undefined.

3.   Operating leverage is present anytime the percentage change in EBIT divided by the percentage change in sales is greater than one.

4.   The degree of operating leverage can be attributed to the business risk that a firm faces.

195

IV. Financial leverage

A. Financial leverage, as defined earlier, is the practice of financing a portion of the firm's assets with securities bearing a fixed rate of return in hopes of increasing the ultimate return to the common stockholders. To see if financial leverage has been used to benefit the common shareholders, the discussion here will focus on the responsiveness of the company's earnings per share (EPS) to changes in its EBIT. It should be noted here that not all analysts rely exclusively on this type of relationship. In fact, the weakness of such an approach will be examined in the following chapter.

B. The firm is using financial leverage and is exposing its owners to financial risk when:

$$\frac{\% \text{ change in EPS}}{\% \text{ change in EBIT}} \text{ is greater than } 1.00$$

C. A precise measure of the firm's use of financial leverage can be expressed in the following relationship:

$$\left( \begin{array}{c} \text{degree of financial} \\ \text{leverage from the} \\ \text{base EBIT level} \end{array} \right) = \text{DFL}_{\text{EBIT}} = \frac{\% \text{ change in EPS}}{\% \text{ change in EBIT}}$$

1. As was the case with operating leverage, the degree of financial leverage concept can be in the negative direction as well as in the positive direction.

2. You should also note that the greater the degree of financial leverage, the greater the fluctuations (positive or negative) in EPS.

D. An easier way of measuring the degree of financial leverage that produces the same results without computing percentage changes in EBIT and EPS is:

$$\text{DFL}_{\text{EBIT}} = \frac{\text{EBIT}}{\text{EBIT - I}}$$

where I is the sum of all fixed financing costs.

V. Combining operating and financial leverage

    A. Since changes in sales revenues cause greater changes in EBIT, and if the firm chooses to use financial leverage, changes in EBIT turn into larger variations in both EPS and EAC (earnings available to common shareholders). Then, combining operating and financial leverage causes rather large variations in EPS.

    B. One way to measure the combined leverage can be expressed as:

$$\left( \begin{matrix} \text{degree of combined} \\ \text{leverage from the} \\ \text{base sales level} \end{matrix} \right) = DCL_S = \frac{\% \text{ change in EPS}}{\% \text{ change in sales}}$$

If the DCL is equal to 5.0 times, then it is important to understand that a 1% change in sales will result in a 5% change in EPS.

    C. The degree of combined leverage is actually the product of the two independent leverage measures. Thus, we have:

$$DCL_S = (DOL_S) \times (DFL_{EBIT})$$

    D. As you might have guessed, there is still another way to compute $DCL_S$. It is a more direct way in that no percentage fluctuations or separate leverage values have to be determined. You need only substitute the appropriate values into the following equation:

$$DCL_S = \frac{Q(P - V)}{Q(P - V) - F - I}$$

All variables have previously been defined.

    E. Implications of combining operating and financial leverage

        1. The total risk exposure that the firm assumes can be managed by combining operating and financial leverage in different degrees.

        2. Knowledge of the various leverage measures that have been examined here aids the financial officer in his or her determination of the proper level of overall risk that should be accepted.

VI.  Introduction to financing mix determination

   A.  A distinction can be made between the terms financial structure and capital structure.

      1.  Financial structure is the mix of all items that appear on the right-hand side of the firm's balance sheet.

      2.  Capital structure is the mix of the long-term, sources of funds used by the firm.

      3.  In this chapter, we do *not* dwell on the question of dealing with an appropriate maturity composition of the firm's sources of funds. Our main focus is on capital structure management, i.e., determining the proper proportions relative to the total in which the permanent forms of financing should be used.

   B.  The *objective* of capital structure management is to mix the permanent sources of funds in a manner that will maximize the company's common stock price. This will minimize the firm's composite cost of capital. This proper mix of funds sources is referred to as the *optimal capital structure*.

VII.  Capital structure theory

   A.  The cost of capital-capital structure argument may be characterized by this question:

      1.  Can the firm affect its overall cost of funds, either favorably or unfavorably, by varying the mixture of financing sources used?

   B.  The argument deals with the postulated effect of the use of financial leverage on the overall cost of capital of the company.

   C.  If the firm's cost of capital can be affected by the degree to which it uses financial leverage, then capital structure management is an important subset of business financial management.

VIII. Capital structure theory: A moderate position

    A.    The moderate position on capital structure importance admits to the facts that (1) interest expense is tax-deductible in the world of corporate activity and (2) the probability of the firm's suffering bankruptcy costs is directly related to the company's use of financial leverage.

    B.    When interest expense is tax-deductible, the *sum* of the cash flows that the firm could pay to *all* contributors of corporate capital (debt investors and equity investors) is affected by its financing mix. This is *not* the case when an environment of no corporate taxation is presumed.

        1.    The amount of the *tax shield on interest* may be calculated as:

$$\text{Tax shield} = r_d(M)(t)$$

where $r_d$ = the interest rate paid on outstanding debt,

$M$ = the principal amount of the debt,

$t$ = the firm's tax rate.

        2.    The moderate position presents the view that the tax shield must have value in the marketplace. After all, the government's take is decreased, and the investor's take is increased because of the deductibility of interest expense.

        3.    Therefore, according to this position, financial leverage affects firm value, and it must also affect the cost of corporate capital.

    C.    To use too much financial leverage, however, would be imprudent. It seems reasonable to offer that the probability that the firm will be unable to meet the financial obligations contained in its debt contracts will increase the more the firm uses leverage-inducing instruments in its capital structure (debt). The likelihood of firm failure, then, carries with it certain costs (bankruptcy costs) that rise as leverage use increases. There will be some point at which the expected cost of default will be large enough to outweigh the tax shield advantage of debt financing. At that point, the firm will turn to common equity financing.

D.    Figure 12.1 depicts the moderate view on capital structure importance. This view of the cost of capital-capital structure argument produces a saucer-shaped or U-shaped average cost of capital curve. In Figure 10.5, the firm's optimal range of financial leverage use lies between points A and B. It would be imprudent for the firm to use additional financial leverage beyond point B because (1) the average cost of capital would be higher than it has to be and (2) the firm's common stock price would be lower than it has to be. Therefore, we can say that the degree of financial leverage use signified by point B represents the firm's *debt capacity*.

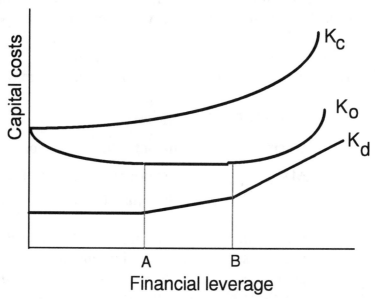

Figure 12.1
Capital Costs and Financial Leverage: The Moderate View Which Considers Taxes and Financial Distress

E.    We conclude that the determination of the firm's financing mix *is* centrally important to both the financial manager and the firm's owners.

IX.    Basic tools of capital structure management

A.    Recall that the use of financial leverage has two effects on the earnings stream flowing to the firm's common stockholders: (1) the added variability in the earnings per share (EPS) stream that accompanies the use of fixed-charge securities and (2) the level of

EPS at a given earnings before interest and taxes level (EBIT) associated with a specific capital structure. The first effect is quantified by the degree of financial leverage measure. The second effect is analyzed by means of what is generally referred to as *EBIT-EPS* analysis.

B.    The objective of EBIT-EPS analysis is to find the EBIT level that will equate EPS regardless of the financing plan chosen (from among two plans) by the financial manager.

    1.    A graphic analysis or an algebraic analysis can be used.

    2.    By allowing for sinking fund payments, the analysis can focus upon uncommitted earnings per share (UEPS).

    3.    Study problems at the end of this chapter illustrate the nature of EBIT-EPS analysis.

    4.    EBIT-EPS analysis considers only the level of the earnings stream and ignores the variability (riskiness) in it. In other words, this tool of capital structure management disregards the implicit costs of debt financing. Therefore, it must be used with caution and in conjunction with other basic tools of capital structure management.

C.    *Comparative leverage ratios* provide another tool of capital structure management. This involves the computation of various balance sheet leverage ratios and coverage ratios. Information for the latter comes essentially from the income statement. The ratios that would exist under alternative financing plans can then be computed and examined for their suitableness to management.

D.    The use of *industry norms* in conjunction with comparative leverage ratios can aid the financial manager in arriving at an appropriate financing mix. Industry norms can be thought of as standards for comparison. We recognize that industry groupings contain firms whose basic business risk may differ widely. Nevertheless, corporate financial analysts, investment bankers, commercial loan officers, and bond rating agencies rely on industry classes in order to compute such "normal" ratios. Since so many observers are interested in industry standards, the financial officer must be too.

E.    Finally, the financial officer can study the projected impact of capital structure decisions on corporate cash flows. This is often called *cash flow analysis* or the study of *company-wide cash flows*. This involves the preparation of a series of cash budgets under (1) different economic conditions and (2) different rent capital structures. The net cash flows under these different situations can be examined to determine if the financing requirements expose the firm to such a high degree of default risk that it is unbearable. According to this tool, the appropriate level of financial leverage use is reached when the chance of running out of cash is exactly equal to that which management will assume. An underlying assumption is that management's risk-bearing preferences are conditioned by the investing marketplace.

X.    A glance at actual capital structure management

A.    The opinions and practices of financial executives reinforce the major topics covered in this chapter. Most senior financial officers, for example, *do* believe there is an optimum capital structure for the corporation.

B.    *Target debt ratios* are widely used by financial officers. Surveys indicate that the firm's actual target debt ratio is affected by several factors including (1) the firm's ability to adequately meet its financing charges, (2) maintaining a desired bond rating, (3) providing an adequate borrowing reserve, and (4) exploiting the perceived advantages of financial leverage. In practice, the firm's *own management group and staff of analysts* seem to be the most important influence on actually setting the target debt ratio.

C.    In this chapter, we defined *debt capacity* as the maximum proportion of debt that the firm can include in its capital structure and still maintain its lowest composite cost of capital. Executives operationalize this concept in different ways. The most popular approach is to define the firm's debt capacity as a target percent of total capitalization (i.e., total long-term debt divided by the sum of all long-term debt, preferred equity, and common equity).

D.    In the opinion of your authors, the single most important factor that should affect the firm's financing mix is the underlying nature of the business in which it operates. This means the firm's *business risk* must be carefully assessed. This means the firm's capital structure cannot be properly designed without a thorough understanding of its commercial (business) strategy.

## Study Problems

1.    Columbia Products will earn $231,000 next year after taxes. Sales for Columbia will be $4,400,000. The firm operates in modern facilities near Columbia, South Carolina. The firm specializes in the production of furniture for lawyers' offices, accountants' offices, and college dormitories. The average unit sells for $220 and has an associated variable cost per unit of $165. Columbia experiences a 30% tax rate.

   (a)    What will fixed costs (in total) be next year for Columbia?

   (b)    Calculate Columbia's break-even point both in units and dollars.

   (c)    Generate the analytical income statement at the break-even level of sales dollars.

## SOLUTION

   (a)    All that we have to do here is use our knowledge of the break-even model *and* the analytical income statement model (both are discussed in detail in Chapter 8 of your text). The calculations follow:

$$\{(P \cdot Q) - [V \cdot Q + (F)]\}\ (1\text{-}T) = \$231{,}000$$

$$[(\$4{,}400{,}000) - (\$3{,}300{,}000) - F]\ (.7) = \$231{,}000$$

$$(\$1{,}100{,}000 - F)\ (.7) = \$231{,}000$$

$$\$770{,}000 - .7F = \$231{,}000$$

$$.7F = \$539{,}000$$

$$F = \underline{\$770{,}000}$$

(b) $\quad Q_B \;=\; \dfrac{F}{P-V} \;=\; \dfrac{\$770{,}000}{\$55} \;=\; 14{,}000 \text{ units}$

$\quad S^* \;=\; \dfrac{F}{1 - \dfrac{VC}{S}} \;=\; \dfrac{\$770{,}000}{1 - .75} \;=\; \dfrac{\$770{,}000}{.25}$

$\qquad\quad =\quad \$3{,}080{,}000$

We have shown that the firm will break even (i.e., EBIT= 0) when it sells 14,000 units. With a selling price of $220 per unit, the break-even sales level is $3,080,000.

(c) The analytical income statement at the break-even level of sales would appear as follows:

| | |
|---|---|
| Sales | $3,080,000 |
| Variable costs | 2,310,000 |
| Revenue before fixed costs | $ 770,000 |
| Fixed costs | 770,000 |
| EBIT | $ 0 |

2. Woody's Carry-Out Pizza expects to earn $16,000 next year before interest and taxes. Sales will be $130,000. The store is the only pizza parlor near the fraternity-row district of Gardiner University. The owner, Eric Nemeth, makes only one variety and size of pizza (the House Special) and it sells for $10. The variable cost per pizza is $6. Woody's Carry-Out Pizza experiences a 48% tax rate.

(a) What are the pizza parlor's fixed costs expected to be next year?

(b) Calculate the parlor's break-even point in units and dollars.

SOLUTION

(a)    To compute fixed costs:

$$S - (VC + FC) = EBIT$$

$$\$130,000/\$10 = 13,000 \text{ units sold}$$

$$\$130,000 - [(13,000)(\$6) + X] \quad = \$16,000$$

$$\$130,000 - \$78,000 - X \quad = \$16,000$$

$$X \quad = \$36,000$$

(b)    First, the break-even point in units:

$$Q_B \;=\; \frac{F}{P - V} \;=\; \frac{\$36,000}{\$10 - \$6} \;=\; 9,000 \text{ units}$$

Then, the break-even point in dollars:

$$S^* \;=\; \frac{F}{1 - VC/S} \;=\; \frac{\$36,000}{1 - \dfrac{\$78,000}{\$130,000}} \;=\; \$90,000$$

3.    The ESM Corporation projects that next year its fixed costs will total $120,000. Its only product sells for $17 per unit, of which $9 is a variable cost. The management of ESM is considering the purchase of a new machine that will lower the variable cost per unit to $7. The new machine, however, will add to fixed costs through an increase in depreciation expense.

(a)    How large can the addition to fixed costs be in order to keep the firm's break-even point in units produced and sold unchanged?

SOLUTION

(a)    Compute the present level of break-even output:

$$Q_B = \frac{F}{P - V}$$

$$= \frac{\$120,000}{8} = 15,000 \text{ units}$$

Compute the new level of fixed costs at the break-even output:

$$F + (7)(15,000) \quad = \quad (17)(15,000)$$

$$F + 105,000 \quad = \quad 255,000$$
$$F \qquad\qquad = \quad \$150,000$$

Compute the addition to fixed costs:

$150,000 - \$120,000 = \$30,000$ *addition*

4.  The management of ESM Corporation decided not to purchase the new piece of equipment. Using the existing cost structure, calculate the degree of operating leverage at 35,000 units of output.

SOLUTION

$$\text{DOL at 35,000 units} = \frac{35,000(\$17 - \$9)}{35,000(\$17 - \$9) - \$120,000}$$

$$= \frac{\$280,000}{\$160,000} = 1.75 \text{ times}$$

This indicates, for example, that a 10% increase in sales for the ESM Corporation will result in a 17.5% increase in EBIT, provided the assumptions of cost-volume-profit analysis hold.

5.  The Moose Hobby Company manufactures a full line of gold-plated model airplanes. The average selling price of a finished unit is $25. The associated variable cost is $15 per unit. Fixed costs for the company average $70,000 per year.

    (a) What would be the company's profit or loss at the following units of production sold? 5,000; 7,000; 9,000 units.

    (b) Find the degree of operating leverage for the production and sales given in part a above.

SOLUTION

(a)    The company's profit or loss:

|  | @ 5,000 units | @ 7,000 units | @ 9,000 units |
|---|---|---|---|
| Sales (P X Q) | $125,000 | $175,000 | $225,000 |
| - VC (VC/unit X Q) | 75,000 | 105,000 | 135,000 |
| - FC | 70,000 | 70,000 | 70,000 |
| Profit (loss) | ($ 20,000) | -0- | $ 20,000 |

(b)    The degree of operating leverage at the different levels of output

$$DOL_S = \frac{Q(P-V)}{Q(P-V) - F}$$

$$DOL_S \text{ at 5,000 units} = \frac{5,000(\$25-\$15)}{5,000(\$25-\$15) - \$70,000}$$

$$= \frac{\$50,000}{-20,000} = -2.5 \text{ times}$$

$$DOL_S \text{ at 7,000 units} = \frac{7,000(\$25-\$15)}{7,000(\$25-\$15) - \$70,000}$$

$$= \frac{\$50,000}{0} = \text{undefined}$$

$$DOL_S \text{ at 9,000 units} = \frac{9,000(\$25-\$15)}{9,000 (\$25-\$15) - \$70,000}$$

$$= \frac{\$90,000}{\$20,000} = 4.5 \text{ times}$$

6. An analytical income statement for the D. A. Bauer Corporation is shown below. It is based on an output level of 69,000 units.

| | |
|---|---|
| Sales | $1,035,000 |
| Variable costs | 552,000 |
| Revenue before fixed costs | $ 483,000 |
| Fixed costs | 183,000 |
| EBIT | $ 300,000 |
| Interest expense | 80,000 |
| Earnings before taxes | $ 220,000 |
| Taxes | 110,000 |
| Net income | $ 110,000 |

(a) Calculate the degree of operating leverage at this output level.

(b) Calculate the degree of financial leverage at this level of output.

(c) Determine the combined leverage effect at this output level.

SOLUTION

(a) DOL at 69,000 units $= \dfrac{69{,}000(\$15\text{-}\$8)}{69{,}000(\$15\text{-}\$8) - \$183{,}000}$

$= 1.61$ times

(b) DFL at EBIT of $300,000 $= \dfrac{\$300{,}000}{\$300{,}000 - \$80{,}000}$

$= 1.364$ times

(c) $\left(\begin{array}{c}\text{combined}\\ \text{leverage effect}\end{array}\right) = \dfrac{69{,}000(\$15\text{-}\$8)}{69{,}000(\$15\text{-}\$8)-\$183{,}000-\$80{,}000}$

$= 2.195$ times

Notice that the combined leverage effect is the product of the degrees of operating and financial leverage. A 1% increase in sales for D. A. Bauer Corporation would be magnified into a 2.195% increase in net income because of the combined leverage effect.

7.   You are supplied with the following analytical income statement for C. J. Omelette Shoppe. It reflects last year's operations.

| | |
|---|---|
| Sales | $75,000 |
| Variable costs | 37,000 |
| Revenue before fixed cost | $38,000 |
| Fixed costs | 19,000 |
| EBIT | $19,000 |
| Interest expense | 7,000 |
| Earnings before taxes | $12,000 |
| Taxes | 6,000 |
| Net income | $ 6,000 |

(a)   What is the degree of operating leverage at this level of output?

(b)   What is the degree of financial leverage?

(c)   What is the degree of combined leverage?

(d)   If sales should increase by 30%, by what percent would earnings before interest and taxes increase?

(e)   What is C. J.'s break-even point in sales dollars?

SOLUTION

(a)   The degree of operating leverage:

$$\text{DOL at } \$75,000 = \frac{\text{Revenue before fixed costs}}{\text{EBIT}} = \frac{S-VC}{S-VC-F}$$

$$= \frac{\$38,000}{\$19,000} = 2 \text{ times}$$

(b)   The degree of financial leverage:

$$\text{DFL at } \$19,000 \text{ EBIT} = \frac{\text{EBIT}}{\text{EBIT-I}} = \frac{\$19,000}{\$19,000 - \$7,000}$$

$$= 1.58 \text{ times}$$

(c)   The degrees of combined leverage:

$$\text{DCL}_S = (\text{DOL}_S)(\text{DFL}_{\text{EBIT}}) = (2)(1.58) = 3.16 \text{ times}$$

(d)   An increase in sales of 30% would result in a 60% increase in EBIT.

(e)    Break-even level in sales dollars:

$$S^* = \frac{F}{1 - VC/S} = \frac{\$19,000}{1 - \dfrac{\$37,000}{\$75,000}} = \$37,500$$

8.    Delphi Parts produces three different lines of boating accessories for several Florida boat manufacturers. The product lines are numbered. Their sales mix and contribution margin ratios appear in the chart below.

| Product Line | % of Total Sales | Contribution Margin Ratio |
|---|---|---|
| 1 | 17 | 44% |
| 2 | 53 | 30% |
| 3 | 30 | 22% |

Forecasted sales for the coming year are $1,200,000. The firm's fixed costs are $300,000.

(a)    Prepare a table showing sales, total variable costs, and the total contribution margin (dollars) associated with each line.

(b)    What is the aggregate contribution margin ratio indicative of this mix?

(c)    What is the break-even point in dollars for this particular sales mix?

SOLUTION

(a)

| Product | 1 | 2 | 3 | Total |
|---|---|---|---|---|
| Sales | 204,000 | 636,000 | 360,000 | 1,200,000 |
| VC* | 114,240 | 445,200 | 280,800 | 840,240 |
| Contr. Margin | 89,760 | 190,800 | 79,200 | 359,760 |

(b)

| Contr. Margin Ratio | 44% | 30% | 22% | 30.0% |
|---|---|---|---|---|

210

(c) $S^* = FC/(1 - VC/S) = 300,000/.300$

$S^* = \$1,000,000$

9. If Delphi (see problem 8) decides to change the sales mix for the next year to 40%, 33%, and 27% for products 1, 2, and 3, respectively, how will this affect their break-even point in dollars? Which mix do you think they would prefer?

SOLUTION

| Product Line | % of Total Sales | Contribution Margin Ratio |
|---|---|---|
| 1 | 40 | 44% |
| 2 | 33 | 30% |
| 3 | 27 | 22% |

Overall Contr. Ratio Margin $= .40(44) + .33(30) + .27(22)$

$= 33.4\%$

$S^* = 300,000/.334 = \$898,204$

This second mix would be preferred, since the overall contribution margin ratio is higher and the break-even point in dollars is now lower. The contribution to fixed costs is higher with the second mix.

10. E. Wrok and Associates, Inc., are planning to open a small manufacturing corporation. The company will manufacture a full line of solar-energized home products. The investors of the company have proposed two financing plans. Plan I is an all common equity alternative. Under this plan, 200,000 common shares will be sold to net the firm $20 per share. Financial leverage is stipulated in Plan II, and 100,000 shares will be sold. A debt issue with a 30-year maturity period will be privately placed. The interest rate on the debt issue will be 18% while the principal borrowed will amount to $2,000,000. The corporate tax rate is 50%.

(a) Find the EBIT indifference level associated with the two financing proposals.

(b) Prepare an analytical income statement that proves EPS will be the same regardless of the plan chosen at the EBIT level found in part a.

211

(c)     If a detailed financial analysis projects that long-term EBIT will always be close to $100,000 annually, which plan would be chosen? Why?

SOLUTION

(a)     In the following equation, E = EBIT.

$$\frac{(E - \$0)(1 - 0.5) - 0}{200,000} = \frac{(E - \$360,000)(1 - 0.5) - 0}{100,000}$$

$$\frac{0.5E}{200,000} = \frac{0.5E - \$180,000}{100,000}$$

$$\$50,000E = 100,000E - \$36,000,000,000$$

$$E = \underline{\$720,000}$$

(b)                          *Analytical Income Statement*

|  | *With C/S Financing* | *Financing With C/S and Debt* |
|---|---|---|
| EBIT | $720,000 | $720,000 |
| Less: Interest Expense | 0 | 360,000 |
| Earnings before taxes | $720,000 | $360,000 |
| Less: Taxes @ 50% | 360,000 | 180,000 |
| Earnings available to common | $360,000 | $180,000 |
|  |  |  |
| C/S Outstanding | 200,000 | 100,000 |
| EPS | $1.80 | $1.80 |

(c)     Plan II, because at any level above the indifference point, the more heavily levered financing plan will generate a higher EPS.

12. Albina's Ice Cream Factory's capital structure for the past year of operations is shown below:

| | |
|---|---|
| First Mortgage bonds at 15% | $ 4,000,000 |
| Debentures at 17% | 3,500,000 |
| Common stock (1,500,000 shares) | 10,500,000 |
| Retained earnings | 2,000,000 |
| Total | $20,000,000 |

The federal income tax rate is 50%. Albina's Ice Cream Factory, home-based in San Antonio, wants to raise an additional $1,500,000 to open new facilities in Houston and Dallas. The firm can accomplish this via two alternatives. That is, it can sell a new issue of 20-year debentures with 18% interest; alternatively, 30,000 new shares of common stock can be sold to the public to net the ice cream factory $50 per share. A recent study performed by an outside consulting organization projected Albina's Ice Cream's long-term EBIT level at approximately $13,575,000.

(a) Find the indifference level of EBIT (with regard to earnings per share) between the suggested financing plans.

(b) Which alternative do you recommend that Albina's Ice Cream Factory pursue?

SOLUTION

(a) In the following equations, E = EBIT

$$\frac{(E - \$1,195,000)(0.5)}{1,530,000} = \frac{(E - \$1,465,000)(0.5)}{1,500,000}$$

$$\frac{0.5E - \$597,500}{153} = \frac{0.5E - \$732,500}{150}$$

$$75E - \$89,625,000 = 76.5E - \$112,072,500$$

$$E = \underline{\$14,965,000} \text{ indifference level of EBIT}$$

(b) The consulting firm projected Albina's Ice Cream Factory's long-term EBIT at $13,575,000. Since this projected level of EBIT is less than the indifference level of $14,965,000, the earnings per share of the firm will be greater if the common stock is issued.

TRUE-FALSE

_____ 1. Dispersion in operating income causes business risk.

_____ 2. Your firm adds to its facilities a completely automated product line. This will have no effect on the break-even point (in units of output).

_____ 3. Variable costs are fixed per unit of output but vary in total as output changes.

_____ 4. Your firm expects a 7% increase in sales for the next year. The degree of operating leverage will decrease for your firm.

_____ 5. If the degree of operating leverage increases and if all else remains unchanged, the degree of combined leverage will decrease.

_____ 6. When the firm uses more financial leverage, its stockholders expect a greater return.

_____ 7. The break-even model enables the financial officer to determine the quality of output that must be sold to cover all operating costs.

_____ 8. If EBIT were to remain constant while the firm incurred additional interest expense, the degree of financial leverage would increase.

_____ 9. If future sales are expected to increase, then decreasing the degree of operating leverage would be a wise decision.

_____ 10. Financial risk can be defined as the variability of the firm's expected earnings before interest and taxes (EBIT).

_____ 11. The incurrence of fixed operating costs in the firm's income stream is referred to as financial leverage.

_____ 12. Break-even analysis is a long-run concept since all costs are variable in the long run.

_____ 13. Operating leverage is the responsiveness of the firm's EBIT to fluctuations in profit.

_____ 14. Earnings per share is the most appropriate criterion for all financing decisions.

_____ 15. The decision to use financial leverage by the firm magnifies its variation in earnings per share, compared to the use of no financial leverage.

_____ 16. Variable costs are fixed per unit of output.

_____ 17. Fixed costs per unit vary with units of output.

_____ 18. Combining operating and financial leverage magnifies variations in earnings per share.

_____ 19. A firm faces a greater chance of insolvency with an increase in the use of financial leverage (other factors held constant).

_____ 20. The decision to use debt or preferred stock in the financial structure of a corporation means that those who own the common shares are exposed to financial risk.

_____ 21. The contribution margin is the difference between the unit selling price and the unit fixed cost.

_____ 22. Business risk provides a link between a firm's asset and financial structures.

_____ 23. Semi-variable costs may be fixed over a range of output then rise sharply as a higher output level is reached and remain fixed over this higher range of output.

_____ 24. Break-even analysis *must* include allowance for all non-cash expenses.

_____ 25. Financial Risk is a direct result of the firm's investment decision.

_____ 26. Financial Leverage is the financing of the firm's assets with securities bearing a fixed rate of return over a specific time period.

_____ 27. Firms can affect their total risk exposures by combining operating and financial leverage in different degrees.

28. The ratio of total variable costs to total sales is presumed constant in ordinary break-even analysis.

29. Capital structure is the mix of all items that appear on the right-hand side of the firm's balance sheet.

30. The major influence on the maturity structure of the financing plan is the nature of the assets owned by the firm.

31. The optimal capital structure can be defined as the mix of permanent sources of funds that minimize the company's common stock price.

32. The EBIT-EPS analysis measures the variability (riskiness) of the earnings stream, thereby recognizing the implicit costs of debt financing.

33. According to cash flow analysis, the appropriate level of financial leverage use is reached when the chance of running out of cash is exactly equal to that which management will assume.

34. In computing the firm's tax bill, the interest expense is assumed not to be tax-deductible.

35. Inputs to the coverage ratios generally come from the firm's balance sheet.

36. According to the moderate position of capital structure theory, financial leverage affects firm value but not the cost of corporate capital.

37. Above a critical level of EBIT, the firm's earnings per share will be lower if greater degrees of financial leverage are employed.

38. Industry norms, used with other tools of capital structure management, can be helpful in determining an appropriate financing mix.

39. If capital structures consist only of debt instruments and common equity and both $K_c$ and $K_d$ are the same, then a change in the capital structure would _not_ affect the firm's stock price.

_____ 40. Whether or not corporate income is taxed, the sum of the cash flows made to all contributors of corporate financial capital is not affected by the firm's financing mix.

_____ 41. In practice, as more financial leverage is used, it will increase the firm's value indefinitely and lower its cost of capital continuously.

_____ 42. The EBIT-EPS analysis chart tells us that EPS will be greater than zero, if the EBIT level just covers the plan's financing cost.

_____ 43. At a point below the EBIT indifference level, the financing plan involving less leverage will generate a higher EPS.

_____ 44. Capital structure is equal to the financial structure less current liabilities.

_____ 45. Debt capacity is the maximum proportion of debt that a company can include in its capital structure without affecting the cost of common equity.

_____ 46. A sinking fund is a real cash reserve used to buy back common equity in the event of a hostile takeover.

_____ 47. Agency costs refer to those expenses paid to lawyers, accountants, etc. during bankruptcy proceedings.

_____ 48. Financial managers must frequently use coverage ratios to operationalize debt capacity concepts.

_____ 49. External economic factors are an important influence on determining a firm's target debt ratio, but firm-specific factors have to be considered as well.

_____ 50. The purpose of EBIT-EPS analysis is to determine the level of operating income at which EBIT equals EPS for a single financing plan.

_____ 51. Most senior financial officers believe there is an _optimum capital structure_ for the corporation.

MULTIPLE CHOICE

1. Which of the following is *not* a limitation of break-even analysis?

   a. The price of the product is assumed to be constant.
   b. In multiple product firms, the product mix is assumed to be constant.
   c. It provides a method for analyzing operating leverage.
   d. Variable costs per unit are assumed to be constant.

2. Which of the following is not considered a fixed cost?

   a  Depreciation
   b. Rent
   c. Electricity
   d. Administrative salaries

3. At each point above the break-even level, the degree of operating leverage

   a. increases; that is, the greater the sales level, the lower the $DOL_S$.
   b. decreases; that is, the greater the sales level, the lower the $DOL_S$.
   c. increases; that is, the greater the sales level, the greater the $DOL_S$.
   d. decreases; that is, the greater the sales level, the greater the $DOL_S$.

4. The greater the degree of financial leverage, the greater the fluctuation in

   a. variable costs.
   b. administrative salaries.
   c. earnings per share.
   d. none of the above.

5. At the break-even level of sales, the degree of operating leverage is

   a. zero.
   b. undefined.
   c. a positive number.
   d. not enough information is given.

6.   An operating leverage factor of 8.00 indicates that if sales increase by

     a.   1%, EBIT will increase by 1%.
     b.   1%, EBIT will increase by 8%.
     c.   8%, EBIT will fall by 1%.
     d.   8%, EBIT will rise by 8%.

7.   In the context of break-even point in sales dollars, if the variable cost per unit rises and if all other variables remain constant, the break-even level of sales will

     a.   fall.
     b.   rise.
     c.   stay the same.
     d.   either a or c.

8.   The combined effect of financial and operating leverage is

     a.   the sum of the degree of financial leverage and the degree of operating leverage.
     b.   the product of the two degrees.
     c.   the product of the degrees minus the sum of the degrees.
     d.   none of the above.

9.   The firm is exposing itself to financial risk when its % change in EPS ÷ % change in EBIT is

     a.   less than 1.
     b.   greater than 1.
     c.   equal to 1.
     d.   between 0 and 1.

10.  Given that the degree of operating leverage is 10 and sales over the coming period are expected to increase by 5%, then the % change in EBIT would be

     a.   2%.
     b.   5%.
     c.   2.5%.
     d.   none of the above.

11. A firm that incurs a low level of fixed operating costs might prudently use

    a.   a low degree of financial leverage.
    b.   a high degree of financial leverage.
    c.   a low degree of combined leverage.
    d.   none of the above.

12. As the firm's sales revenue increases over time,

    a.   it can lessen its business risks.
    b.   it can lessen its operating leverage.
    c.   both a and b.
    d.   none of the above.

13. A combined leverage measure of 6.5 indicates that

    a.   a 1% increase in sales would increase EPS by 6.5%.
    b.   a 1% increase in sales would increase EBIT by 6.5%.
    c.   a 1% increase in EPS would increase sales by 6.5%.
    d.   a 1% increase in EBIT would increase sales by 6.5%.

14. The practice of financing a portion of a firm's assets with securities bearing a fixed rate of return in hopes of increasing the ultimate return to shareholders refers to

    a.   operating leverage.
    b.   financial leverage.
    c.   break-even sales level.

15. The selling price of a product is $25, and the unit variable cost is $17. If a firm's fixed costs are $20,000, what is the break-even level in units?

    a.   800 units
    b.   2,000 units
    c.   2,500 units
    d.   4,300 units

16. Business risk is the residual effect of

    a.   the company's cost structure.
    b.   product demand characteristics.
    c.   intra-industry competitive position.
    d.   all of the above.
    e.   none of the above.

17. The break-even model assumes that if sales increase by 10%, variable costs

    a.   remain unchanged.
    b.   rise by 10%.
    c.   rise by 20%.
    d.   the break-even model makes no assumptions about variable costs and sales.

18. The break-even level for the number of units sold is defined as

    a.   (unit sales price minus unit variable cost) divided by total fixed costs.
    b.   unit sales minus (unit variable costs divided by total fixed costs).
    c.   (total fixed costs divided by unit sales price) minus unit variable costs.
    d.   trial and error analysis.
    e.   All are acceptable techniques.

19. Break-even analysis can be accomplished through each of the following techniques except

    a.   contribution margin analysis.
    b.   algebraic analysis.
    c.   risk analysis.
    d.   trial and error analysis.
    e.   All are acceptable techniques.

20. The degree of combined leverage can be defined as

    a. the percentage change in EPS divided by the percentage change in sales.
    b. the degree of operating leverage divided by the degree of financial leverage.
    c. the percentage change in sales divided by the percentage change in EPS.
    d. the degree of financial leverage divided by the degree of operating leverage.

21. As the quantity of product increases, the fixed cost per unit of output

    a. increases.
    b. decreases.
    c. remains constant.
    d. increases to a certain level and then decreases.

22. The degree of operating leverage can be attributed to _____ that a firm assumes.

    a. the financial risk
    b. the business risk
    c. both a and b
    d. none of the above

23. Break-even analysis and its assumptions can help the financial officer determine the

    a. level of output that must be sold to recover all operating costs.
    b. EBIT that will be achieved at various output levels.
    c. Both of the above.
    d. None of the above.

24. The firm's capital structure consists of

    a. long-term debt.
    b. common equity.
    c. preferred equity.
    d. only b and c.
    e. all of the above.

25. A firm will turn to common equity financing when

    a.  the stock market is looking favorable.
    b.  the expected cost of default is greater than the tax advantage of debt financing.
    c.  it reaches optimal capital structure.
    d.  only a and b.

26. The objective of capital structure management is to

    a.  minimize the composite cost of capital.
    b.  determine the optimal capital structure.
    c.  maximize the common stock price.
    d.  all of the above.

27. The implicit cost of debt is the change in the cost of common equity brought on by using

    a.  operating leverage.
    b.  financial leverage.
    c.  stock options.
    d.  all of the above.

28. Which of the following assumptions does capital structure theory not include?

    a.  Corporate income is not subject to any tax.
    b.  Transaction costs of selling securities are prevalent.
    c.  The expected values of all investors' forecasts of the future levels of EBIT for each firm are identical.
    d.  The capital structures consist only of stocks and bonds.

29. According to the independence hypothesis

    a.  the firm's cost of capital and stock price is unaffected by the degree of financial leverage.
    b.  the firm's total market value is affected by the manner in which the right-hand side of the balance sheet is arranged.
    c.  both a and b.
    d.  none of the above.

30. Which of the following is not a limitation of EBIT-EPS analysis?

    a.   It disregards the explicit cost of debt financing.
    b.   It ignores the level of the firm's earnings stream.
    c.   Both a and b are limitations.
    d.   None of the above.

31. Which of the following is not true about capital structure theory (moderate position)?

    a.   Firm's bankruptcy cost is related to its use of financial leverage.
    b.   The sum of the cash flows that the firm could pay to all contributors of corporate capital is not affected by its financing mix.
    c.   Financial leverage affects the firm's value.
    d.   a and c.

32. Which of the following is *not* a basic tool of capital structure management?

    a.   EBIT-EPS analysis
    b.   Comparative leverage ratios
    c.   Use of industry norms
    d.   None of the above

33. Which of the following is/are a way of analyzing capital structure:

    a.   EBIT-EPS analysis
    b.   Comparative leverage ratios
    c.   Analysis of cash flows
    d.   a and b
    e.   All of the above

34. Within prudent limits, which factor influencing optimal capital structure can increase the firm's share price?

    a.   Agency relationships
    b.   Bankruptcy costs
    c.   Debt tax shields
    d.   All of the above

35. The optimal capital structure refers to a capital structure that

    a.  is comprised of 99.9% debt capital.
    b.  will minimize the composite cost of a firm's capital for raising a given amount of funds.
    c.  will minimize the firm's common stock price.
    d.  All of the above.

36. The target debt ratio is affected by the firm's ability to

    a.  adequately meet its financing charges.
    b.  maintain a desired bond rating.
    c.  provide an adequate borrowing reserve.
    d.  exploit the perceived advantages of financial leverage.
    e.  All of the above.

37. *The most* important factor that affects the firm's financing mix is

    a.  the underlying nature of the business in which it operates.
    b.  the industry financing norms.
    c.  the firm's debt capacity.
    d.  none of the above.

# CHAPTER 13

# Dividend Policy

Orientation: In determining the firm's dividend policy, two issues are important: the dividend payout ratio and the stability of the dividend payment over time. In this regard, the financial manager should consider the investment opportunities available to the firm and any preference that the company's investors have for dividend income or capital gains. Also, stock dividends, stock splits, or stock repurchases can be used to supplement or replace cash dividends.

I.      The tradeoffs in setting a firm's dividend policy

      A.      If a company pays a large dividend, it will thereby:

            1.      Have a low retention of profits within the firm.

            2.      Need to rely heavily on a new common stock issue for equity financing.

      B.      If a company pays a small dividend, it will thereby:

            1.      Have a high retention of profits within the firm.

            2.      Will not need to rely heavily on a new common stock issue for equity financing. The profits retained for reinvestment will provide the needed equity financing.

II.     The importance of a firm's dividend policy depends on the impact of the dividend decision on the firm's stock price. That is, given a firm's capital budgeting and borrowing decisions, what is the impact of the firm's dividend policies on the stock price?

III.   Three views about the importance of a firm's dividend policy.

A.   View 1:   Dividends do not matter

1.   Assume that the dividend decision does not change the firm's capital budgeting and financing decisions.

2.   Assume perfect markets which means:

a.   There are no brokerage commissions when investors buy and sell stocks.

b.   New securities can be issued without incurring any flotation cost.

c.   There is no income tax—personal or corporate.

d.   Information is free and equally available to all investors.

e.   There are no conflicts of interest between management and stockholders.

3.   Under the foregoing assumptions, it may be shown that the market price of a corporation's common stock is unchanged under different dividend policies. If the firm increases the dividend to its stockholders, it has to offset this increase by issuing new common stock in order to finance the available investment opportunities. If, on the other hand, the firm reduces its dividend payment, it has more funds available internally to finance future investment projects. In either policy, the present value of the resulting cash flows to be accrued to the current investors is independent of the dividend policy. By varying the dividend policy, only the type of return is affected (capital gains versus dividend income), not the total return.

B.   View 2:  High dividends increase stock value

1.   Dividends are more predictable than capital gains because management can control dividends, while they cannot dictate the price of the stock. Thus, investors are less certain of receiving income from capital gains than from dividend income. The incremental risk associated with capital gains relative to dividend income should, therefore, cause us to use a higher required rate in discounting a dollar of capital gains than the rate used for discounting a dollar of dividends. In so doing, we would give a higher value to the dividend income than we would the capital gains.

2.   Criticisms of view 2

a.   Since the dividend policy has no impact on the volatility of the company's overall cash flows, it has no impact on the riskiness of the firm.

b.   Increasing a firm's dividend does not reduce the basic riskiness of the stock; rather, if dividend payment requires management to issue new stock, it only transfers risk *and* ownership from the current owners to new owners.

C.   View 3:  Low dividends increase value

Stocks that allow us to defer taxes (low dividends-high capital gains) will possibly sell at a premium relative to stocks that require us to pay taxes currently (high dividends-low capital gains). Only then will the two stocks provide comparable after tax returns, which suggests that a policy to pay low dividends will result in a higher stock price. That is, high dividends hurt investors, while low dividends-high retention help the firm's investors.

D.   Additional thoughts about the importance of a firm's dividend policy

1.   Residual dividend theory: Because of flotation costs incurred in issuing new stock, firms must issue a larger amount of securities in order to receive the amount of capital required for investments. As a result, new equity capital will be more expensive than capital raised through retained earnings. Therefore, financing investments internally (and decreasing dividends) instead of issuing new stock may be favored. This is embodied in the *residual dividend theory*, where a dividend would be paid only when any internally generated funds remain after financing the equity portion of the firm's investments.

2.   The clientele effect: If investors do in fact have a preference between dividends and capital gains, we could expect them to seek out firms that have a dividend policy consistent with these preferences. They would in essence "sort themselves out" by buying stocks which satisfy their preferences for dividends and/or capital gains. In other words, there would be a "clientele effect," where firms draw a given clientele, given the stated dividend policy. However, unless there is a greater aggregate demand for a particular policy than is being satisfied in the market, dividend policy is still unimportant, in that one policy is as good as the other. The clientele effect tells us only to avoid making capricious changes in a company's dividend policy.

3.   Information effect

   a.   We know from experience that a large, unexpected change in dividends can have significant impact on the stock price. Despite such "evidence," it is not unreasonable to hypothesize that dividend policy only appears to be important, because we are not looking at the real cause and effect. It may be that investors use a change in dividend policy as a *signal* about the firm's "true" financial condition, especially its earning power.

b. Some would argue that management frequently has inside information about the firm that it cannot make available to the investors. This difference in accessibility to information between management and investors, called *information asymmetry*, may result in a lower stock price than would be true if we had conditions of certainty. Dividends become a means in a risky market place to minimize any "drag" on the stock price that might come from differences in the level of information available to managers and investors.

4. Agency costs: Conflicts between management and stockholders may exist, and the stock price of a company owned by investors who are separate from management may be less than the stock value of a closely-held firm. The difference in price is the cost of the conflict to the owners, which has come to be called *agency costs*. A firm's dividend policy may be perceived by owners as a tool to minimize agency costs. Assuming the payment of a dividend requires management to issue stock to finance new investments, then new investors will be attracted to the company only if management provides convincing information that the capital will be used profitably. Thus, the payment of dividends indirectly results in a closer monitoring of management's investment activities. In this case, dividends may provide a meaningful contribution to the value of the firm.

5. Expectations theory: As the time approaches for management to announce the amount of the next dividend, investors form expectations as to how much the dividend will be. When the actual dividend decision is announced, the investor compares the actual decision with the expected decision. If the amount of the dividend is as expected, even if it represents an increase from prior years, the market price of the stock will remain unchanged. However, if the dividend is higher or lower than expected, the investors will reassess their perceptions about the firm and the value of the stock.

E. The empirical evidence about the importance of dividend policy

1. Statistical tests: To test the relationship between dividend payments and security prices, we could compare a firm's dividend yield (dividend/stock price) and the stock's total return; the question being, "Do stocks that pay high dividends provide higher or lower returns to the investors?" Such tests have been conducted using a variety of the most sophisticated statistical techniques available. Despite the use of these extremely powerful analytical tools involving intricate and complicated procedures, the results have been mixed. However, over long periods of time, the results have given a slight advantage to the low-dividend stocks; that is, stocks that pay lower dividends appear to have higher prices. The findings are far from conclusive, however, owing to the relatively large standard errors of the estimates.

2. Reasons for inconclusive results from the statistical tests

   a. To be accurate, we would need to know the amount of dividends investors *expect* to receive. Since these expectations cannot be observed, we can use only historical data, which may or may not relate to expectations.

   b. Most empirical studies have assumed a linear relationship between dividend payments and stock prices. The actual relationship may be nonlinear, possibly even with discontinuities in the relationship.

3. Since our statistical prowess does not provide us with any conclusive evidence, researchers have surveyed financial managers about their perceptions of the relevance of dividend policy. In such surveys, the evidence favors the relevance of dividend policy, but not just overwhelmingly so. For the most part, managers are divided between believing that dividends are important and having no opinion in the matter.

F. Conclusions about the importance of dividend policy

1. As a firm's investment opportunities increase, the dividend payout ratio should decrease.

2. The firm's dividend policy appears to be important; however, appearances may be deceptive. The real issue may be the firm's *expected* earnings power and the riskiness of these earnings.

3. If dividends influence stock price, it probably comes from the investor's desire to minimize and/or defer taxes and from the role of dividends in minimizing agency costs.

4. If the expectations theory has merit, which we believe it does, it behooves management to avoid surprising the investors when it comes to the firm's dividend decision.

IV. Dividend policy decisions

A. Other practical considerations

1. Legal restrictions

a. A corporation may not pay a dividend

(1) If the firm's liabilities exceed its assets.
(2) If the amount of the dividend exceeds the accumulated profits (retained earnings).
(3) If the dividend is being paid from capital invested in the firm.

b. Debtholders and preferred stockholders may impose restrictive provisions on management, such as common dividends not being paid from earnings prior to the payment of interest or preferred dividends.

2. Liquidity position: The amount of a firm's retained earnings and its cash position are seldom the same. Thus, the company must have adequate *cash* available as well as retained earnings to pay dividends.

3. Absence or lack of other sources of financing: All firms do not have equal access to the capital markets. Consequently, companies with limited financial resources may rely more heavily on internally generated funds.

4. Earnings predictability: A firm that has a stable earnings trend will generally pay a larger portion of its earnings in dividends. If earnings fluctuate significantly, a larger amount of the profits may be retained to ensure that enough money is available for investment projects when needed.

5. Ownership control: For many small firms, and certain large ones, maintaining the controlling vote is very important. These owners would prefer the use of debt and retained profits to finance new investments rather than issue new stock.

6. Inflation: Because of inflation, the cost of replacing equipment has increased substantially. Depreciation funds tend to become insufficient. Hence, greater profit retention may be required.

B. Alternative dividend policies

1. Constant dividend payout ratio: The percentage of earnings paid out in dividends is held constant. Therefore, the dollar amount of the dividend fluctuates from year to year.

2. Stable dollar dividend per share: Relatively stable dollar dividend is maintained. The dividend per share is increased or decreased only after careful investigation by the management.

3. Small, regular dividend plus a year-end extra: Extra dividend is paid out in prosperous years. Management's objective is to avoid the connotation of a permanent dividend increase.

C. Bases for stable dividends

1. Investors may use the dividend policy as a surrogate for information that is not easily accessible. The dividend policy may be useful in assessing the company's long-term earnings prospects.

2. Many investors rely on dividends to satisfy personal income need. If dividends fluctuate from year to year, investors may have to sell or buy stock to satisfy their current needs, thereby incurring expensive transaction costs.

3. Legal listings stipulate that certain types of financial institutions may invest only in companies that have a consistent dividend payment.

4. Conclusion: An investor who prefers stable dividends will assign a lower required rate of return (a higher P/E ratio) for a stock paying a stable dividend. This results in a higher market price for the stock.

V. Dividend payment procedures

   A. Dividends are generally paid quarterly.

   B. The *declaration date* is the date on which the firm's board of directors announces the forthcoming dividends.

   C. The *date of record* designates when the stock transfer books are to be closed (who is entitled to the dividend).

   D. Brokerage firms terminate the right of ownership to the dividend four working days prior to the date of record. This date is called the *ex-dividend date*.

   E. Dividend checks are mailed on the *payment date*.

VI. Stock dividends and stock splits

   A. Both a stock dividend and a stock split involve issuing new shares of stock to current stockholders.

   B. The investors' percentage ownership in the firm remains unchanged. The investor is neither better nor worse off than before the stock split/dividend.

   C. On an economic basis, there is no difference between a stock dividend and a stock split.

   D. For accounting purposes, the stock split has been defined as a stock dividend exceeding 25%.

E.    Accounting treatment

    1.    For a stock dividend, the dollar amount of the dividend is transferred from retained earnings to the capital accounts.

    2.    In the case of a split, the dollar amounts of the capital accounts do not change. Only the number of shares is increased, while the par value of each share is decreased proportionately.

F.    Rationale for a stock dividend or split

    1.    The price of stock may not fall precisely in proportion to the share increase; thus, the stockholders' value is increased.

    2.    If a company is encountering cash problems, it can substitute a stock dividend for a cash dividend. Investors will probably look beyond the dividend to determine the underlying reasons for conserving cash.

VII.    Stock repurchases

A.    A number of benefits exists justifying stock repurchases instead of dividend payment. Included in these are:

    1.    To provide an internal investment opportunity.

    2.    To modify the firm's capital structure.

    3.    To impact earnings per share, thus increasing stock price.

B.    Share repurchase as a dividend decision

    1.    A firm may decide to repurchase its shares, increasing the earnings per share which should be reflected in a higher stock price.

    2.    The investor's choice

        a.    For tax purposes, the investor may prefer the firm to repurchase stock in lieu of a dividend. Dividends are taxed as ordinary income, whereas any price appreciation resulting from the stock repurchase would be taxed as a capital gain.

b. The investor may still prefer dividend payment because

    (1) Dividends are viewed more dependable than stock repurchases.

    (2) The price the firm must pay for its stock may be too high.

    (3) Riskiness of the firm's capital structure may increase, lowering the P/E ratio and, thus, the stock price.

C. Financing or investment decision

1. A stock repurchase effectively increases the debt-equity ratio towards higher debt; thus, repurchase is viewed as a financing decision.

2. Buying its own stock at depressed prices, a firm may consider the repurchase as an investment decision. However, this action is not a true investment opportunity, as the extreme result would mean the company would consume itself.

D. The repurchase procedure

1. A public announcement should be made detailing the amount, purpose, and procedure for the stock repurchase.

2. Open market purchase—at the current market price.

3. Tender offer—more formal and at a specified price.

4. Negotiated basis—repurchasing from specific large shareholders.

1. The Harvestor Corporation has the following capital structure:

| | |
|---|---|
| Common stock ($5 par; 300,000 shares) | $1,500,000 |
| Paid-in capital | 2,500,000 |
| Retained earnings | 4,000,000 |
| Total net worth | $8,000,000 |

(a) If the company issues a 20% stock dividend, how would the new capital structure appear? The market price per share for the stock is $10.

(b) How would the capital accounts appear after a 2-for-1 split?

SOLUTION

(a)

| | |
|---|---|
| Decrease in retained earnings ($10 x 60,000 shares) | $600,000 |
| Increase in par value of common stock ($5 x 60,000 shares) | 300,000 |
| Remainder to increase capital surplus | $300,000 |

The new capital structure after a 20% stock dividend:

| | |
|---|---|
| Common stock ($5 par; 360,000 shares) | $1,800,000 |
| Paid-in capital | 2,800,000 |
| Retained earnings | 3,400,000 |
| Total net worth | $8,000,000 |

(b) The new capital structure after a 2-for-1 split:

| | |
|---|---|
| Common stock ($2.50 par; 600,000 shares) | $1,500,000 |
| Capital surplus | 2,500,000 |
| Retained earnings | 4,000,000 |
| Total net worth | $8,000,000 |

2.  The Mansville Corporation's capital structure is as follows:

| | |
|---|---|
| Common stock ($4 par; 5,000,000 shares outstanding) | $20,000,000 |
| Paid-in capital | 1,000,000 |
| Retained earnings | 9,000,000 |
| Total net worth | $30,000,000 |

The firm's earnings after taxes are $2 million, of which the company paid out 25% in cash dividends. The price of the firm's common stock was $8.

(a)  If the firm declares a 20% stock dividend, how would the capital structure appear?

(b)  If the firm declares a 30% stock dividend, what would be the end result on the capital structure? (Hint: Stock dividends in excess of 25% should be calculated on the basis of book value less retained earnings instead of market value.)

(c)  If a 20% stock dividend is assumed, what would be the earnings per share and dividends per share?

SOLUTION

(a)  Capital structure after a 20% stock dividend:

Increase in the shares outstanding:

20% x 5,000,000 shares = 1,000,000 shares

Increase in the par value:

$4 x 1,000,000 = $4,000,000

Increase in the capital surplus account:

($8 - $4) x 1,000,000 = $4,000,000

Result:

| | |
|---|---|
| Common stock (6,000,000 shares) | $24,000,000 |
| Capital surplus | 5,000,000 |
| Retained earnings | 1,000,000 |
| Total net worth | $30,000,000 |

(b)    Capital structure after a 30% stock dividend:

Increase in shares outstanding:
30% x 5,000,000 = 1,500,000 shares

| | |
|---|---:|
| Increase in par value:<br>1,500,000 shares x $4 par value | $6,000,000 |
| Increase in capital surplus:<br>$1,000,000 x 30% | 300,000 |
| Amount transferred from<br>    retained earnings: | $6,300,000 |

Revised capital structure:

| | |
|---|---:|
| Common stock ($4 par value;<br>    6,500,000 shares) | $26,000,000 |
| Paid-in capital | 1,300,000 |
| Retained earnings | 2,700,000 |
| Total net worth | $30,000,000 |

(c)    Earnings per share after a 20% stock dividend:

$$\frac{\text{Earnings}}{\text{Number of Shares}} = \frac{\$2,000,000}{6,000,000} = \$0.33$$

Dividends per share after a 20% stock dividend:

$$\frac{\text{Dividends}}{\text{Number of Shares}} = \frac{\$500,000}{6,000,000} = \$0.083$$

3.    Philips Limited treats dividends as a residual variable in its financial decisions (see residual dividend theory). Net income has been forecasted for the upcoming year to be $600,000, which may be used for reinvesting in the firm or for paying dividends. The firm has only equity in its capital structure, and its cost of internally generated equity capital is 10%. If, however, new common stock were issued, flotation costs would raise this cost to 11%. If the firm considers the 10% cost of internal equity to be the opportunity cost of retained earnings,

(a)    (l)    How much in dividends should be paid if the company has $500,000 in projects with expected returns exceeding 10%?

(2) How much should the dividend be if $600,000 in investments are available having expected returns greater than 10%?

(b) How much should be paid in dividends if the firm has $1 million in projects whose expected returns exceed 11%?

(c) How would your answer change in part b if the firm's optimal debt-equity mix is 40% debt and 60% common and the cost of capital remains the same?

## SOLUTION

(a) (l) According to the residual dividend theory, the firm should pay dividends only when it has exhausted its investments whose returns exceed the firm's cost of capital. Therefore, the firm should pay $100,000 in dividends ($600,000 income available for investing less $500,000 investments).

(2) The firm should use all of the $600,000 for investing in the projects and should not pay any dividends.

(b) If the firm has investment opportunities with returns exceeding the cost of capital, the firm should undertake these investments. In this example, the cost of capital increases (to 11%) when new equity is issued. Since the returns on the available investment projects (totaling $1 million) exceed the cost of equity capital, the firm should use up its internally generated funds ($600,000) and raise the remaining $400,000 by issuing new common stock. Therefore, no dividends would be paid.

(c) We would need $400,000 in new debt, i.e., 40% of $1 million. The remaining $600,000 (which is 60% of the needed capital) will be supplied by internally generated funds. No dividend will be paid.

4. Beardsell Products and Voltas Products are identical firms in terms of (l) being in the same industry, (2) producing the same products, (3) being subject to the same risks, and (4) having equivalent earnings per share. Beardsell pays a constant cash dividend, whereas Voltas follows a constant percentage payout ratio of 50%. However, Voltas' common stock price has been lower than Beardsell's in spite of Voltas' dividend being substantially larger than Beardsell's in certain years. Given the data below:

| | Beardsell Products | | | Voltas Products | | |
|---|---|---|---|---|---|---|
| Year | EPS | Dividend | Market Price | EPS | Dividend | Market Price |
| 1988 | $2.50 | $0.65 | 9 | $2.50 | $1.25 | 6 ¾ |
| 1989 | -0.25 | 0.65 | 8 ¾ | -0.25 | 0 | 6 ½ |
| 1990 | 3.00 | 0.65 | 9 ¼ | 3.00 | 1.50 | 9 |
| 1991 | 2.00 | 0.65 | 9 | 2.00 | 1.00 | 10 |

(a)   What might account for the differences in the market prices of the two companies?

(b)   What might both companies do in order to enhance the market prices of their respective shares?

SOLUTION

(a)   The dissimilarity between market prices might be a function of the different dividend policies, with a lower capitalization rate, and, accordingly, a higher price being assigned to Beardsell as a result of the stable dividend stream.

(b)   It appears that neither company would appear to be growth-oriented. If both firms are valued in terms of their dividend yield, which seems to be the case, higher dividend payouts might produce higher prices.

5.   Rexall Corporation is considering 5 investment opportunities. The required investment outlays and expected rates of return for these investments are shown below. The cost of capital for the firm is 13%. Investments are to be financed with 30% debt and 70% equity. Internally generated funds available for reinvestment equal $1 million.

(a)   Which investments should be accepted?

(b)   According to the residual dividend theory, what amount should be paid out in dividends?

| Investment | Cost | Internal Rate of Return |
|------------|------|-------------------------|
| A | $200,000 | 20% |
| B | 300,000 | 15 |
| C | 900,000 | 14 |
| D | 100,000 | 10 |
| E | 400,000 | 7 |

SOLUTION

(a) Investments A, B, and C should be accepted because their expected returns exceed the firm's cost of capital.

(b) Dividends to be paid:

Total cost of three projects:

| | | |
|---|---|---|
| $200,000 + $300,000 + $900,000 | = | $1,400,000 |
| Equity financing: $1,400,000 x 70% | = | 980,000 |
| Debt financing: $1,400,000 - $980,000 | = | 420,000 |

| | |
|---|---|
| Internally generated funds available: | $1,000,000 |
| Less equity necessary for projects: | 980,000 |
| Funds available for dividend payment: | $ 20,000 |

Self Tests

TRUE-FALSE

_____ 1. If dividend policy is treated as a passive residual, dividends are paid only if the firm has any remaining capital after financing attractive investments.

_____ 2. In practice, the firm should invest retained earnings as long as the required rate of return exceeds the expected rate of return from the investment.

_____ 3. The greater the ability of a firm to borrow, the less is its ability to pay a cash dividend.

_____ 4. If a firm has sporadic investment opportunities, it might be expected to pay out more dividends.

_____ 5. A stock dividend results in a recapitalization of retained earnings.

_____ 6. In a stock split, the only accounting change is the shifting of amounts from retained earnings to the common stock (par) account.

_____ 7. The introduction of flotation costs to the "dividend irrelevance" concept favors the retention of earnings in the firm.

_____ 8. The only wealth-creating activity under "perfect market" conditions for an all-equity firm is the management's investment decisions.

_____ 9. Dividend income and capital gains from the sale of stock are taxed at the same personal income tax rate. Thus, there is no advantage to capital gains over dividend income for the investor.

_____ 10. An "expected" change in the dividend policy of a firm may not affect the price of the firm's stock when the change is actually announced.

_____ 11. A stock repurchase increases the debt-to-equity ratio.

_____ 12. Stock repurchases offer an attractive investment alternative any time prices are depressed.

_____ 13. The "bird-in-the-hand" theory assigns a higher value to capital gains than to dividend income.

_____ 14. A firm's dividend policy affects the variability of the firm's overall cash flows, even when we do not allow the dividend policy to impact investment decisions.

_____ 15. Stocks that allow us to defer taxes will not sell at a premium.


MULTIPLE CHOICE

1. Which of the following is not an assumption of the "dividend irrelevance" theory?

   a. No taxes
   b. Efficient capital markets
   c. No flotation costs
   d. Costless information

2. An argument for the relevance of dividends would be

   a. informational content.
   b. resolution of uncertainty
   c. preference for current income.
   d. all of the above.
   e. none of the above.

3. An advantage of a stock dividend is that it

   a. may help to conserve cash.
   b. tends to increase the market price.
   c. keeps the price of the stock within a desired trading range.
   d. does all of the above.

4. When the assumption of no taxes is removed from the "dividend irrelevance" theory

   a. there is a preference for the retention of earnings.
   b. there is a preference for paying out dividends.
   c. the preference depends on the individual investor's tax status, but generally there is a preference for retention of earnings.

5. The following factors may influence the dividend policy that a firm undertakes:

   a. The liquidity of the firm.
   b. Capital structure.
   c. Legal restrictions.
   d. a and c.
   e. a and b.

6. Advantages of a stock repurchase may be

   a. a means to modify capital structure.
   b. to impact earnings per share.
   c. the elimination of a particular minority group.
   d. all of the above.

7. A firm may not legally pay dividends if

   a. its liabilities exceed its assets.
   b. the dividend is being paid from capital invested in the firm.
   c. debtholders' contracts are not satisfied.
   d. all of the above.
   e. a and b.

8. For tax purposes, a corporation may exclude _____% of the dividend income received from another corporation.

   a. 0
   b. 10
   c. 50
   d. 80
   e. 100

9. When real-world considerations are taken into account, the amount of a firm's dividend payment depends on the following factors:

   a. Profitability of investment opportunities.
   b. Investor's preference for capital gains or dividend income.
   c. Debt-to-equity ratio.
   d. Trading range of the firm's stock.
   e. a and b.

10. Small-sized firms generally use retained earnings for investment purposes because

   a. they do not have easy access to the capital markets.
   b. ownership control is an important factor.
   c. their earnings fluctuate widely.
   d. inflation has greater impact on small companies.
   e. none of the above.
   f. a and b.

11. Which one of the following dividend policies is the most popular?

   a. Constant dividend payout ratio
   b. Stable dividend (dollar) per share
   c. Small, regular dividend plus a year-end extra

12. The ex-dividend date is

    a. the same as the date of record.
    b. four working days prior to date of record.
    c. eight days prior to the payment date.
    d. five days after the declaration date.
    e. none of the above.

13. Properly viewed, a stock repurchase should be used as:

    a. a dividend decision.
    b. an investment decision.
    c. a refinancing decision.
    d. both a and c.
    e. all of the above.

# CHAPTER 14

# Introduction to Working-Capital Management

Orientation: In this chapter, we introduce working-capital management in terms of managing the firm's liquidity. Specifically, net working capital is defined as the difference in current assets and current liabilities. The hedging principle is offered as one approach to addressing the firm's liquidity problems. In this chapter, we also discuss sources of short-term financing that must be repaid within 1 year.

I.    Managing current assets

    A.    The firm's investment in current assets (like fixed assets) is determined by the marginal benefits derived from investing in them compared with their acquisition cost.

    B.    However, the current-fixed asset mix of the firm's investment in assets is an important determinant of the firm's liquidity. That is, the greater the firm's investment in current assets, other things remaining the same, the greater the firm's liquidity. This is generally true, since current assets are usually more easily converted into cash.

    C.    The firm can invest in marketable securities to increase its liquidity. However, such a policy involves committing the firm's funds to a relatively low-yielding (in comparison to fixed assets) investment.

II.   Managing the firm's use of current liabilities

    A.    The greater the firm's use of current liabilities, other things being the same, the less will be the firm's liquidity.

    B.    There are a number of *advantages* associated with the use of current liabilities for financing the firm's asset investments.

        1.    *Flexibility.* Current liabilities can be used to match exactly the timing of a firm's short-term financing needs.

2.  *Interest cost.* Historically, the interest cost on short-term debt has been lower than that on long-term debt.

C.  Following are the *disadvantages* commonly associated with the use of short-term debt:

   1.  Short-term debt exposes the firm to an increased *risk of illiquidity* because short-term debt matures sooner and in greater frequency, by definition, than does long-term debt.

   2.  Since short-term debt agreements must be renegotiated from year to year, the *interest cost* of each year's financing *is uncertain.*

III.  Determining the appropriate level of working capital

A.  Pragmatically, it is impossible to derive the "optimal" level of working capital for the firm. Such a derivation would require estimation of the potential costs of illiquidity which cannot be precisely measured.

B.  However, the "hedging principle" provides the basis for the firm's working-capital decisions.

   1.  The *hedging principle* or *rule of self- liquidating debt* involves the following: Those asset needs of the firm not financed by spontaneous sources (i.e., payables and accruals) should be financed in accordance with the following rule: Permanent asset investments are financed with permanent sources, and temporary investments are financed with temporary sources of financing.

   2.  A *permanent investment in an asset* is one which the firm expects to hold for a period longer than 1 year. Such an investment may involve current or fixed assets.

   3.  *Temporary asset investments* comprise the firm's investment in current assets that will be liquidated and *not* replaced during the year.

4. *Spontaneous sources of financing* include all those sources which are available upon demand (e.g., trade credit--accounts payable) or which arise naturally as a part of doing business (e.g., wages payable, interest payable, taxes payable, etc.).

5. *Temporary sources of financing* include all forms of current or short-term financing not categorized as spontaneous. Examples include bank loans, commercial paper, and finance company loans.

6. *Permanent sources of financing* include all long-term sources such as debt having a maturity longer than 1 year, preferred stock, and common stock.

C. Although the hedging principle provides a useful guide to the firm's working-capital decisions, no firm will follow its tenets strictly. At times, a firm may find itself overly reliant on temporary financing, but, at other times, it may have excess cash as a result of excessive use of permanent financing.

IV. Selecting a source of short-term financing

A. In general, there are three basic factors that should be considered in selecting a source of short-term financing;

1. The effective cost of the credit source.

2. The availability of credit.

3. The effect of the use of a particular source of credit on the cost and availability of other sources.

B. The basic procedure used in estimating the cost of short-term credit utilizes the basic interest equation, i.e., interest = principal x rate x time.

C. The problem faced in assessing the cost of a source of short-term financing involves estimating the annual effective rate (RATE) where the interest amount, the principal sum, and the time for which financing will be needed is known. Thus, the basic interest equation is "rearranged" as follows where we refer to the interest rate as the annual percentage rate or APR:

$$APR = RATE = \frac{interest}{principal} \times \frac{1}{time}$$

D. Compound interest was not considered in the simple APR calculation. To consider compounding, the following relation is used:

$$APY = \left(1 + \frac{R}{M}\right)^M - 1$$

where APR is the *annual percentage rate*, R is the nominal rate of interest per year, and M is the number of compounding periods within 1 year. The effect of compounding is, thus, to raise the effective cost of short-term credit.

V. Sources of short-term credit

A. The two basic sources of short-term credit are unsecured and secured credit.

1. Unsecured credit consists of all those sources which have as their security only the lender's faith in the ability of the borrower to repay the funds when due.

2. Secured funds include additional security in the form of assets that are pledged as collateral in the event the borrower defaults in payment of principal or interest.

B. There are three major sources of unsecured short-term credit: trade credit, unsecured bank loans, and commercial paper.

1. Trade credit provides one of the most flexible sources of financing available to the firm. To arrange for credit, the firm need only place an order with one of its suppliers. The supplier then checks the firm's credit, and if the credit is good, the supplier sends the merchandise.

2. Commercial banks provide unsecured short-term credit in two basic forms: lines of credit and transaction loans (notes payable). Maturities of both types of loans are usually 1 year or less with rates of interest depending on the creditworthiness of the borrower and the level of interest rates in the economy as a whole.

3.  A line of credit is generally an informal agreement or understanding between the borrower and the bank as to the maximum amount of credit that the bank will provide the borrower at any one time. There is no "legal" commitment on the part of the bank to provide the stated credit. There is another variant of this form of financing referred to as a *revolving credit agreement* whereby such a legal obligation is involved. The line of credit generally covers a period of 1 year corresponding to the borrower's "fiscal" year.

4.  Transaction loans are another form of unsecured short-term bank credit; the transaction loan, in contrast to a line of credit, is made for a specific purpose.

5.  Only the largest and most creditworthy companies are able to use commercial paper which consists of unsecured promissory notes in the money market.

    a.  The maturities of commercial paper are generally 6 months or less with the interest rate slightly lower than the prime rate on commercial bank loans. The new issues of commercial paper are either directly placed or dealer placed.

    b.  There are a number of advantages that accrue to the user of commercial paper: Interest rates are generally lower than rates on bank loans and comparable sources of short-term financing. No minimum balance requirements are associated with commercial paper. Commercial paper offers the firm with very large credit needs a single source for all its short-term financing needs. Since it is widely recognized that only the most creditworthy borrowers have access to the commercial paper market, its use signifies a firm's credit status.

    c.  However, a very important "risk" is involved in using this source of short-term financing; the commercial paper market is highly impersonal and denies even the most credit worthy borrower any flexibility in terms of repayment.

C.    Secured sources of short-term credit have certain assets of the firm, such as accounts receivable or inventories pledged as collateral to secure a loan. Upon default of the loan agreement, the lender has first claim to the pledged assets.

    1.    Generally, a firm's receivables are among its most liquid assets. Two secured loan arrangements are generally made with accounts receivable as collateral: (a) Under the arrangement of *pledged accounts receivable*, the amount of the loan is stated as a percent of the face value of the receivables pledged. (b) Factoring accounts receivable involves the outright sale of a firm's accounts receivables to a factor.

    2.    Four secured loan arrangements are generally made with inventory as collateral: (a) Under the *floating lien agreement*, the borrower gives the lender a lien against all his or her inventories. (b) The *chattel mortgage agreement* involves having specific items of inventory identified in the security agreement. (c) The *field warehouse financing agreements* means that the inventories used as collateral are physically separated from the firm's other inventories and are placed under the control of a third-party field warehousing firm. (d) *Terminal warehouse agreements* involve transporting the inventories pledged as collateral to a public warehouse which is physically removed from the borrower's premises.

## Study Problems

1.    In order to meet a temporary need for working capital during an upcoming seasonal peak in sales, Gregory Sales Co. needs $500,000. Gregory's bank has agreed to lend the funds for the necessary 3-month interval at a rate of 12% with a 20% compensating balance. Gregory Sales Co. normally maintains a demand deposit amount of $20,000. Estimate the annual (effective) cost of the loan to Gregory.

# SOLUTION

To obtain the needed $500,000 and meet the compensating balance requirement, Gregory must borrow X dollars, where X is found as follows:

$$X - [0.20X - 20,000] = 500,000$$

$$0.80X = 480,000$$

$$X = \$600,000$$

Thus, Gregory borrows $600,000 for which it must maintain a compensating balance of 0.20 x 600,000 = $120,000, of which $20,000 will come from its normal demand deposit and $100,000 must be borrowed. This will leave the firm with the use of $500,000. The interest cost of the loan is computed as follows:

$$\text{Interest} = 0.12 \times 600,000 \div 4 = \$18,000$$

We divide by 4 since the loan is for only 3 months or one-fourth of a year. The _effective_ annual cost of the loan is:

$$\text{Rate} = \frac{\$ \text{ loan cost}}{\$ \text{funds available}} \times \begin{array}{c} \text{loan maturity as a} \\ \text{fraction of 1 year} \end{array}$$

$$= \frac{18,000}{500,000} = \underline{0.144} \text{ or } \underline{14.4\%}$$

2. A factor has agreed to buy Thomas Brothers' receivables ($250,000 per month) which have an average collection period of 90 days. The factor will advance up to 80% of the face value of the receivables for an annual charge of 10% of the funds advanced. The factor also charges a handling fee of 5% of the face value of all accounts purchased. What is the effective annual cost of the factoring arrangement to Thomas Brothers if the maximum advance is taken every month?

SOLUTION

With an average collection period of 90 days and monthly credit sales, Thomas Brothers could build up a loan advance over 3 months of 0.80 x 750,000 = $600,000. This loan would be constantly rolling over as accounts were being collected and as new credit sales were being made. The 90-day interest cost of the loan would be computed:

$$\text{Interest} = \$600,000 \ x \ \frac{0.10}{4} = \$15,000$$

The factor's fee is calculated as follows:

$$\text{Fee} = 0.05 \ x \ \$750,000 = \$37,500$$

Thus, the effective annual cost of the 90-day loan would be:

$$\text{Rate} = \frac{\$15,000 + \$37,500}{\$600,000} \div \frac{3}{12}$$

$$= \underline{0.35} \text{ or } \underline{35\%}$$

3. For the past 7 years, Warden Company has been factoring its accounts receivables. The factor's fee is 3%, and the factor will lend up to 90% of the volume of receivables purchased for an additional 1% per month. The firm typically has sales of $200,000 per month; 75% are on credit. Warden Company will save credit department costs of $3,500, since it will no longer need to operate a credit department. In addition, there will no longer be bad-debt losses which previously were 1 ¼% per month.

The firm's bank has recently offered to lend the firm up to 90% of the face value of the receivables shown on the schedule of accounts. The bank would charge 9% per annum interest plus a 2% processing charge per dollar of receivables pledged. The firm extends terms of net 30, and all customers who plan to pay will do so by the thirtieth of the month. Should the firm discontinue its factoring arrangement in favor of the bank's offer if the firm borrows, on the average, $100,000 per month on its receivables?

SOLUTION

The cost of factoring is:

| | |
|---|---:|
| Fee (0.03 x $200,000 x .75) | $4,500 |
| Interest cost (0.01 x $100,000) | 1,000 |
| | $5,500 |

The cost of the bank loan is:

| | |
|---|---:|
| Fee (0.02 x $100,000/.90) | $2,222 |
| Interest (0.09 x $200,000 x 1/12) | 1,500 |
| | $3,722 |

Plus:

| | |
|---|---:|
| Credit department cost per month | $3,722 |
| Bad-debt losses ($200,000 x .75 x 0.0125) | 1,875 |
| Total cost | $5,597 |

No, in this case, factoring is slightly cheaper.

4.  Calculate the effective cost of the following trade credit terms where payment is made on the net due date.

a.  2/10, net 30

b.  3/15, net 30

c.  3/15, net 45

d.  2/15, net 60

SOLUTION

a.  $\dfrac{0.02}{0.98} \times \dfrac{1}{20/360} = 0.36734$ or 36.73%

b.  $\dfrac{0.03}{0.97} \times \dfrac{1}{15/360} = 0.74226$ or 74.23%

c. $\dfrac{0.03}{0.97} \times \dfrac{1}{30/360} = 0.37113$ or $37.11\%$

d. $\dfrac{0.02}{0.98} \times \dfrac{1}{45/360} = 0.16327$ or $16.33\%$

5. Luft, Inc., recently acquired production rights to an innovative sailboard design but needs funds to pay for the first production run, which is expected to sell briskly. The firm plans to issue \$450,000 in 180-day maturity notes. The paper will carry an 11% rate with discounted interest and will cost Luft \$13,000 (paid in advance) to issue.

a. What is the effective cost of credit to Luft?

b. What other factors should the company consider in analyzing whether to issue the commercial paper?

SOLUTION

a. $\text{RATE} = \dfrac{\text{interest}}{\text{principal}} \times \dfrac{1}{\text{time}}$

$\text{RATE} = \dfrac{\$24,750^* + 13,000}{\$450,000 - 13,000 - 24,750} \times \dfrac{1}{180/360}$

$= .1831$ or $18.31\%$

$^*\text{Interest} = .11 \times \$450,000 \times \tfrac{1}{2}$

b. The risk involved with the issue of commercial paper should be considered. This risk relates to the fact that the commercial paper market is highly impersonal and denies even the most creditworthy borrower any flexibility in terms of when repayment is made.

In addition, commercial paper is a viable source of credit to only the most creditworthy borrowers. Thus, it may simply not be available to the firm.

6. DST, Inc., a producer of inflatable river rafts, needs $400,000 for the three-month summer season, ending September 30, 199X. The firm has explored two possible sources of credit.

1. DST has arranged with its bank for a $400,000 loan secured by accounts receivable. The bank has agreed to advance DST 80% of the value of its pledged receivables at a rate of 11% plus a 1% fee based on all receivables pledged. DST's receivables average a total of $1 million year-round.

2. An insurance company has agreed to lend the $400,000 at a rate of 9% per annum, using a loan secured by DST's inventory. A field warehouse agreement would be used, which would cost DST $2,000 a month.

Which source of credit should DST select? Explain.

## SOLUTION

Pledged Receivables (A/R):

0.80 A/R = $400,000 loan

A/R = $400,000/.80 = $500,000

Fee = (0.01) ($500,000) = $5,000

Interest cost = (0.11) ($400,000) x ¼ = $11,000

$$\text{Effective rate} = \left(\frac{\$11,000 + 5,000}{\$400,000}\right)\left(\frac{1}{90/360}\right) = .16 \text{ or } 16\%$$

Inventory loan:

Warehousing cost = $2,000 x 3 months = $6,000

Interest cost = 0.09 x $400,000 x ¼ = $9,000

$$\text{Effective rate} = \left(\frac{\$6,000 + 9,000}{\$400,000}\right)\left(\frac{1}{90/360}\right) = .15 \text{ or } 15\%$$

The inventory loan would be preferred since its cost is lowest under the conditions presented.

TRUE-FALSE

_____  1.  Working capital has traditionally been defined as the firm's investment in assets.

_____  2.  Generally, interest rates on short-term debt are higher than they are on long-term debt for a given borrower.

_____  3.  The guiding principle for the firm's working capital policies is referred to as the "principle of self-liquidating debt" or the "hedging principle."

_____  4.  The use of short-term sources of financing enhances the firm's liquidity and reduces the firm's rate of return on assets.

_____  5.  There are two basic problems encountered in attempting to manage the firm's use of short-term financing: determining how much short-term debt to use and determining what sources to select.

_____  6.  Investment decisions are undertaken in the expectation of receiving future benefits.

_____  7.  In order to reduce the risk of illiquidity, a firm should decrease its investment in cash and marketable securities.

_____  8.  Current liabilities provide a flexible source of financing.

_____  9.  The "hedging principle" is founded in valuation theory.

_____  10.  Spontaneous financing consists of trade credit and other accounts payable which arise "automatically" in the firm's day-to-day operations.

_____  11.  The amount of trade credit available to the firm varies inversely with the size of the cash discount.

_____  12.  Compensating balances are never required when a firm has a line of credit with a bank.

_____  13.  A transaction loan is made for a specific purpose or use for the funds involved.

_____ 14.	An advantage of commercial paper to a creditworthy borrower is that repayment can be postponed if necessary.

_____ 15.	Pledging involves selling accounts receivable to a factor.

_____ 16.	The primary sources of collateral for secured short-term credit are accounts receivable and inventories.

_____ 17.	Field warehouse financing agreements involve physically moving the pledged inventories to a public warehouse.

_____ 18.	Commercial paper and trade credit are both forms of secured credit.

_____ 19.	An advantage of trade credit is that the amount of credit extended expands and contracts with the needs of the firm.


MULTIPLE CHOICE

1.	Which of the following is an advantage associated with the use of current liabilities?

	a.	The use of current liabilities subjects the firm to greater risk of illiquidity.
	b.	The firm's interest costs can vary from year to year.
	c.	All of the above.
	d.	None of the above.

2.	Spontaneous financing consists of

	a.	accounts payable.
	b.	trade credit.
	c.	short-term notes payable.
	d.	common stock.
	e.	all of the above.
	f.	a and b only.

3.  Which of the following accounts would *not* be a prime consideration in working-capital management?

    a.  Cash
    b.  Accounts payable
    c.  Bonds payable
    d.  Marketable securities
    e.  Accounts receivable

4.  The greatest margin of safety for a firm would be provided by

    a.  more current assets and less current liabilities.
    b.  more current assets and more current liabilities.
    c.  less current assets and more current liabilities.
    d.  less current assets and less current liabilities.

5.  Which asset-liability combination would result in the firm having the greatest risk of technical insolvency?

    a.  More current assets and less current liabilities
    b.  More current assets and more current liabilities
    c.  Less current assets and more current liabilities
    d.  Less current assets and less current liabilities

6.  Which of the following illustrates the use of the hedging approach?

    a.  Temporary assets financed with long-term liabilities
    b.  Permanent assets financed with long-term liabilities
    c.  Temporary assets financed with short-term liabilities
    d.  All of the above
    e.  b and c

7.  Which of the following is not a form of secured short-term credit?

    a.  General lien
    b.  Chattel mortgages
    c.  Commercial paper
    d.  Terminal warehouse receipt
    e.  Factoring

8.  Under which of the following agreements does the borrower retain physical possession of the inventory used as collateral for a loan?

    a.  Field warehouse financing
    b.  Chattel mortgage
    c.  Terminal warehouse
    d.  All of the above
    e.  None of the above

9.  An informal agreement between a bank and its customer with respect to the maximum amount of unsecured credit the bank will permit the firm to owe at any one time is a

    a.  line of credit.
    b.  revolving credit agreement.
    c.  transaction loan.
    d.  none of the above.

10. When a firm needs short-term funds for only one purpose, it usually obtains a

    a.  line of credit.
    b.  revolving credit agreement.
    c.  transaction loan.
    d.  compensating balance.
    e.  none of the above.

11. If a firm borrows $1 million at 8% and is required to maintain $100,000 in a compensating balance, the effective annual interest cost is

    a.  8%
    b.  8.88%
    c.  7.27%
    d.  9.5%
    e.  none of the above

# CHAPTER 15

# Liquid Asset Management

Orientation: This chapter initiates our study of liquidity management. Here, we focus on the cash flow process and the reasons why a firm holds cash balances. The objectives of a sound cash management system are identified. The concept of float is defined. Several techniques that firms can use to favorably affect their cash receipts and disbursement patterns are examined. Finally, the composition of the firm's marketable securities portfolio is discussed.

Additionally, the risk-return tradeoff associated with the firm's investment in accounts receivable is discussed. For accounts receivable this tradeoff occurs as less creditworthy customers with a higher probability of bad debts are taken on to increase sales. The analysis is similar for sound inventory management. Here, a larger investment in inventory leads to more efficient production and speedier delivery; this should result in increased sales. However, additional financing costs to support the increase in inventory and increased handling and carrying costs is required.

I.    Why a company holds cash

    A.    The firm's cash balance is constantly affected by a variety of influences. Sound cash management techniques are based on a thorough understanding of the cash flow process.

        1.    On an irregular basis, cash holdings are increased from several external sources, such as from the sale of securities.

        2.    In a similar fashion, irregular cash outflows reduce the firm's cash balance. Typical examples include cash dividend payments and the interest requirements on debt agreements.

3.    Other major sources of cash arising from internal operations occur on a rather regular basis. Accounts receivable collections are an example.

B.    Three motives for holding cash balances have been identified by Keynes.[1]

1.    The *transactions motive* is the need for cash to meet payments that arise in the ordinary course of doing business. Holding cash to meet a payroll or to acquire raw materials characterizes this motive.

2.    The *precautionary motive* describes the investment in liquid assets that are used to satisfy possible, but as yet indefinite, needs for cash. Precautionary balances are a buffer against all kinds of things that might happen to drain the firm's cash resources.

3.    The *speculative motive* describes holding cash to take advantage of hoped-for, profit-making situations.

II.    Variations in liquid asset holdings

A.    Considerable variation is present in the liquid asset holdings of major industry groups and individual firms.

1.    This is because (1) not all of the factors noted above affect every firm, and (2) the executives in different firms who are ultimately responsible for cash management tasks have different risk-bearing preferences.

2.    Some industries invest very heavily in liquid assets. For example, the total-liquid-assets-to-total-assets ratio of the contract construction industry greatly exceeds that of the utility industry.

B.    Because assets are acquired, wasted, and sold every day, the management of liquid assets must be viewed as a dynamic process. The cash flow process is complex. In order to cut through this complexity, it is necessary that the firm's cash management system operate within clearly defined objectives.

---

[1] John Maynard Keynes, *The General Theory of Employment Interest and Money* (New York: Harcourt Brace Jovanovich, Inc., 1936).

III. Cash management objectives and decisions

    A. A properly designed cash management program forces the financial manager to come to grips with a risk-return tradeoff.

        1. He or she must strike an acceptable balance between holding too much cash and holding too little cash.

        2. A large cash investment minimizes the chances of insolvency, but it penalizes company profitability.

        3. A small cash investment frees excess (cash) balances for investment in longer-lived and more profitable assets, which increases the firm's profitability.

    B. The firm's cash management system should strive to achieve two prime objectives:

        1. Enough cash must be on hand to dispense effectively with the disbursal needs that arise in the course of doing business.

        2. The firm's investment in idle cash balances must be reduced to a minimum.

    C. In the attempt to meet the two objectives noted above, certain decisions dominate the cash management process. These decision areas can be reduced to the three following questions:

        1. What can be done to speed up cash collections and slow down or better control cash outflows?

        2. What should be the composition of the marketable securities portfolio?

        3. How should the investment in liquid assets be split between actual cash holdings and marketable securities? This is covered in the Appendix to this chapter.

IV. Collection and disbursement procedures

   A. Cash acceleration and deceleration techniques revolve around the concept of *float*. Float can be broken down into four elements:

      1. *Mail float* refers to funds that are tied up as a result of the time that elapses from the moment a customer mails his or her remittance check until the firm begins to process the check.

      2. *Processing float* refers to funds that are tied up as a result of the firm's recording and processing remittance checks prior to their deposit in the bank.

      3. *Transit float* refers to funds that are tied up as a result of the time needed for a deposited check to clear through the commercial banking system and become "usable" funds to the firm.

      4. *Disbursing float* refers to funds that are technically usable to the firm until its *payment* check has cleared through the banking system and has been charged against its deposit account.

   B. Float reduction can result in considerable benefits in terms of (1) usable funds that are released for company use and (2) in the returns produced on these freed-up balances. A study problem at the end of this chapter illustrates the calculation of such savings.

   C. Several techniques are available to improve the management of the firm's cash inflows. These techniques may also provide for a reduction in float.

      1. The lock-box arrangement is a widely used commercial banking service for expediting cash gathering.

         a. The objective is to reduce *both* mail and processing float.

b. The procedure behind a lock-box system is very simple. The firm rents a local post office box and authorizes a local bank in which a deposit account is maintained to pick up remittances from the box.

    (1) Customers are instructed to mail their payments to the numbered post office box.

    (2) A deposit form is prepared by the *bank* for each batch of processed checks.

    (3) The bank may notify the firm daily as to the amount of funds deposited on the firm's behalf.

    (4) The firm that receives checks from all over the country establishes several lock boxes.

c. A lock-box arrangement provides for (1) increased working cash, (2) elimination of clerical functions, and (3) early knowledge of dishonored checks.

d. The firm must carefully evaluate whether this or any cash management service is worth the added costs. Usually, the bank levies a charge for each check processed through the system. The marginal income generated from released funds must exceed the added costs of the system to make it economically beneficial. A study problem at the end of this chapter illustrates this kind of calculation.

2. *Pre-authorized checks* (PACs) are another method for speeding up the conversion of receipts into working cash.

a. The objective of the PAC is to reduce mail and processing float.

b. A PAC (1) is created with the individual's legal authorization, (2) resembles an ordinary check, and (3) does *not* contain the signature of the person on whose account it is being drawn.

c.   PAC systems are most useful to firms that (1) regularly receive a large volume of payments of a fixed amount (2) from the same customers. Insurance companies and savings and loan associations are prominent examples.

d.   The principle behind the PAC system is straightforward. The firm simply obtains an authorization from its customers to draw checks (at specified times and for specified amounts) on their (the customers') demand deposit accounts.

e.   Figure 15.1 shows the operation of a PAC system.

f.   The benefits derived from a PAC system include (1) highly predictable cash flows, (2) reduced billing, postage, and clerical expenses, (3) customer preference, and (4) increased working cash stemming from reduced mail and processing float.

3.   *Depository transfer checks* are used in conjunction with *concentration banking*. A concentration bank is one in which the firm maintains a major disbursing account.

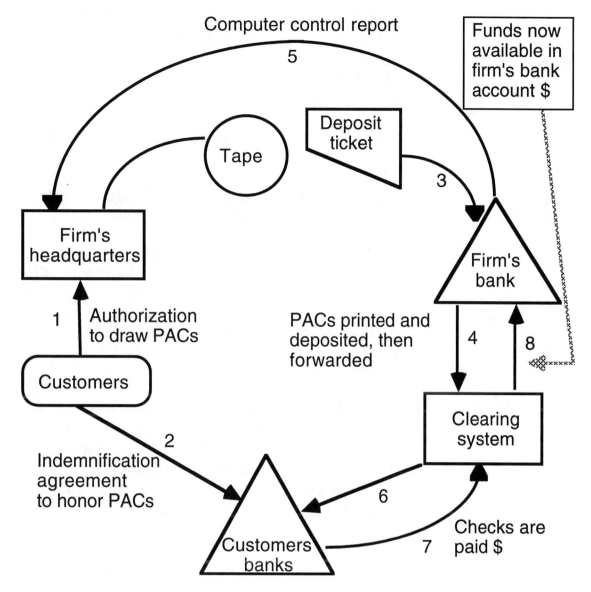

FIGURE 15.1
Pre-Authorized Check Systems (PAC)

a. The major objective of using depository transfer checks (DTCs) is to eliminate excess cash balances held by the firm in its several regional banks. A secondary objective, which is achieved through use of the <u>automated depository transfer check</u> (ADTC) is to reduce float incurred by mailing (ordinary) DTCs from a regional bank to a concentration bank.

b. The DTC provides a means for moving (transferring) funds from a local bank to a concentration bank.

b. The DTC provides a means for moving (transferring) funds from a local bank to a concentration bank.

    (1) The DTC is an unsigned, non-negotiable instrument.

    (2) The DTC is payable only to the bank of ultimate deposit.

    (3) DTCs can operate through the use of the U.S. mail system or an automated system (ADTC).

c. With the conventional DTC, a company employee deposits the day's cash receipts in a local bank, fills out a DTC for the amount of the deposit, and mails the DTC to the concentration bank. When the DTC is received at the concentration bank, the transferred funds are credited to the firm's demand deposit account.

d. The ADTC eliminates the time required for the conventional DTC to travel through the mails and physically reach the concentration bank. The deposit information is transmitted electronically at the concentration bank, which results in the saved time. This system is shown in Figure 15.2.

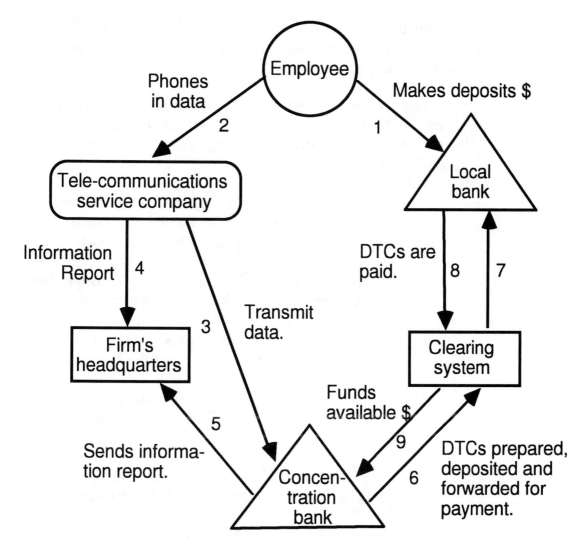

FIGURE 15.2
Automated Depository Transfer Check System (ADTC)

4.    *Wire transfers* offer the fastest method for moving funds between
      commercial banks. Usable ("good") funds are transferred and
      thereby immediately become usable funds at the receiving bank.
      There is no *transit* float with wire transfers. Two major
      communication facilities are used to accommodate wire transfers: (1)
      bank wire, which is privately operated by about 250 major
      commercial banks in the United States, and (2) Federal Reserve wire
      system, which is accessible to members of the Federal Reserve
      system. The movement of small dollar amounts does not usually
      justify use of this system.

D. Techniques used by firms that hope to improve the management of their cash outflows include: (1) zero balance accounts, (2) payable-through drafts, and (3) remote disbursing.

1. *Zero balance accounts* (ZBAs) permit centralized control (i.e., at the head office) over cash disbursements, but, at the same time, they allow the firm to maintain disbursing authority at the local or divisional level.

   a. The major objective of a ZBA system is to achieve better control over cash payments. A secondary benefit of this technique *might* be an increase in disbursement float.

   b. Under a ZBA system, each profit center (division) has a disbursing account located in the *same* concentration bank.

      (1) The firm's authorized employees write payment checks in the usual manner.

      (2) These checks then clear through the banking system and are presented to the firm's concentration bank for payment.

      (3) The checks are paid by the bank, and negative balances build up in the appropriate disbursing accounts.

      (4) Daily, the negative balances are restored to a zero level by means of credits to the various ZBAs and a corresponding reduction in the firm's master demand deposit account in the concentration bank.

   c. For the firm that has several operating units, the benefits from using a ZBA system include:

      (1) Centralized control over disbursements.

      (2) Reduction of time spent on superficial cash management activities.

      (3) Reduction of excess cash balances held in outlying accounts.

      (4) An increase in disbursement float.

2. *Payable-through drafts* (PTDs) have the physical appearance of ordinary checks but they are drawn on and paid by the issuing firm instead of the bank. The bank serves as a collection point for the documents and passes the documents on to the firm for inspection and authorization for payment.

   a. The objective of a payable-through draft system is to provide for effective control of field-authorized payments. An example would be a claim settlement authorized by an insurance agent.

   b. Stop payment orders can be initiated by the firm's headquarters on any drafts considered inappropriate.

   c. Legal payment of *individual* drafts takes place *after* review and approval of the drafts by the company. Disbursing float, however, is usually *not* increased by the use of drafts. For purposes of measuring usable funds to the firm, drafts presented daily for payment are charged in *total* against the corporate master demand deposit account.

3. *Remote disbursing*, rather obviously, is intended to increase disbursing float.

   a. To implement such a procedure, the firm needs only to open and use a deposit account located in a city distant from its customers' banks.

   b. Since checks written on that account take longer to clear, the firm has use of its funds for a longer period of time.

   c. The major constraint on this procedure is the possible alienation of important customers who must wait longer for their remittance checks to become usable funds.

4. *Electronic funds transfer* methods are serving to reduce transit, mail, and processing float

   a. If Firm A owes money to Firm B, this situation ought to be immediately reflected on both the books and bank accounts of these companies.

b. This ideal within the U.S. financial system has not been reached; the trend towards it is readily observable. Business firms, for example, are using systems such as terminal-based wire transfers to move funds within their cash management systems.

c. The heart of electronic funds transfer (EFT) is the elimination of the check as a method of transferring funds. The process of EFT should provide for a more efficient economy, since funds (cash) will be released for more productive purposes.

V. Evaluating the costs of cash management services

A. Whether a particular cash management system will provide an economic benefit to the firm can be evaluated by use of this relationship:

added costs = added benefits

B. Clearly, if the benefits exceed the costs of using the system, then the system is economically feasible

C. On a per-unit basis, this relationship can be expressed as follows:

$$P = (D)\,(S)\,(i)$$

where $P$ = increase in per-check processing cost, if the new system is adopted,
$D$ = days saved in the collection process, i.e., float reduction,
$S$ = average check size in dollars,
$i$ = the daily, before-tax opportunity cost (rate of return) of carrying cash.

D. The sum of $(D)\,(S)\,(i)$ must exceed $P$ for the system to be beneficial to the firm. A study problem at the end of this chapter provides an example of this logic.

VI. Composition of the marketable securities portfolio

A. When selecting a proper marketable securities mix, five factors should be considered.

1.  *Financial risk* is the uncertainty of expected returns from a security due to unforeseeable changes in the financial capacity of the security issuer to make future payments to the security owner.

2.  *Interest rate* risk is the uncertainty in expected returns caused by possible changes in interest rates. This is particularly important for securities that have long, as opposed to short, terms of maturity. (See study problem 5 for an illustration of this point.)

3.  *Liquidity* is the ability to transform a security into cash. Consideration should be given to (1) the time needed to sell the security and (2) the likelihood that the security can be sold at or near its prevailing market price.

4.  The *taxability* of interest income and capital gains is seriously considered by some corporate treasurers.

    a.  The interest income from *municipal obligations* is tax-exempt.

    b.  The following equation may be used to determine an equivalent before-tax yield on a taxable security.

        (1)  Notation:

             $r$ = equivalent before-tax yield
             $r^*$ = after-tax yield on tax-exempt security
             $T$ = firm's marginal income tax rate

        (2)  Computation

             $$r = \frac{r^*}{(1 - T)}$$

        (3)  Example:  Suppose a firm has a choice between investing in a 1-year tax-free debt issue yielding 6% on a $1,000 outlay or a 1-year taxable issue that yields 7% on a $1,000 outlay.  The firm pays federal taxes at the rate of 34%.  Which security is more beneficial to the firm?

             $$r = \frac{0.06}{(1 - 0.34)} = 9.09\%$$

277

(4)   Clearly, this firm should choose the tax-exempt security.

5.   The *yield* criterion involves a weighing of the risks and benefits inherent in the four previously mentioned factors. The higher the risks associated with a particular security, the higher the expected yield (risk-return tradeoff).

B.   Marketable security alternatives

1.   A *Treasury bill* is a direct obligation of the U.S. government sold on a regular basis by the U.S. Treasury.

a.   These bills may be purchased in denominations of $10,000, $15,000, $50,000, $100,000, $500,000, and $1,000,000.

b.   The bills are currently offered with maturities of 91, 182, and 365 days.

c.   Since Treasury bills are sold on a discount basis, the investor does not receive an actual interest payment.

d.   Since Treasury bills are backed by the U.S. government, they are considered risk-free and consequently sell at lower yields than those obtainable on other marketable securities.

e.   The income from Treasury bills is subject only to federal income taxes and is always taxed as an ordinary gain.

2.   *Federal agency securities* represent debt obligations of federal government agencies and were created to carry out lending programs of the U.S. government.

a.   The Federal National Mortgage Association (FNMA) renders supplementary assistance to the secondary market for mortgages.

b.   The Federal Home Loan Banks (FHLB) function as a credit reserve system for member banks.

c. The Federal Land Banks grant loans to members of Federal Land Bank Associations who are engaged in agriculture, provide agricultural services, or own rural homes.

d. The Federal Intermediate Credit Banks grant loans to and purchase notes originating from loans made to farmers by other financial institutions.

e. The Banks for Cooperatives make loans to cooperative associations which are owned and controlled by individuals involved in general farm business.

f. Securities of these "big five" federally sponsored agencies are *not* directly backed by the U.S. government.

g. The maturities available range from 30 days to 15 years, with most (80%) maturing in 5 years or less.

h. The yields available always exceed those of Treasury bills of comparable maturity and are taxable at the federal, state, and local level.

3. *Bankers' acceptances* are largely concentrated in the financing of foreign transactions; this acceptance is a draft (order to pay) drawn on a specific bank by an exporter in order to obtain payment for goods shipped to a customer who maintains an account with that bank.

a. The maturities run mostly from 30 to 180 days, with the most common period being 90 days.

b. Like Treasury bills, the acceptances are sold on a discount basis.

c. Income generated from acceptances is fully taxable at all governmental levels.

d. Acceptances provide investors with a higher yield than do Treasury bills and agency obligations of comparable maturity.

4. A <u>negotiable</u> <u>certificate</u> <u>of</u> <u>deposit</u> (CD), is a marketable receipt for funds that have been deposited in a bank for a fixed time period at a fixed interest rate.

    a. CDs are offered in denominations ranging from $25,000 to $10,000,000, with popular sizes of $100,000, $500,000 and $1,000,000.

    b. Original maturities on CDs range from 1 to 18 months.

    c. Yields on CDs are higher than yields on Treasury bills, and, in recent years, they have exceeded those available on acceptances.

    d. The income received from CDs is taxed at all governmental levels.

5. *Commercial paper* refers to short-term, unsecured promissory notes sold by large businesses in order to raise cash.

    a. Paper is usually sold in relatively large denominations, typically in excess of $25,000, and ranging up to $1,000,000.

    b. The notes are sold on a discount basis with maturities ranging from 3 to 270 days.

    c. It is the only investment instrument discussed here that has no *active* trading in a secondary market.

    d. The return on commercial paper is fully taxable at all governmental levels.

6. *Repurchase agreements* are legal contracts that involve the actual sale of securities by a borrower to the lender, with a commitment on the part of the borrower to repurchase the securities at the contract price plus a stated interest charge.

a. These agreements are usually executed in sizes of $500,000 or more.

b. The maturity is either for a specified time period (tailored to the needs of the investor) or there is no fixed maturity date.

c. The yields are generally less than those of Treasury bill rates of comparable maturities and are taxable at all governmental levels.

7. *Money market mutual funds* usually invest in a diversified portfolio of short-term, high-grade debt instruments like those described in this section.

   a. These funds sell their shares to a large number of small investors in order to raise cash.

   b. The funds offer the investing firm a high degree of liquidity and investment expertise.

   c. The returns earned from owning shares in a money market fund are taxable at all governmental levels.

   d. Table 15.1 summarizes the salient features of the major money market instruments important to businesses.

Table 15-1  Features of Selected Money Market Instruments

| Instrument | Denominations | Maturities | Basis | Liquidity | Taxability |
|---|---|---|---|---|---|
| U.S. Treasury Bills: Direct obligations of the U.S. government | $10,000<br>15,000<br>50,000<br>100,000<br>500,000<br>1,000,000 | 91 days<br>182 days<br>365 days<br>9-month not presently issued | Discount | Excellent secondary market | Exempt from state and local income; do not qualify for favorable capital gains rate |
| Federal Agency Securities: Obligations of corporations and agencies created to affect the federal government's lending programs. | Wide variation from $1,000 to $1,000,000 | 5 days* to more than ten years (*Farm Credit consolidated system-wide discount notes) | Discount or coupon; usually on coupon | Good for issues of "Big Five" agencies | Generally exempt at local level; FNMA issues are not |
| Bankers' Acceptances: Drafts accepted for future payment by commercial banks | No set size; typically range from $25,000 to $1,000,000 | Predominantly from 30 to 180 days | Discount | Good for acceptances of large "money market" banks | Taxed at all levels of government |
| Negotiable Certificates of Deposit: Marketable receipts for funds deposited in a bank for a fixed time period. | $15,000 to $10,000,000 | 1 to 18 months | Accrued interest | Fair to good | Taxed at all levels of government |
| Commercial Paper: Short-term, unsecured promissory notes. | $5,000 to $5,000,000; $1,000 and $5,000 multiples above the initial offering size are sometimes available | 3 to 270 days | Discount | Poor; no active, secondary market in usual sense | Taxed at all levels of government |
| Repurchase Agreements: Legal contracts between a borrower (security seller) and lender (security buyer). The borrower will repurchase at the contract price plus an interest charge | Typical sizes are $500,000 or more | According to terms of contract | Not applicable | Fixed by the agreement, i.e., borrower will repurchase | Taxed at all levels of government |
| Money Market Mutual Funds: Hold a diversified portfolio of short-term, high-grade debt instruments | Some require an initial investment as small as $1,000. | Shares can be sold at any time | Net asset value | Good; provided by the fund itself | Taxed at all levels of government |

8. *Money market deposit accounts* became available to the public on December 14, 1982, on authorization of the Depository Institutions Deregulatory Committee.

   a. These accounts are offered by commercial banks and thrift institutions. The intent is to compete with money market mutual funds, but they *do* differ in significant ways from the funds.

   b. One characteristic of the money market deposit accounts (MMDAs) that makes them inappropriate for *most* businesses is that the number of transactions per month on each account is limited. Firms generally do not want to be restricted on the number of times per month that they can tap their liquid asset reserves. That runs counter to the very logic of holding a buffer stock of liquidity.

   c. Alternatively, the MMDAs have become very popular with *individual* investors.

VII. Accounts receivable

   A. Typically, accounts receivable accounts for just over 25%of a firm's assets.

   B. The size of the investment in accounts receivable varies from industry to industry and is affected by several factors including the percentage of credit sales to total sales, the level of sales, and the credit and collection policies, more specifically, the terms of sale, the quality of customer, and collection efforts.

   C. Although all these factors affect the size of the investment, only the credit and collection policies are decision variables under the control of the financial manager.

   D. The terms of sale are generally stated in the form a/b net c, indicating that the customer can deduct a percentage if the account is paid within b days; otherwise, the account must be paid within c days.

E.  If the customer decides to forgo the discount and not pay until the final payment date, the annualized opportunity cost of passing up this a% discount and withholding payment until the cth day is determined as follows:

annualized opportunity

$$\text{cost of foregoing the discount} = \frac{a}{1-a} \times \frac{360}{c-b}$$

Example: Given the trade credit terms of 3/20 net 60, what is the annualized opportunity cost of passing up the 3% discount and withholding payment until the 60th day?

Solution: Substituting in the values from the example, we get

$$27.8\% = \frac{0.03}{1-0.03} \times \frac{360}{60-20}$$

F.  A second decision variable in determining the size of the investment in accounts receivable in addition to the trade credit terms is the type of customer.

1.  The costs associated with extending credit to lower-quality customers include:

    a.  Increased costs of credit investigation
    b.  Increased probability of customer default
    c.  Increased collection costs

G.  Analyzing the credit application is a major part of accounts receivable management.

1.  Several avenues are open to the firm in considering the credit rating of an applicant. Among these are financial statements, independent credit ratings and reports, bank checking, information from other companies, and past experiences.

2.  One commonly used method for credit evaluation is called credit scoring and involves the numerical evaluation of each applicant in which an applicant receives a score based upon the answers to a simple set of questions. The score is then evaluated relative to a predetermined standard, its level

relative to that standard determining whether or not credit scoring should be extended to the applicant. The major advantage of credit scoring is that it is inexpensive and easy to perform.

    3.    Once the decision to extend credit has been made, and, if the decision is yes, a maximum credit line is established as a ceiling on the amount of credit to be extended.

H.    The third and final decision variable in determining the size of the investment in accounts receivable is the firm's collection policies.

    1.    Collection policy is a combination of letter-sending, telephone calls, personal visits, and legal actions.

    2.    The greater the amount spent on collecting, the lower the volume of bad debts.

        a.    The relationship is not linear, however, and beyond a point is not helpful.

        b.    If sales are independent of collection efforts, then methods of collection should be evaluated with respect to the reduction in bad debts against the cost of lowering those bad debts.

I.    Credit should be extended to the point that marginal profitability on additional sales equals the required rate of return on the additional investment in receivables necessary to generate those sales.

J.    Credit policy changes involve direct tradeoffs between costs and benefits. Determining whether the increased sales contribute more towards profits than the increased costs take away from them is the job of marginal or incremental analysis. Marginal analysis is performed as follows:

    1.    Estimate the change in profits from the new policy. This is equal to the increased sales times the profit contribution less any additional bad debts incurred.

    2.    Estimate the cost of the additional investment in accounts receivable and inventory.

3.   Estimate the change in the cost of the cash discount (if a change in the cash discount is enacted).

4.   Compare the incremental revenues with the incremental costs.

VIII.   Inventory

A.   Typically, inventory accounts for about 4.88% of a firm's assets.

B.   The purpose of carrying inventories is to uncouple the operations of the firm, that is, to make each function of the business independent of each other function.

C.   As such, the decision with respect to the size of the investment in inventory involves a basic tradeoff between risk and return.

D.   The risk comes from the possibility of running out of inventory if too little inventory is held, while the return aspect of this tradeoff results because increased inventory investment costs money.

E.   There are several general types of inventory.

1.   Raw materials inventory consists of the basic materials that have been purchased from other firms to be used in the firm's productions operations. This type of inventory uncouples the production function from the purchasing function.

2.   Work-in-process inventory consists of partially finished goods that require additional work before they become finished goods. This type of inventory uncouples the various production operations.

3.   Finished goods inventory consists of goods on which the production has been completed but the goods are not yet sold. This type of inventory uncouples the production and sales function.

4.   Stock of cash inventory, already discussed in some detail in preceding chapters, serves to make the payment of bills independent of the collection of accounts due.

F. In order to effectively manage the investment in inventory, two problems must be dealt with: the order quantity problem and the order point problem.

G. The order quantity problem involves the determination of the optimal order size for an inventory item given its expected usage, carrying, and ordering costs.

H. The economic order quantity (EOQ) model attempts to determine the order size that will minimize total inventory costs. The EOQ is given as:

$$Q^* = \sqrt{\frac{2SO}{C}}$$

where C = carrying costs per unit
O = ordering costs per order
S = total demand in units over the planning period
Q* = the optimal order quantity in units

I. The order point problem attempts to answer the following question: How low should inventory be depleted before it is reordered?

J. In answering this question, two factors become important:

1. What is the usual procurement or delivery time, and how much stock is needed to accommodate this time period?

2. How much safety stock does the management desire?

K. Modification for safety stocks is necessary since the usage rate of inventory is seldom stable over a given timetable.

L. This safety stock is used to safeguard the firm against changes in order time and receipt of shipped goods.

M. The greater the uncertainty associated with forecasted demand or order time, the larger the safety stock.

1. The costs associated with running out of inventory will also determine the safety stock levels.

2. A point is reached where it is too costly to carry a larger safety stock given the associated risk.

N. Inflation can also have an impact on the level of inventory carried.

   1. Goods may be purchased in large quantities in anticipation of price rises.

   2. The cost of carrying goods may increase causing a decline in $Q^*$, the optional order quantity.

O. The just-in-time inventory control system is more than just an inventory control system; it is a production and management system.

   1. Under this system, inventory is cut down to a minimum, and the time and physical distance between the various production operations is also minimized.

   2. Actually, the just-in-time inventory control system is just a new approach to the EOQ model, which tries to produce the lowest average level of inventory possible.

   3. Average inventory is reduced by locating inventory supplies in convenient locations and setting up restocking strategies that cut time, thereby reducing the needed level of safety stock.

Study Problems

1. Buckeye Equipment has $3,000,000 in excess cash that it might invest in marketable securities. In order to buy and sell the securities, though, the company must pay a transactions fee of $67,500.

   (a) Would you recommend purchasing the securities if they yield 13% annually and are held for:

      1. 1 month?
      2. 2 months?
      3. 3 months?
      4. 6 months?
      5. 1 year?

(b)     What minimum required yield would the securities have to return for the firm to hold them for 3 months?

SOLUTION

(a)     It is necessary to calculate the dollar value of the estimated return for each holding period and compare it with the transactions fee. This will allow you to determine if a gain can be made by investing in the securities. The calculations and recommendations are shown below:

|  |  |  |  | Recommendation |
|---|---|---|---|---|
| 1. | $3,000,000(.13)(1/12) | = | $32,500 < $67,500 | No |
| 2. | $3,000,000(.13)(2/12) | = | $65,000 < $67,500 | No |
| 3. | $3,000,000(.13)(3/12) | = | $97,500 > $67,500 | Yes |
| 4. | $3,000,000(.13)(6/12) | = | $195,000 > $67,500 | Yes |
| 5. | $3,000,000(.13)(12/12) | = | $390,000 > $67,500 | Yes |

(b)     Now we find the break-even yield for a 3-month holding period. Let (%) be the required yield. With $3,000,000 to invest for three months, we have:

$$\$3,000,000 \ (\%) \ (3/12) = \$67,500$$
$$\$3,000,000 \ (\%) = \$270,000$$
$$(\%) = \$270,000/\$3,000,000 = \underline{9\%}$$

2.     Portland Energy Products is evaluating whether or not to use an additional lock box. If the lock box is used, check processing costs will rise by $.20 a check. The average check size that will be mailed to the lock-box location is $1,000. Funds that are freed by using the lock box will be invested in marketable securities to yield an *annual* before-tax return of 7%. The firm uses a 365-day year in its analysis procedures. What reduction in check-collection time is required to justify use of the lock box?

SOLUTION

Solve the following relationship for D:

$$P = (D) \quad (S) \ (i)$$

$$\$.20 = (D)(\$1,000)\left(\frac{0.07}{365}\right)$$

$$\$.20 = (D) \quad (\$.192)$$

$$\frac{\$.20}{\$.192} = D = \underline{1.0417 \text{ days}}$$

Thus, the lock box is justified if it can speed up collections by *more* than 1.0417 days.

3.   Annual sales for Austin Drilling Supply will total $250,000,000 next year. What would be the annual value of 1 day's float reduction to this firm if it could invest the freed-up balances at 8% per year?

SOLUTION

Compute Austin's sales per day:

$$\frac{\text{annual revenues}}{\text{days in years}} = \frac{250,000,000}{365} = \$684,932$$

Compute the annual value of the 1-day float reduction:

$$(\$684,932)\,(0.08) = \underline{\$54,795}$$

4.   The corporate treasurer of Buckeye Bottling is considering purchasing a municipal obligation with a 7% coupon and a $1,000 par value. Mr. Inside Info has telephoned the treasurer about another $1,000 par value offering which provides a 12% yield. This latter offering is, however, fully taxable. Buckeye is taxed at a 48% rate.

(a)   Should the treasurer take Mr. Info's advice and purchase the 12% security?

(b)   What is the equivalent before-tax yield on the municipal, assuming Buckeye is in a 48% tax bracket?

SOLUTION

(a)   The after-tax yield to Buckeye on the 12% offering is $(0.12)\,(1-0.48)$ = 6.24%. Since the yield on the municipal is already stated on an after-tax basis, the treasurer should ignore Mr. Info's advice and purchase the municipal offering.

290

(b)     The equivalent before-tax yield is:

$$r = \frac{0.07}{(1-0.48)} = \underline{13.46\%}$$

Thus, the taxable issue would have to yield in excess of 13.46% to be more attractive than the municipal to Buckeye.

5.     Tech Electronics, manufacturers of fine calculators, has recently purchased 10-year bonds at their par value of $1,000 per security. Texas Parts, a close competitor, has just purchased 5-year bonds at their $1,000 par value. Both securities have a coupon rate set at 8%, are compounded annually, and have a maturity value of $1,000. Suppose the prevailing interest rate 1 year from now rises to 10%. What would the decline in market price be for each bond in 1 year?

SOLUTION

One year from now, the 5-year issue has 4 years remaining to maturity. The market price in 1 year can be found by computing P according to the following:

$$P = \sum_{T=1}^{4} \frac{\$80}{(1+0.10)^T} + \frac{\$1,000}{(1+0.10)^4} = \$936.60$$

where $80 = (0.08) ($1,000). Similarly, for the 10-year issue, which now has 9 years to maturity,

$$P = \sum_{T=1}^{9} \frac{\$80}{(1+0.10)^T} + \frac{\$1,000}{(1+0.10)^9} = \$884.82$$

Thus the 10-year security declines in price $115.18 ($1,000 - $884.82), while the 5-year security declines in price by only $63.40 ($1,000-$936.60). This illustrates the concept of *interest rate risk*, discussed in the text in Chapter 15.

6. Gavin International expects to generate sales of $74,000,000 in the coming year. All sales are done on a credit basis, net 30 days. Gavin has estimated that it takes an average of 4 days for payments to reach their central office and an additional day to process the payments. What is the opportunity cost of the funds tied up in the mail and processing? Gavin uses a 360-day year in all calculations and can invest free funds at 7%.

SOLUTION

Daily collections = 74,000,000/360 = $ 205,555.56

Opportunity Cost = (205,555.56) (5) (.07) = <u>$71,944</u>

7. The corporate treasurer of Chester Motors is considering the purchase of either an offering carrying a 7.6% coupon or a municipal obligation with a 5% coupon. Both bonds have a $1,000 par value. The company is currently in the 34% marginal tax bracket. Which security should the treasurer recommend?

SOLUTION

The after-tax yield to Chester Motors on the 7.6% offering is (1-.34) (.076) = 5%. The municipal's after-tax rate is the stated 5%. There is no difference in yield. If the risk is considered equal for each security, then the treasurer would be indifferent between the two.

8. The Swank Furniture Company is trying to determine the optimal order quantity for sofas. Annual sales for sofas are 800, and the retail price is $300 per sofa. The cost of carrying sofas is $50 per sofa per year. It costs $35 to prepare and receive an order. The inventory planning period is one year.

   a. Determine the EOQ (assuming a one-year planning period).

   b. If the annual sales are 1200, what is the EOQ? If the annual sales are 300, what is the EOQ?

SOLUTION

   a. $\text{EOQ} = \sqrt{\dfrac{2(800)(55)}{50}} = \sqrt{1120} = 33.47 = 33$ sofas

b. $\quad EOQ = \sqrt{\dfrac{2(1200)(35)}{50}} = \sqrt{1680} = 40.99 = 41$ sofas

$$\sqrt{\dfrac{2(300)(35)}{50}} = \sqrt{420} = 20.49 = 20 \text{ sofas}$$

9. What is the effective annualized cost of forgoing a trade discount with terms 4/40, net 60?

SOLUTION

The annualized opportunity cost of foregoing the trade discount $= \dfrac{a}{1-a} \times \dfrac{360}{c-b}$

where the terms of sale are stated in the form a/b net c, indicating that they can deduct a% if the account is paid within b days; otherwise, the account must be paid within c days.

Thus,

$$\text{annualized opportunity cost of foregoing the trade discount} = \dfrac{a}{1-a} \times \dfrac{360}{c-b}$$

$$= \dfrac{.04}{1-.04} \times \dfrac{360}{60\ 40}$$

$$= 0.75$$
$$= 75\%$$

Self Tests

TRUE-FALSE

_____ 1. Accounts receivable are usually referred to as "near-cash assets."

_____ 2. Holding cash to pay for next week's labor bill (payroll) is an example of the precautionary motive for holding cash.

_____ 3. Ready borrowing power enables the firm to reduce the cash balances actually held for precautionary purposes.

_____ 4.   Technical insolvency means that the firm is able to meet its short-term obligations on time but that its long-term obligations are in jeopardy.

_____ 5.   Cash flow forecasting is the initial step in any effective cash management program.

_____ 6.   Wire transfers provide the fastest and least costly method of transferring funds among depository institutions.

_____ 7.   A possible benefit stemming from the use of pre-authorized checks is that cash flows can be more predictable.

_____ 8.   The major objective of using payable-through drafts is to extend disbursing float.

_____ 9.   The major reason for using lock boxes is to enjoy a reduction in transit float.

_____ 10.  Zero balance accounts are used to accelerate cash receipts.

_____ 11.  Although they have a lower yield, agency securities are more readily marketable by the purchasing corporation than are Treasury bills.

_____ 12.  Bankers' acceptances generally mature from 9 to 12 months after "sight."

_____ 13.  Commercial paper is backed by specific assets of the firm.

_____ 14.  The most common denomination for the negotiable CD is $10,000.

_____ 15.  The longer the term of maturity, the less sensitive the price of a security to changes in interest rates.

_____ 16.  Long-term bonds may serve as a useful (comfortable) hedge against interest rate risk.

_____ 17.  Because of their higher financial risk, agency securities always yield more than Treasury securities of a comparable maturity do.

_____ 18.  The higher the marginal tax bracket, the lower the after-tax rate of return on a taxable security.

_____ 19. Bankers' acceptances provide for a steady flow of interest payments to the investor in the form of coupon payments.

_____ 20. With respect to interest risk, Treasury securities are risk-free.

_____ 21. Money market deposit accounts (MMDAs) are more suited to individual investors than business firms as a tool of liquid asset management.

_____ 22. The lock-box system is the most widely used commercial banking service for expediting cash gathering.

_____ 23. A concentration bank is one where the firm generally maintains several minor disbursing accounts.

_____ 24. There is an inverse relationship between a financial instrument's chance of default and financial risk.

_____ 25. The contract price of the securities that make up the repurchase agreement is fixed for the duration of the transaction.

_____ 26. According to Keynes, the demand for cash can be divided into three categories: transactions, precautionary, and speculative.

_____ 27. A PAC or pre-authorized check does not ordinarily bear the name of the person on whose account the check was drawn.

_____ 28. To calculate the annual savings due to float reduction, you would multiply the sales per day by the days of float reduction.

_____ 29. Payable-through drafts provide control over field payments.

_____ 30. A liquid asset is an asset that can be sold regardless of the time it takes to make the sale and the price concession suffered to make the sale.

_____ 31. Commercial paper is sometimes described as short term, corporate IOUs.

_____ 32. Increases in cash holdings from external sources of funds tend to be more regular than internal generation of cash.

_____ 33. The motives for holding cash apply equally to all firms. Variations in cash holdings from firm to firm result from differing management risk preferences.

_____ 34. The prime objectives of cash management are to reduce idle cash balances and to have sufficient cash on hand to meet disbursal needs.

_____ 35. Under the lock-box arrangement, a deposit form is prepared by the *depositor* for each batch of processed checks.

_____ 36. Most cash management techniques should be adopted regardless of their economic benefits, in order to financially aid commercial banks.

_____ 37. The use of payable-through drafts will usually increase disbursing float to the issuing firm.

_____ 38. Commercial paper refers to short-term, unsecured promissory notes sold by *government agencies* to raise cash.

_____ 39. The objective in credit policy management is to minimize losses.

_____ 40. An increase in the time period over which credit must be repaid will increase demand.

_____ 41. Receivables arise from credit sales.

_____ 42. To speed up the turnover of receivables, a firm may either shorten the discount term or increase the discount offered.

_____ 43. The expression "5/10, net 30" means that the customers receive a 10% discount if they pay within 5 days; otherwise, they must pay within 30 days.

_____ 44. There is no one level of inventory that is efficient for all firms.

_____ 45. In determining the level of safety stock, it is important to evaluate the tradeoff between the cost of carrying the additional inventory with the risk of running out of inventory.

_____ 46. Lead time in determining the reorder point refers to the time between the receipt of a customer's order and the shipment of that order.

_____ 47.    Large safety stocks tend to reduce the possibility of stockouts.

_____ 48.    The EOQ provides for an optimal safety stock determination.


## MULTIPLE CHOICE

1.    Indicate the item that is not an advantage of the lock-box system.

   a.    The cost is minimal.
   b.    Speeds up the flow of cash to the firm.
   c.    Remittances are collected sooner.
   d.    All of the above are advantages.

2.    Which of the following is not a cash acceleration technique?

   a.    Lock boxes
   b.    Automated depository transfer checks
   c.    Pre-authorized checks
   d.    Payable-through drafts
   e.    All of the above *are* cash acceleration techniques

3.    Depository transfer checks mainly

   a.    reduce mail and processing float.
   b.    extend disbursing float.
   c.    provide a method of moving funds from local banks to concentration banks.
   d.    centralize disbursing authority.

4.    Zero balance accounts:

   a.    Permit centralized control over disbursements.
   b.    Provide for effective control over field payments.
   c.    Are an integral part of the lock-box system.
   d.    Are the same thing as pre-authorized checks.

5.    A pre-authorized check system

      a.     reduces mail float.
      b      reduces processing float.
      c.     extends disbursing float.
      d.     a and b.
      e.     b and c.

6.    Generally, the least important component of a firm's preference for liquidity is

      a.     the transaction motive.
      b.     the precautionary motive.
      c.     the speculative motive.
      d.     all motives are of equal importance.

7.    Which of the following is *not* an objective of the lockbox system?

      a.     Reduce mail float.
      b.     Reduce processing float.
      c.     Reduce transit float.
      d.     Reduce disbursing float.

8.    The advantages of a pre-authorized check system include:

      a.     reduced expenses.
      b.     highly predictable cash flows.
      c.     increased working cash.
      d.     customer preference.
      e.     all of the above are benefits of a PAC.

9.    The uncertainty of expected returns from a security attributable to possible changes in the financial capacity of the security issuer to make future payments to the security owner refers to

      a.     interest rate risk.
      b.     liquidity.
      c.     financial risk.
      d.     taxability.
      e.     yield.

10.   Which short-term investment has, for all practical purposes, *no* active trading in a secondary market?

a.   Treasury bills
b.   Federal agency securities
c.   Negotiable certificates of deposit
d.   Commercial paper
e.   Banker's acceptances

11.   Which of the following is a benefit of centralizing the firm's pool of cash?

a.   Lower levels of excess cash
b.   Stricter control over available cash
c.   More efficient investments in near-cash assets
d.   a and b
e.   All of the above

12.   The fact that funds are available in the company's bank account until its payment check has cleared through the banking system refers to

a.   mail float.
b.   processing float.
c.   transit float.
d.   disbursing float.

13.   Which is *not* an objective of zero balance accounts?

a.   Achieve better control over cash payments.
b.   Reduce excess cash balances held in regional banks for disbursing purposes.
c.   Decrease disbursing float.

14.   Firms use remote disbursements to

a.   decrease mail float.
b.   increase disbursing float.
c.   decrease disbursing float.
d.   increase processing float.

15. Interest rate risk is of concern to a firm's financial officer, because

a. it is more difficult to issue securities when interest rates are low.
b. changes in interest rates affect the expected return of financial instruments.
c. federal government taxation increases as interest rates rise, reducing the cash available to the firm.
d. inflationary periods may reduce the real earnings of the firm.

16. Which of the following does *not* describe U.S. Treasury bills?

a. Maturities include 3-month, 6-month, and 1-year securities.
b. Discount instrument
c. Issued only in bearer form
d. Income subject to federal, state and local income tax
e. All of the above describe U.S. Treasury bills.

17. Which security (assuming identical maturities) would be expected to have the highest yield based on recent experience?

a. Banker's acceptances
b. Agencies
c. CDs
d. Commercial paper
e. Treasury bills

18. Which of the following is *not* a motive for holding cash balances?

a. Transactions motive
b. Speculative motive
c. Convenience motive
d. Precautionary motive

19. A concentration bank is:

a. a bank that has the most deposit accounts.
b. a bank that concentrates its service in one geographic area.
c. a bank that concentrates on one type of service.
d. a bank in which the firm maintains a major disbursing account.

20. Wire transfers can be used to

a. move steel wire between two utility companies.
b. move funds between two industrial companies.
c. move funds between commercial banks.
d. move funds between investment banks.
e. b, c, and d above.
f. none of the above.

21. The major objective of a credit policy is to

a. maximize sales.
b. minimize losses.
c. maximize profits.
d. None of the above.

22. Which of the following is not part of the firm's credit and collection policy decisions?

a. The credit period
b. The cash discount given
c. The dividend decision
d. The level of collection expenditures
e. The quality of account accepted

23. Which of the following would be a source of credit information?

a. Firm's financial statement
b. Credit ratings from Dun & Bradstreet
c. A credit check through a bank
d. The company's past experience
e. All of the above

24. Which of the following is a cost associated with relaxed credit standards?

a. Enlarged credit department
b. Increased probability of bad debt
c. Additional investment in receivables
d. All of the above
e. None of the above

25.    All of the following are relationships that exist for safety stock, except

    a.    The greater the risk of running out of stock, the larger the safety stock.
    b.    The larger the opportunity cost of the funds invested in inventory, the smaller the safety stock.
    c.    The greater the uncertainty associated with future forecasts of use, the larger the safety stock.
    d.    The higher the profit margin per unit, the lower the safety stock necessary.

26.    In the basic model, the optimal inventory level is the point at which

    a.    total depreciation is minimized.
    b.    total cost is minimized.
    c.    total revenue is maximized.
    d.    carrying costs are minimized.
    e.    ordinary costs are minimized.

27.    Determine the effective annualized cost of forgoing the trade discount on terms 2/10, net 45 (round to nearest .01%).

    a.    21.0%
    b.    16.3%
    c.    16.0%
    d.    20.6%

28.    The Janjigian Company uses approximately 4,000 oxygen tanks in its manufacturing process each year. The carrying cost of the oxygen tanks inventory is $.60 per tank, and the ordering cost per order is $20. What is Janjigian's economic ordering quantity of tanks (round to the nearest unit)?

    a.    15
    b.    365
    c.    417
    d.    516

# CHAPTER 16

# International Business Finance

Orientation: This chapter introduces some of the financial techniques and strategies necessary to the efficient operation of an international business. Problems inherent to these firms include multiple currencies, differing legal and political environments, differing economic and capital markets, and internal control problems. The difficulties arising from multiple currencies are stressed here, including the dimensions of foreign exchange risk and strategies for reducing this risk. We also cover working-capital management and direct foreign investment for international firms.

I.     The globalization of product and financial markets

    A.     World trade has grown faster over the last few decades than has aggregate world GNP.

    B.     In less-developed countries, long-run overseas investments of the United States' companies have yielded high returns.

    C.     Many American *multinational corporations* (MNC) have significant assets, sales, and profits attributable to foreign investments.

    D.     Many foreign MNCs have significant operations in the United States.

    E.     Many firms, investment companies, and individuals invest in the capital markets of foreign companies in the hopes of realizing

        1.     higher returns than those available in domestic capital markets, and

        2.     reduced portfolio risk through international diversification.

F.  Companies are increasingly turning to the Eurodollar market to raise funds.

II.  Exchange rates

A.  Recent history of exchange rates

1.  Exchange rates between the major currencies were fixed from 1949 and 1970.

2.  Countries were required to set a *parity rate* with the U.S. dollar, around which the daily exchange rate could narrowly fluctuate.

3.  In order to effect a major adjustment, a currency had to undergo either a *devaluation* (reducing the cost relative to the dollar) or an *up-valuation/revaluation* (increasing the cost relative to the U.S. dollar).

4.  Since 1973, a *floating rate* international currency system has operated, wherein the currencies are allowed to fluctuate freely.

5.  Two major types of transactions now occur in the foreign exchange markets: *spot* and *forward transactions*.

B.  Spot exchange rates

1.  The rate at which one currency can be immediately exchanged for another currency

2.  *Direct quote* expresses the exchange rate in the units of home currency required to buy one unit of foreign currency. For example, 1.4845 U.S. dollars per pound.

3.  *Indirect quotes* indicate the number of foreign currency units needed to purchase one unit of home currency. For example, .6691 pounds per U.S. dollar.

EXAMPLE

Using the rates listed above, how many dollars would a U.S. manufacturer pay for a part costing 250 pounds?

250 (pounds) x 1.4845 ($/pound) = $371.13

4.   The direct and indirect quotes should have a reciprocal relationship. In formula

$$Direct\ Quote = \frac{1}{Indirect\ Quote}$$

or

$$Indirect\ Quote = \frac{1}{Direct\ Quote}$$

5.   When these quotes are not equal, *arbitrage* will occur, where a trader (or arbitrageur) makes a riskless profit, by exchanging currency in two markets.

6.   The *asked rate* is the rate which the bank or foreign exchange trader "asks" the buyer to pay for the foreign currency.

7.   The *bid rate* is the rate at which the bank or foreign exchange trader buys the foreign currency from the customer.

8.   The *spread* is the difference in the bid and the asked rates.

9.   The narrower the spread, the greater is the efficiency in the spot exchange market.

10.   A *cross rate* is the result of an indirect computation of one currency's exchange rate from the exchange rate of two other currencies. For example, the calculation of marks per pound from U.S. dollars per pound and marks per U.S. dollars.

11.   Triangular arbitrage will occur when the cross rates are not equal to the exchange rates offered.

C.   Forward exchange rates

1.   A *forward exchange rate* specifies *today* the rate at which currencies will be exchanged in the future, usually 30, 90, or 180 days from today.

2. Rates are quoted in both the direct and indirect form.

3. Forward rates are often quoted at a *premium* or a *discount* to the existing spot rate. This is also referred to as the forward-spot differential.

4. These differentials may be stated either in absolute terms or as an annualized percent premium or discount.

5. The use of forward contracts allows for risk reduction, in that future cash outlays are known with certainty.

III. Interest rate parity

A. Theorem states that the forward premium or discount should be equal and opposite in sign to the difference in the national interest rates for securities of the same maturity (except for the effects of small transaction costs). Notationally, this is expressed as

$$P \text{ (or D)} = -\left(\frac{I^f - I^d}{1 + I^f}\right) = \left(\frac{I^d - I^f}{1 + I^f}\right)$$

where

$P$ (or D) = the percent-per-annum premium or discount on the forward rate

$I^f$ = the annual interest rate on a foreign instrument having the same maturity as the forward contract

$I^d$ = the annualized interest rate on a domestic instrument having the same maturity as the forward contract

EXAMPLE

The premium (P) on 30-day forward mark contracts is 4.368%. If the 30-day T-bill is yielding 10%, what must the 30-day German instrument yield?

$$P = \frac{I^f - I^d}{1 + I^f}$$

$$0.04368 = \frac{I^f - .10}{1 + I^f}$$

$$I^f = .1502 \text{ or } 15.02\%$$

B. If the forward differentials are not those predicted by the interest parity theorem, then *covered interest arbitrage* can occur and be profitable at no risk.

IV. Purchasing power parity

A. According to purchasing power parity, exchange rates will adjust over time so that the currencies of different countries will have the same purchasing power. The exchange rates will adjust to cover the inflation rate differential between the two countries.

B. Purchasing power parity can be demonstrated by the equation

$$S_{t+1} = S_t (1 + P_d) / (1 + P_f)^n$$

$$= S_t (1 + P_d - P_f)^n$$

where

$S_t$ = units of domestic currency per unit of the foreign currency at time t,

$P_f$ = the foreign inflation rate,

$P_d$ = the domestic inflation rate, and

n = the number of time periods.

## EXAMPLE

The inflation rate in Great Britain is 6%, and, in the United States, it is 10%. The current spot rate of the pound is $2.00. According to purchasing power parity, what will be the expected value of the pound at the end of the year?

$$S = \$2.00 \, (1 + .10 - .06)^1$$

$$= \$2.00 \, (1.04)^1$$

$$= \$2.08$$

C.  The law of one price

The law of one price underlies purchasing power parity. This law suggests that where there are no transportation costs or barriers to trade, the same good sold in different countries should sell for the same price if all the different prices are expressed in terms of the same currency.

D.  International Fisher effect

1.  According to the Fisher effect, interest rates reflect not only the real rate of return but also the expected inflation rate.

2.  The Fisher effect can be expressed as

$$= P + I_r + (P)(I_r)$$
$$r_{nom} = r_{inf} + r_{real} + (r_{inf})(r_{real})$$

where

$r_{nom}$ = the nominal interest rate

$r_{real}$ = the real rate of return

$r_{inf}$ = the expected inflation rate

3.  The international Fisher effect suggests that the exchange rate adjusts to cover the interest rate differential between two countries.

4.  This theory suggests that in efficient markets, with rational expectations, the forward rate is an unbiased forecast of the future spot rate.

V.  Exchange rate risk

A.  Risk arises from not knowing today the value of the future spot rate.

B.  Types of exchange risk

1.  Risk in international trade contracts: when an agreement exists to purchase some good at a future date in foreign currency, uncertainty exists as to the future cash outlay.

2.  Risk in foreign portfolios: because of exchange rate fluctuations in foreign securities, the returns are more variable and, thus, more risky than investment in domestic securities.

3.  Risk in direct foreign investment (DFI): the balance sheet and income statement are dominated in foreign currency. Thus, for the parent company, risk arises from the fluctuations in both the asset's value and the profit streams.

C.  Exposure to exchange rate risk

1.  Transaction exposure refers to the net total foreign currency transactions whose monetary value was fixed at a time different from when the transactions are actually completed. Examples of transactions exposed to this kind of risk are receivables, payables, and fixed price sales or purchase contracts. Fluctuations in exchange rates can affect the value of these assets and liabilities.

2.  Translation exposure is actually a paper gain or loss. Translation exposure refers to gains or losses caused by the translation of foreign currency assets and liabilities into the currency of the parent company for accounting purposes.

3. Economic exposure refers to the extent to which the economic value of a company can decline due to exchange rate changes. It is the overall impact of exchange rate changes on the value of the firm. A decline in value can be attributed to an exchange-rate-induced decline in the level of expected cash flows and/or by an increase in the riskiness of these cash flows.

D. Hedging strategies

1. The standard procedure to hedge is to match the amount and the duration of the asset (liability) position.

2. The *money market hedge* offsets the exposed position in a foreign currency by borrowing or lending in the foreign and domestic money markets. This may be costly for small or infrequent users.

3. The *forward market hedge* matches the asset (liability) position with an offsetting forward contract of equal value and maturity. Generally, this is less costly than the money market hedge.

4. Foreign currency futures contracts and foreign currency options are two relatively new instruments used for hedging. Futures contracts are similar to forward contracts in that they provide a fixed price for the required delivery. Options, on the other hand, *permit* a fixed price anytime before their expiration date. Options and futures both differ from forward contracts in that they are traded in standardized amounts with standardized maturity dates and are traded through organized exchanges and individual dealers. The difference between the futures contract and the currency option is that the option requires delivery only if it is exercised. The option can be exercised anytime before its maturity date; this can provide additional flexibility for a company.

VI. Multinational working-capital management

A. The MNC must be careful to make decisions concerning working-capital management that are optimal for the corporation as a whole and not just the best for the individual entities.

B. *Leading* and *lagging* are important risk reduction techniques for a MNC's working-capital management.

    1. When holding an _asset_ in a:

        a. strong (appreciating) currency, we should lag (delay) conversion to the domestic currency.

        b. weak (depreciating) currency, we should lead (expedite) conversion to the domestic currency.

    2. When holding a *liability* in a:

        a. strong currency, we should lead (expedite) payment of the liability.

        b. weak currency, we should lag (delay) payment of the liability.

C. Cash management

    1. A MNC may wish to position funds in a specific subsidiary in another country such that the foreign exchange exposure and the tax liability of the MNC are minimized as a whole. This strategy may not, however, be the optimal strategy for the subsidiary.

    2. The transfer of funds is effected by royalties, fees, and transfer-pricing. The *transfer price* is the price charged for goods or services transferred from a subsidiary or parent company to another subsidiary.

VII. International financing decisions

A. A multinational corporation (MNC) may have a lower cost of capital than a domestic firm due to its ability to tap a larger number of financial markets.

    1. A multinational company has access to financing sources in the countries in which it operates.

    2. Host countries often provide access to low-cost subsidized financing to attract foreign investment.

3. A MNC may enjoy preferential credit treatment due to its size and investor preference for its home currency.

4. A MNC may be able to access third country capital markets.

5. A MNC has access to external currency markets variously known as Eurodollar, Eurocurrency, or Asiandollar markets. These markets are unregulated and, because of their lower spread, can offer attractive rates for financing and investment.

B. To increase their visibility in foreign capital markets, MNCs are increasingly listing their stocks in the foreign capital markets.

C. A MNC's capital structure should reflect its wider access to financial markets, the ability to diversify economic and political risks, and several of its other advantages over domestic firms.

VIII. Direct foreign investment

A. Risk in international capital budgeting

1. Political risk arises from operating a business in a different and possibly less stable business climate than the United States.

2. Exchange risk incorporates changes in the future earnings stream because of currency fluctuations, possibly in both foreign and domestic currencies.

3. Business risk is affected by the response of business and the MNC to economic conditions within the foreign country.

4. Financial risk arises from the financial structure of the firm and its effect on the profit stream.

B. Cash flows must be estimated considering the potential effects of exchange rate changes, governmental policy, and other items that determine product demand and sales.

C.    A foreign investment can be evaluated from either a parent or a local firm perspective. If a firm uses a local perspective, the initial investment and all of its cash flows should be discounted at a rate that reflects the local inflation rate and the riskiness of the project. When using the parent company perspective, the discount rate should reflect the expected inflation rate in the parent currency, and foreign currency cash flows should be converted to the parent currency cash flows using projected exchange rates.

D.    The net present value (NPV) must be calculated using the preceding factors.

    1.    If NPV is greater than zero, accept direct foreign investments.

    2.    If NPV is less than zero, the MNC may decide to

        a.    Reject direct foreign investment.

        b.    Establish a sales office in the foreign country.

        c.    License a local company to manufacture the product, where the MNC receives royalty payments.

## Study Problems

1.    An American manufacturer owes 5,000 marks to a German supplier. How much does he owe in U.S. dollars, if the exchange rate is 0.661 U.S. dollars per mark?

SOLUTION

Exchange rate = 0.6601 U.S. dollar per mark

5,000 (marks) x 0.6601 (U.S. dollar/mark) = $3,300.50 U.S. dollars

2.    A fashion designer in France owes $65,000, due in 30 days, to a counterpart in the United States How much is the foreign liability today if the exchange rates for 30-day forward contracts is 5.2070 francs per U.S. dollar?

SOLUTION

30-day forward exchange rate - 5.2070 francs per U.S. dollar

65,000 ($) x 5.2070 (francs per U.S. dollar) = 338,455 francs

3.  You own $20,000. The dollar rate in London is 0.5201. The pound rate is given in the textbook. Are arbitrage profits possible? Set up an arbitrage scheme with your capital. What is the gain (loss) in dollars?

SOLUTION

The London rate is 0.5201 pounds/U.S. dollar. The indirect New York rate is 0.5349 pounds/U.S. dollar.

Assuming no transaction costs, the rates between London and New York are out of line. Arbitrage profits are possible.

Pounds are cheaper in New York. Buy pounds in New York with the $20,000.

20,000 ($) x .5349 (pounds/dollars) = 10,698 pounds.

Sell pounds in London.
10,698 (pounds) ÷ .5201 (pounds/U.S. dollars) = $20,569.12.

Your net gain is $20,569.12 - $20,000 = $569.12

4.  Interest rates on the 30-day instruments in the United States and Germany are 12 and 10% (annualized), respectively. What is the correct price of the 30-day forward mark? Use spot rates from textbook.

SOLUTION

The spot rate is .6601 U.S. dollar per mark. The annual premium via equation discussed on page 276 is

$$= \frac{.12 - .10}{1 + .10} = \frac{.02}{1.10} = .0182$$

$$P = 1.82\%$$

Using this premium in equation (16-2), compute the "correct" forward price.

$$\frac{F - .6601}{.6601} \times \frac{12}{1} = .0182 \quad \underline{F = .6611}$$

TRUE-FALSE

_____ 1. One of the most difficult aspects of operating a business in a foreign country is the problem of multiple currencies.

_____ 2. International business affairs affect very few firms and, therefore , are of little concern to most businesses.

_____ 3. Exchange rates are fixed according to the U.S. dollar and must be maintained within the narrow margins unless a major adjustment is enacted.

_____ 4. The forward contract states the exchange rate to be used in the spot market on a specific date in the near future.

_____ 5. A narrow spread between the bid and asked rates indicates an efficient spot market.

_____ 6. The interest parity theorem states that (except for effect of transaction costs) the forward premium or discount should be equal and opposite in sign to the difference in the respective country's interest rates for securities of the same maturities.

_____ 7. Extensive profit opportunities exist for arbitrageurs in the foreign exchange markets.

_____ 8. Exchange rate risk constitutes only a small portion of the risk associated with international business.

_____ 9. An investor with foreign currency liabilities may want to hedge against exchange rate changes in the money markets.

_____ 10. Leading and lagging are strategies for optimal working capital management.

_____ 11. Covered interest arbitrage can be taken advantage of when the premiums in the forward rate are not equal to the interest rate differentials.

_____ 12. Purchasing power parity suggests that exchange rates in countries with high inflation rates tend to decline.

_____ 13. Translation exposure results in exchange-rate-related losses or gains that have little or no impact on taxable income.

_____ 14. Futures contracts are customized with regard to the amount and maturity date of the contract.

_____ 15. Receivables and payables are subject to transaction exposure.

_____ 16. The objective of a hedging strategy is to have a positive net asset position in the foreign currency.

MULTIPLE CHOICE

1. A direct 30-day forward quote of 1.4957 U.S. dollars per pound is equivalent to what 30-day indirect quote?

   a. .6686 U.S. dollars per pound
   b. .6671 pounds per U.S. dollar
   c. 1.4957 U.S. dollars per pound
   d. .6686 pounds per U.S. dollar
   e. .6671 pounds per U.S. dollar

2. An example of a cross rate, when the exchange rates are given in U.S. dollars, would be

   a. marks per U.S. dollar.
   b. pounds per yen.
   c. yen per mark.
   d. U.S. dollars per yen.
   e. both b and c.

3. Forward rate contracts are used in international transactions to

   a. reduce the risk for the buyer.
   b. reduce the risk for the seller.
   c. both a and b.
   d. neither a nor b.

4.  If an investor noticed a discrepancy in the exchange rates of two countries and acted upon it, he would be engaging in

    a.  money market hedging.
    b.  forward hedging.
    c.  arbitrage.
    d.  sabotage.
    e.  leading strategies.

5.  If your firm held liabilities in a strong currency, it would be wise to

    a.  lead.
    b.  lag.
    c.  engage in money market hedging.
    d.  engage in forward hedging.
    e.  all of the above.

6.  Direct foreign investment involves

    a.  political risk.
    b.  business risk.
    c.  financial risk.
    d.  exchange rate risk.
    e.  all of the above.

7.  If the net present value of a direct foreign investment project for a MNC is less than zero, they should

    a.  reject it.
    b.  open a sales office.
    c.  license a foreign company.
    d.  accept it.
    e.  a, b, and c are all possibilities.

8.  If the U.S. experiences a 7% inflation rate while France is experiencing a 4% inflation rate, then according to purchasing power parity

    a.  the value of the U.S. dollar should increase by approximately 3% against the French franc.
    b.  the U.S. dollar should decline against the French franc by 3%.
    c.  the French franc would decline by 3% against the U.S. dollar.
    d.  there would be no change in either currency.

9. A paper loss/gain best describes which type of risk:

   a. economic.
   b. transaction.
   c. interest rate.
   d. translation.

10. Which of the following do not provide a hedge against some risk?

    a. Forward contract
    b. Money market hedge
    c. Currency options
    d. Futures contracts
    e. All are forms of hedging

# CHAPTER 17

# Changes and Challenges in Finance

Orientation: The purpose of this chapter is to examine how the practice of finance is evolving and to pay special attention to the challenges involved in the current practice of finance. In so doing, we examine recent innovations in risk management, raising capital, corporate restructuring, the agency problem, and challenges from academia.

I. Futures and options can be used by the financial manager to reduce the risks associated with interest and exchange rate and commodity price fluctuations.

    A. A futures contract is a contract to buy or sell a stated commodity (such as soybeans or corn) or a financial claim (such as U.S. Treasury bonds) at a specified price at some future specified time.

        1. For the financial manager, financial futures provide an excellent way of controlling risk in interest rates, foreign exchange rates, and stock fluctuations.

    B. There are two basic types of options: puts and calls. A call option gives its owner the right to purchase a given number of shares of stock or some other asset at a specified price over a specified time period. A put gives its owner the right to sell a given number of shares of common stock or some other asset at a specified price over a given time period.

        1. The popularity of options can be explained by their leverage, financial insurance, and investment alternative expansion features.

        2. Recently, four new variations of the traditional option have appeared: the stock index option, the interest rate option, the foreign exchange option and the Treasury bond futures option.

a. Stock index options are merely options with the underlying asset being the value or price of an index of stocks--for example, the S&P 100.

b. Interest rate and foreign exchange options are also merely options with the underlying asset being the Treasury bonds or a specific foreign currency.

c. Options on Treasury bond futures are different from other bond options in that they involve the acquisition of a futures position rather than the delivery of actual bonds. The buyer of an option on a futures contract achieves immunization against any unfavorable price movements, whereas the buyer of a futures contract achieves immunization against any price movements regardless of whether they are favorable or unfavorable.

II. During the 1980s, corporate restructuring dramatically changed the number and structure of the corporate landscape. In the United States alone, the total value of assets changing hands in the 1980s was $1.3 trillion, and of the 500 largest industrial corporations in the U.S. in 1980, 28% had been acquired by other firms by 1989.

   A. Why might mergers create wealth?

      1. If a firm has lost money and does not have current earnings on which to write off this loss, the tax credits which have no value to the current firm may take on value if the firm is acquired.

      2. Agency costs can be reduced if the new management does a better job of monitoring the management of the company being taken over.

      3. If the merger reduces free cash flow, wealth can be created.

      4. Wealth can be created through economies of scale, perhaps in administrative or accounting areas.

      5. If the acquired firm has unused debt capacity, the new firm can issue additional debt and reap the tax benefits.

      6. When cash-rich bidders and cash-poor targets are combined, wealth may be created as a result of the positive NPV projects taken by the merged firm that the cash-poor firm would have passed up.

7. Removal of ineffective management may create wealth.

8. Increased market power may increase wealth.

9. If the possibility of bankruptcy is reduced, then the merger may create wealth.

B. As part of the restructuring, three popular types of highly levered transactions developed.

1. Management buyouts (MBO): a group of investors forms a shell corporation to acquire the target firm or simply buys the target firm directly where the group of investors includes the members of the management of the target firm. This newly acquired firm is taken private, and the acquisition is financed primarily through debt.

2. Levered buyout (LBO): In a levered buyout, the new owners do not necessarily have to include members of the original management team and the firm is not necessarily taken private following the acquisition.

3. Levered ESOPs: In a levered employee stock ownership plan (ESOP), the rank-and-file employees participate with management in the purchase of stock in their employer corporation.

C. A substantial portion of the borrowing to finance LBOs involved the use of junk bonds.

1. Junk bond is a term used for low-grade bonds that promise high interest payments to their owners. The bonds are rated B+ or lower by the rating agencies, such as Moody's or Standard & Poor's.

D. A tender offer is a bid by an interested party, usually a corporation, to control another corporation. The prospective purchaser approaches the stockholders of the firm, rather than the management.

E. Divestitures, or "reverse mergers," have become important factors in corporate restructuring. A successful divestiture allows the firm to be used more efficiently and, therefore, be assigned a higher value by the market forces. The different types of divestitures may be summarized as follows:

1. *Selloff:* A selloff is the sale of a subsidiary, division, or product line by one company to another.

2. *Spinoff:* A spinoff involves the separation of a subsidiary from its parent, with no change in the equity ownership.

3. *Liquidation:* A liquidation in this context is not a decision to shut down or abandon an asset. Rather, the assets are sold to another company, and the proceeds are distributed to the stockholders.

4. *Going private*: Going private results when a company, whose stock is traded publicly, is purchased by a small group of investors and the stock is no longer bought and sold on a public exchange.

5. *Leveraged buyout:* The leveraged buyout is a special case of going private. The existing shareholders sell their shares to a small group of investors. The purchasers of the stock use the firm's unused debt capacity to borrow the funds to pay for the stock.

III. As the spread between interest rates charged to blue chip and non-blue chip borrowers grew in the late 1980s, firms began issuing securities which were combinations of conventional debt issues and futures or options. These securities allowed non-blue chip firms to borrow at a lower rate than would otherwise be possible. Many of these hybrids were simply variations of convertible securities. A convertible security is a bond or preferred stock that can be exchanged for a stated number of common shares at the option of the holder.

IV. The importance of the agency problem which was first presented in Axiom 7 has become apparent in recent years. In recent years, much debate has taken place on how best to structure executive compensation so that managers act in the best interests of shareholders. Also, addressing the agency problem is the emergence of relationship investing and the active investor.

A. The purpose of an executive compensation play is to align managerial behavior with shareholder objectives. The key to doing this is to tie managerial compensation to changes in shareholder wealth within a plan that is easy to monitor.

B.  Relationship investing involves taking large long-term positions in companies. The advantage to this is that the firm is allowed to take on a long-term perspective with regard to investments. In addition, it allows for increased manager accountability.

V.  Recently, challenges to the CAPM and the concept of market efficiency have come from academia.

A.  The CAPM controversy erupted in 1992 when Eugene Fama and Kenneth French of the University of Chicago published findings that suggested that the beta, the CAPM's measure of systematic risk, had not been related to returns over the past 50 years.

B.  This is not a question that has been fully answered. Challenges to these findings are presently being made. However, because the CAPM provides quantifiable insights into the risk-return tradeoff, it will continue to be used in the absence of a workable alternative that is understandable to managers. However, we must keep in mind the limitations and underlying assumptions of this model.

C.  The concept of market efficiency has come under recent attack with the attacks centering around the existence of pricing bubbles and questioning the rationality of investors. While it is clear that a lot is going on in security pricing, we can feel comfortable that security pricing is guided by the present value principles presented in this text.


Self Tests

TRUE-FALSE

_____  1.  A futures contract requires its holder to buy or sell the asset regardless of what happens to its value during the interim.

_____  2.  An option contract requires its holder to buy or sell the asset regardless of what happens to its value during the interim.

_____  3.  The only time a firm receives any proceeds from issuing convertibles is when the convertibles are initially issued.

_____  4.  When the convertible security is issued, the firm receives the proceeds from the sale less flotation costs.

_____ 5. Once the convertible owner trades his convertibles in for common stock, he can retrade the stock back for the convertibles if he desires.

_____ 6. Synergism is defined as the state wherein the whole is greater than the sum of the parts.

_____ 7. In response to a tender offer, the management of the target firm may seek a more agreeable partner or white knight.

## MULTIPLE CHOICE

1. Convertible bonds

   a. prohibit the issuance of more common stock.
   b. can never be called.
   c. are often an indirect way of selling common stock.
   d. have no advantages to the investor over straight debt.

2. The defensive maneuver that involves the target firm to become the attacker is the

   a. pac-man.
   b. shark repellent.
   c. white Knight.
   d. earn out.

# FINANCIAL PROBLEM-SOLVING
# WITH AN ELECTRONIC CALCULATOR

The article that follows was written by Mark A. White and appeared in *Financial Practice and Education*, Fall/Winter 1991, pp. 73 - 88. The *Journal* is sponsored by the Financial Management Association.

Note: Be aware that a transposition of two numbers occurred in the latter portion of the article when the author is demonstrating the use of particular calculators. In several instances, when computing the "Loan balance after 2nd payment," the answer is given to be $1,638.02. The correct answer in all cases is $1,683.02. This small typographical error does not happen in every case, but is repeated in several examples when showing how to use a particular calculator. It is a small matter, but we thought you should be aware. With this trivial exception, the article is extremely beneficial in introducing us to financial calculators.

# Financial Problem-Solving with an Electronic Calculator

## Mark A. White

*Mark A. White is an Assistant Professor of Commerce at the McIntire School of Commerce, University of Virginia, Charlottesville, VA.*

*"But the age of chivalry is gone. That of sophisters, economists and calculators has succeeded ..."*
*Edmund Burke*

■ Electronic calculating machines have evolved significantly since ENIAC dimmed the lights of Philadelphia in the 1940s, and hand-held calculators are now a common occurrence in the finance classroom.[1] Numerous financial calculator models are available with a wide variety of features, although unfortunately very few models implement these features in similar fashion. Much more frequently, keystroke sequences appropriate for solving a problem with Calculator A do not work with Calculator B, leading to increased frustration and loss of productivity for those accustomed to working with a particular calculator model. Instructors of the introductory finance curriculum are particularly aware of these problems, for it is they who are often called upon for solutions.

Many contemporary textbooks encourage or assume the use of financial calculators [3,4,6,8,9,10,12]. Brigham and Gapenski [4, p. 90] strongly support their use:

> *"... In today's world, it is mandatory that a student obtains a financial calculator and learns how to use it, for calculators - and not clumsy, rounded and incomplete tables - are used exclusively in well-run, efficient businesses."*

Yet none of these authors provides detailed instructions for using these tools to solve financial problems, assuming either that the instruction manual provides sufficient guidance or that students are capable of adapting model-specific keystrokes to their particular situation. Unfortunately, many instruction manuals are poorly written or do not address problems common to the classroom, and textbook authors cannot be expected to provide illustrative solutions for all possible financial calculator models. Third-party manuals [1,7,13] are unavailable for most models or too dated to be of much use. A comparative, concise guide to problem solving has long been needed.

Relatively little inquiry has appeared in the financial education literature, and the few papers which do exist focus primarily on programming techniques for particular methods of investment analysis [5,14,15,16]. A recent paper by White [17] describes the comparative features of several financial calculator models but does not discuss specific methods of problem-solving.

This paper provides a *practical* guide to financial problem-solving with an electronic calculator. It presents illustrative examples drawn from the introductory financial management course and describes *specific* keystroke sequences necessary for their resolution on *specific* calculator models. It should prove useful to individuals wishing to swiftly determine the particular keystroke sequences appropriate for a particular problem and it provides a *comparison* and *contrast* of the different methods of problem solution employed by various financial calculator models. Similarities and inconsistencies between the various models are identified, guiding students and instructors towards a better understanding of

---

[1] ENIAC (Electronic Numerical Integrator and Calculator) is widely regarded as the first successful high-speed electronic digital computer. It was developed by John Eckert and John Mauchly at the University of Pennsylvania and completed in 1946. The computer used over 18,000 vacuum tubes, stood two stories high and occupied 1,500 square feet of floor space. It required so much electricity that surrounding city lights dimmed when it was running.

[2] The author wishes to thank the managements of Hewlett-Packard, Sharp Electronics and Texas Instruments for graciously providing samples of their products for review, and gratefully acknowledges financial support provided by the University of Virginia's McIntire School of Commerce Associates Program. R. DeMong, R. Osborne, J. Todd, T. Crunk, J. Stevens and an anonymous reviewer provided helpful comments and suggestions.

the capabilities and usage of the modern financial calculator.[2]

The ten calculators examined in this paper are Texas Instruments' *BA-35*, *BA-II* and *Financial Investment Analyst*, the *EL-731*, *EL-733* and *EL-735* manufactured by Sharp Electronics, and Hewlett-Packard's *HP-10B*, *HP-12C*, *HP-17B II* and *HP-19B II*. More detailed information on these models can be found in White [17].

## I. USING CALCULATORS TO SOLVE BASIC FINANCIAL PROBLEMS

This section discusses the use of electronic calculators in solving *basic* financial problems. It is organized around examples of the several most common types of problems encountered in the introductory finance course. The reader is assumed to be familiar with the various underlying financial concepts, and emphasis is placed on differences in the implementation, i.e. keystroke sequences, of particular solution techniques. The following conventions are used throughout to identify key sequences:

- *Numerical entries* are shown without modification, e.g. 23.00.
- *Primary keys* have a physical location and appear underlined within square brackets, e.g. [PMT].
- *Secondary keys* are enclosed with curly braces, e.g. {FIN}. Pressing a modifier key, e.g. [2nd], invokes the secondary function generally printed slightly above or below the physical key location.
- *Software keys*, the availability of which depends upon a particular menu selection, are shown enclosed in square brackets, but are not underlined, e.g. [NOM%]. Only a few models use menu systems.

### A. Housekeeping Functions

Students just beginning to use their calculators or users confronted with an unfamiliar model are often perplexed regarding the most basic set of operations, or "housekeeping functions." Exhibit 1 summarizes the keystroke sequences needed to set the display format, clear memory registers, enter financial mode, etc.

**Exhibit 1**. Housekeeping Functions of Financial Calculators

| | Set Display Format to Two Decimal Places | Clear Display | Set Financial Mode | Clear Financial Registers | Set Compounding Frequency to 1x per Period | Adjust for Payment at Beginning of Period |
|---|---|---|---|---|---|---|
| **Texas Instruments** | | | | | | |
| BA-35 | [2nd] {Decimal} | [ON/C] | [2nd] {FIN} | [2nd] {FIN} | N/A | [DUE] [1] |
| BA-II | [FIX] 2 | [ON/C] | [2nd] {MODE} | [2nd] {CMR} | N/A | [DUE] [1] |
| Financial Investment Analyst | [2nd] {FORMAT} 2 [DEC] | [CE/C] | [TVM] | [2nd] {CLR COL} | 1 [P/Y] [2] | [BGN], [END] [2] |
| **Sharp Electronics** | | | | | | |
| EL-731, EL-733 | [2ndF] {TAB} 2 | [C - CE] | [2ndF] {MODE} | [2ndF] {CA} | N/A | [BGN] |
| EL-735 | [2ndF] {TAB} 2 | [C - CE] | N/A | [2ndF] {CA} | N/A | [2ndF] {BEG/END} |
| **Hewlett-Packard** | | | | | | |
| HP-10B | [_] [DSP] 2 | [C] | N/A | [_] {CLEAR ALL} | 1 [_] {P/YR} | [_] {BEG/END} |
| HP-12C | [f] 2 | [CLX] | N/A | [f] CLEAR {FIN} | N/A | [g] {BEG}, [g] {END} |
| HP-17B II & HP-19B II | [DSP] [FIX] 2 [INPUT] [3] | [_] {CLEAR} | [FIN] [TVM] | [_] {CLEAR DATA} | 1 [P/YR] [4] | [BEG], [END] [4] |

1  The [DUE] key must be pressed just *prior* to the last keystroke needed for solution on the *BA-35* and *BA-II*.
2  Select the Time Value of Money worksheet by pressing [TVM], then scroll down twice to change the compounding frequency and/or type of annuity.
3  The [DSP] key is labelled [DISP] on the *HP-19B II*.
4  Press [FIN] [TVM] to obtain the Time Value of Money menus, then choose [OTHER] to access these function.

Most calculators are able to display entries in a number of different formats. Setting the number of decimal places to a fixed number, generally two, improves display readability and helps to minimize errors. Numbers are rounded to appear in the display, although full precision is maintained for calculations. Except for the *BA-35*, displays may be set to any number of decimal places by substituting a different single-digit integer in place of the '2' shown in Exhibit 1.

It is very important to clear previous information from the display and memory registers before beginning a new calculation. Clearing the display register erases only the currently displayed data item and is helpful for correcting data entry errors. All financial calculators have additional sets of memory registers, generally for the financial and statistical functions, which must also be cleared prior to beginning any new time-value-of-money calculation. It is VERY important to clear the financial registers, as leftover data from a previous problem may not otherwise be overwritten, causing an error message or, even worse, an incorrect answer. Sometimes it is possible to clear just the financial registers, but more commonly ALL registers are cleared. If one has entered but a single number incorrectly, it may be more efficient to "zero out" the mistake by entering zero in the appropriate memory location.

On some calculators, the financial functions are not always available, that is one must be in 'financial mode' in order to access (or clear) them. The *BA-35*, *BA-II*, *EL-731* and *EL-733* require one to enter financial mode by pressing a particular key sequence, as shown in Exhibit 1. The *Financial Investment Analyst*, *HP-17B II* and *HP-19B II* use a menu system which is similar in some respects to a modal form of operation.

The last major sources of error for beginning users involve multiple compounding periods and annuities due. Older financial calculator models assume compounding occurred once per period, necessitating students to think in terms of the number of *periods*, and the interest rate *per period*. On newer models, it is possible to set the number of compounding sessions per period to a desired frequency, e.g., 12 payments per year, and in fact this is the default frequency for the *HP-10B*, *HP-17B II* and *HP-19B II*. Generally, students should be encouraged to set the compounding frequency equal to *one payment period per year*, for three reasons: 1) the vast majority of problems assume annual compounding; 2) failure to change the compounding frequency *back* after using the calculator to solve a particular problem can result in serious errors; 3) conceptually, it is often easier to solve problems in terms of compounding periods, rather than using multiperiod compounding.

Almost all problems in the beginning finance course assume payments occur at the END of a period (END mode). The major exceptions are *annuities due*, which assume payment occurs at the *beginning* of a period (BEGIN mode). Most of the models reviewed in this paper toggle between END and BEGIN mode with one or two keystrokes and display a small annunciator indicating the calculator's status. The *BA-35* and *BA-II* handle annuities due by requiring one to press the [DUE] key just prior to the last keystroke needed to solve a problem. On the *HP-17B II*, *HP-19B II* and the *Financial Investment Analyst*, one adjusts the annuity type in a separate menu or worksheet which, unfortunately, is not displayed continuously.

Finally, most errors in calculation can be traced to improper data entry or failure to answer the following questions in the affirmative: 1) Did you clear the financial registers? 2) Is the compounding frequency set to one payment per year? 3) Is the calculator in END mode?

## B. Future Value/Present Value Calculations

The simplest time-value-of-money problems involve computing the present value or future value of a single sum. Example 1 asks one to determine an unknown future value, given a known amount to be deposited *now*.

---

**Example 1.** Determining the Future Value of a Present Sum

*Harry has just deposited $1000 into a savings account paying 6 percent, compounded annually. How much will he have in the account at the end of five years?*

Harry will have accumulated $1,338.23 at the end of five years.

---

Reproducible pages describing specific keystrokes needed to solve Example 1 and other examples discussed in this paper have been attached as Appendix A. Instructors are encouraged to photocopy and distribute them to students requiring additional help with their calculators. Note that most calculators require one to specify the sign (+ or - ) of a particular cash flow, but are generally flexible enough to accept data from either side of the transaction. Thus, the $1,000 initial deposit could have been treated as a *positive* inflow (to the bank), and the resulting *negative* $1,338.23 could have been considered an outflow (from the bank's point of view). Recall that certain calculators must be in "financial mode" to solve problems using the financial registers, and observe that the Texas Instruments and Sharp calculators require one to press a "Compute" key before obtaining the answer. On the *HP-17B II* and *HP-19B II*, press [FIN][TVM] to obtain the Time Value of Money menus before beginning a calculation.

A slightly more complex problem involves determining the present or future value of an ordinary annuity. Example 2 illustrates a problem of this type, with the addition of multiperiod compounding, i.e. interest is compounded more than once per period. The problem's solution defines the periods as *months* and expresses the interest rate on a *monthly* basis ... a 12 percent nominal rate divided by 12 months = 1 percent per month. It would also be possible to solve this example using multiple payment periods per year, but this is not recommended for beginning students.

**Example 2.** Determining the Present Value of an Annuity

*Nancy has obtained an $11,000 bank loan to finance the purchase of a new car. The loan is for 48 months at an interest rate of 12 percent, compounded monthly. What is the amount of her monthly payment?*

Nancy's monthly payment is $289.67.

Numerous permutations of these basic problems could obviously be constructed, using future values, ordinary annuities, and different compounding regimes. The PV/FV tables are generally just as efficient at solving these problems, provided they contain the appropriate interest rates and times to maturity. The value of a financial calculator is much more apparent when solving for unknown *payments*, *interest rates* or *maturities*, for rarely will these results be in whole numbers, requiring users of the PV/FV tables to resort to the tedious and approximate method of linear interpolation.

Unfortunately, some calculators exhibit operational inconsistencies when solving these types of problems. To solve for an unknown number of periods or interest rate on the *BA-35* when the Payment and Future Value are known, one must enter one of the cash flows as a negative number, as the *BA-35* switches to '+/-' mode when evaluating certain types of problems involving the Future Value of an Annuity. Example 3 is concerned with the determination of an unknown interest rate.

**Example 3.** Determining an Unknown Interest Rate

*Exactly five years ago, Dave and Cindy purchased 100 shares of Gro-Tex Corporation at $45 per share. They now wish to sell their holdings at the current market price of $75 per share. What was their average annual rate of return over this period?*

Dave and Cindy earned a 10.76 percent holding period rate of return.

The problem in Example 4 involves determining an unknown number of periods. With one exception, all of the financial calculators reviewed in this paper display the answer exactly, in fractions of a period. The *HP-12C*

rounds *up* the number of periods to the next highest integer, i.e. the end of the period during which the account is exhausted. Unfortunately, there is no way to disable this function.

**Example 4.** Determining an Unknown Number of Periods

*Stacy received her retirement pension in a lump sum, and has invested it in an account which guarantees her a 10 percent annual rate of return. She wishes to make annual withdrawals of $35,000 beginning at the end of this year. If her current account balance is $250,000, how long will it be until she exhausts her account?*

Her account balance will be exhausted in 13.14 periods; her last withdrawal (which will be smaller than her earlier ones) will be made 14 years from today.

### C. Bond Pricing and Yields to Maturity

The time value of money registers may also be used to solve simple bond pricing and yield-to-maturity problems, i.e. problems in which a bond matures **exactly** *n* periods in the future. The introductory finance courses are rife with these problems, though they rarely occur in practice. By combining the annuity registers with the future value register, one can mimic a bond's interest and principal payments. Note that this technique is *not* comparable to the bond pricing functions found on higher-end calculators, which are really too sophisticated to be of use in the introductory class.

Example 5 illustrates the application of this technique to the pricing of a semiannual coupon bond. The general method uses all the financial registers and views the problem in terms of semiannual payment periods. There are 6 years x 2 periods/year = 12 periods in this example. Interest payments of $80 per year divided by 2 periods/year = $40 per period are made at the end of each period, up to and including the maturity date, at which point the bond's par value of $1,000 is repaid. The appropriate discount rate equals 10 percent per year divided by 2 periods/year = 5 percent *per period.*[3] Be aware that the *BA-II* cannot perform this calculation, but rather than displaying an error message, it reports a potentially misleading *incorrect* answer. This problem must be solved in two steps on the *BA-II*, i.e. one must

---

[3] On the *HP-10B*, *HP-17B II* and *HP-19B II*, one may specify *two* compounding periods per year and express the yield as an annual rate, i.e. 10.00 [I/YR] or 10.00 [I%YR]. The remaining entries are unchanged, as the sole effect of the 'P/YR' function is to divide the number in the interest rate register by the number of payment periods per year. This procedure is NOT recommended, as it can create additional errors if one forgets to change the compounding frequency back. Further, it "mixes apples with oranges," for the payment and time to maturity are still entered in terms of semiannual periods, while the yield is expressed in terms of years.

first find the present value of the annuity portion and then add to it the present value of the $1,000 principal amount.

---

**Example 5**. Simple Bond Pricing

*What is the price of an 8 percent semiannual coupon bond maturing EXACTLY six years from now? It has a par value of $1000, and bonds of similar risk are yielding 10 percent.*

The bond should sell for $911.37.

---

This particular pattern of cash flows, i.e. the "bond pattern," appears elsewhere in the introductory finance curriculum. Simple balloon mortgages share this pattern, as do problems in which a person purchases a financial instrument, receives a series of equal payments over time, and then sells the instrument at some future point. The method outlined above is usually quicker than using the cash flow registers, but one must be careful to apply it correctly.

A financial calculator greatly facilitates solving for a bond's yield to maturity. For simple bond problems, the techniques just described work quite well. Example 6 presents keystroke solutions for an annual coupon bond; for semiannual coupon bonds one must carefully specify the amount of interest to be received each *period* and the number of periods. The solution will then be displayed as a *periodic* rate; this number must be *doubled* to express it on an annual basis.[4] The *BA-II* is again unable to perform this calculation, but fortunately responds with an error message, rather than an incorrect answer.

---

**Example 6.** Simple Bond Yields to Maturity

*What is the yield to maturity on a 10 percent annual coupon bond currently selling for $1,038.31? It matures in exactly three years.*

The bond is priced to yield 8.50 percent per year.

---

**D. Interest Rate Conversions**

An alternative method for solving problems involving multiperiod compounding is to determine the effective annual rate. *Nominal rate* refers to the stated or published rate, e.g. "18 percent, compounded monthly." The *effective annual rate* incorporates the effect of multiple compounding periods and is expressed on an annual basis. Interest rate conversions are usually not a major focus in the introductory finance course. Conversion functions are, however, a useful tool for making comparisons among yields on instruments encountered in the

---

[4] More precisely, the annualized yield to maturity equals $(1 + r)^2 - 1$, but this value is sufficiently close to 2r for most purposes. See [2] and [11].

---

'real world.' For this reason, and because there seems to be little pattern among the three manufacturers' implementations of these functions, Example 7 is provided. Conversion functions are not built into the *HP-12C*, and problems of this sort must be solved 'by hand.' On the *HP-17B II* and *HP-19B II*, one must first press [FIN][ICONV] to obtain the Interest Rate Conversion menus.

---

**Example 7.** Interest Rate Conversions

*A furniture store offers loan terms of 18 percent, compounded monthly. What is the loan's effective annual rate?*

The loan has an effective annual rate of 19.56 percent.

---

**II. ADVANCED FEATURES OF FINANCIAL CALCULATORS**

Among the advanced uses of financial calculators are loan amortization, capital budgeting and the estimation of beta coefficients using linear regression. These problems utilize 'hardwired' functions and keystroke sequences designed specifically for their solution. Programmable financial calculators such as the *HP-12C*, *HP-17B II* and *HP-19B II* are of course able to solve a much wider array of problems, although such techniques are beyond the scope of this paper.

**A. Loan Amortization**

Loan amortization problems focus on the preparation of an *amortization schedule*, in which the portions of each payment representing principal and interest vary over the life of the loan. Frequently asked questions include: "What will be the remaining balance after the nth payment?" and "What portion of the nth payment represents principal/interest?" Example 8 requests one to prepare an amortization schedule illustrating the breakdown of each payment into its interest and principal components.

---

**Example 8.** Loan Amortization

*Prepare an amortization schedule for a 1-year, $2,000 computer loan at 12 percent annual interest, compounded monthly. Monthly payments are $177.70.*

|  | 1 | 2 | 3 | 4 | etc. |
|---|---|---|---|---|---|
| Payment | $177.70 | $177.70 | $177.70 | $177.70 | |
| Interest Portion | $20.00 | $18.42 | $16.88 | $15.22 | |
| Principal Portion | $157.70 | $159.28 | $160.87 | $162.48 | |

*Example Continues*

**Example 8** Continued

Remaining  $1,842.30  $1,683.02  $1,522.15  $1,359.67
Balance

Loan amortization is easier on some calculators than on others. The Sharp Corporation's calculators have the cleanest and most intuitive keystroke sequences; there would be little problem in memorizing or understanding their logic. At the other end of the spectrum, the *BA-35's* keystrokes are unreasonably complicated and students are not at all likely to memorize this sequence. Most calculators display payment information in the format, "Interest Principal Remaining Balance." Sharp's calculators interchange the interest and principal payment portions.

**B. Cash Flow Analysis**

One of the most useful and desirable functions of a financial calculator is the ability to analyze uneven streams of cash flows. A special case of uneven cash flows, i.e. the "bond pattern," has already been discussed, but there are an infinite number of cash flow patterns which defy easy description and which are tedious to solve using just the time-value-of-money registers. Cash flow registers alleviate drudgery, improve accuracy and frequently aid in students' basic problem setup. The computation of internal rate of return (IRR) and net present value (NPV) becomes much easier, freeing the instructor to discuss more critical issues concerning the choice of a discount rate, timing of cash inflows, and assumptions regarding the project's termination value. Example 9 presents a cash flow analysis problem in an investment setting.

**Example 9.** Cash Flow Analysis

*An investment project promises the following schedule of cash flows. The project's initial outlay is -$100,000 and the appropriate discount rate is 10%. Use the NPV and IRR criteria to determine acceptance or rejection of this project.*

Year 1:   $15,000     Year 4:   $20,000
Year 2:   $20,000     Year 5:   $20,000
Year 3:   $20,000     Year 6:   $60,000

Tne project should be accepted because its NPV of $5,138.72 is greater than zero and its IRR of 11.42 percent is greater than the discount rate of 10 percent.

Students can analyze the sensitivity of a project's NPV to changes in the discount rate by entering a different value and recomputing NPV. On the *Financial Investment Analyst, HP-10B, HP-12C, HP-17B II* and *HP-19B II* it is possible to recall and modify previously stored *cash*

*flows* and their corresponding frequency occurrences as well, which can be extremely useful for examining a project's sensitivity to critical assumptions. Press [FIN][CFLO] to obtain the Cash Flow menus on the *HP-17B II* and *HP-19B II*, and note that the *HP-19B II* has a key to *plot* an NPV profile.

**C. Estimation of Beta Coefficients Using Linear Regression**

All too frequently students fail to apply knowledge gained in other disciplines to problems in the course at hand. Regression analysis is an excellent case in point. It is an extremely powerful tool, but one which many students fail to work with outside of the introductory quantitative methods class. There is limited application for linear regression in the introductory finance course, and generally even more limited time in which to teach it. Still, it is important for instructors to nurture an understanding of the interrelatedness among business disciplines, and the estimation of beta coefficients as a measure of market risk is a good example with which to work. A security's beta coefficient is defined as the slope of its *characteristic line*, i.e. the line of best fit between the returns on a market index (x-variable) and the returns on the security (y-variable). Using a financial calculator's linear regression functions, students can estimate slope and intercept coefficients; *the slope of the resulting linear relationship is the stock's beta.* Further statistical analyses may also be easily computed. The *correlation coefficient* (r) measures the degree to which two variables (x and y) are related. Squaring the correlation coefficient gives the *coefficient of determination* ($r^2$), which measures how well the 'line of best fit' fits, or the proportion of variation in the stock's returns explained by move-

**Example 10.** Estimation of Beta Coefficients Using Linear Regression

*What is the beta of a security with the following pattern of returns vis-a-vis the market?*

| Return on the Market (x-variable) | Return on the Security (y-variable) |
|---|---|
| 6.5% | 4.8% |
| 11.8% | 14.5% |
| 14.9% | 19.1% |
| 1.1% | 3.7% |
| 12.0% | 15..6% |

The security has a beta coefficient of 1.20. The correlation coefficient of 0.95 is very high and suggests a strong relationship between beta and the security's expected return.

**Exhibit 2.** Estimation of Beta Coefficients Using Linear Regression

| BA-II | | Financial Investment Analyst [1] | | | EL-733, EL-735 [2] | | |
|---|---|---|---|---|---|---|---|
| 6.5 [x ≷ y] | 4.8 [Σ+] | 6.5 [x] | 4.8 [y] | [Σ+] | 6.5 {(x,y)} | 4.8 {DATA} |
| 11.8 [x ≷ y] | 14.5 [Σ+] | 11.8 [x] | 14.5 [y] | [Σ+] | 11.8 {(x,y)} | 14.5 {DATA} |
| 14.9 [x ≷ y] | 19.1 [Σ+] | 14.9 [x] | 19.1 [y] | [Σ+] | 14.9 {(x,y)} | 19.1 {DATA} |
| 1.1 [x ≷ y] | 3.7 [Σ+] | 1.1 [x] | 3.7 [y] | [Σ+] | 1.1 {(x,y)} | 3.7 {DATA} |
| 12.0 [x ≷ y] | 15.6 [Σ+] | 12.0 [x] | 15.6 [y] | [Σ+] | 12.0 {(x,y)} | 15.6 {DATA} |
| | | [↓] [↓] [↓] | [INT] 0.44 | | [2ndF] {a} 0.44 | |
| | | | [SLP] 1.20 | | [2ndF] {b} 1.20 | |
| [2nd] [b/a] 0.44 | | | [COR] 0.95 | | [2ndF] {r} 0.95 | |
| [x ≷ y] 1.20 | | | | | | |
| [2nd] [Corr] 0.95 | | | | | | |

| HP-10B | HP-12C | HP-17B II, HP-19B II [3] |
|---|---|---|
| 6.5 [INPUT] 4.8 [Σ+1] | 4.8 [ENTER] 6.5 [Σ+1] | Use the [SUM] menu to create two lists containing the market returns (x) and stock returns (y). Press [CALC] [MORE] [FRCST], select the x-variable, then press [LIN] to select linear regression. Press [M] to solve for beta, [B] for the intercept and [CORR] to get the correlation coefficient. |
| 11.8 [INPUT] 14.5 [Σ+1] | 14.5 [ENTER] 11.8 [Σ+1] | |
| 14.9 [INPUT] 19.1 [Σ+1] | 19.1 [ENTER] 14.9 [Σ+1] | |
| 1.1 [INPUT] 3.7 [Σ+1] | 3.7 [ENTER] 1.1 [Σ+1] | |
| 12.0 [INPUT] 15.6 [Σ+1] | 15.6 [ENTER] 12.0 [Σ+1] | |
| 0 [_] [ŷ, m] 0.44 | 0 [g] [ŷ, r] [STO] 7 | |
| [_] [SWAP] 1.20 | 1 [g] [ŷ, r] [RCL] 7 [÷] 1.20 | |
| [_][x̂, r] [_][SWAP] 0.95 | [x ≷ y] 0.95 | |

[1] You must first select the statistics worksheets by pressing [Stat].
[2] On the EL-735, the {DATA} key is labelled {S. DATA}.
[3] The HP-19B II assumes the current list is the y-variable and only requires you to specify the x-variable list. On the HP-17B II, you must select both the x-variable and y-varaible lists. To specify a regression model on the HP-17B II, choose [MORE] [MODL] from the menu containing the intercept, slope and correlation coefficients.

ments in the market returns. Example 10 is an over-simplified illustration of beta coefficient estimation in that it uses only five data points; betas are usually estimated using 5 years of monthly returns (60 data points).

Keystroke solutions to Example 10 are not included in Appendix A for space reasons and because some instructors may prefer not to confuse students with advanced applications. Instead, Exhibit 2 presents the key sequences used by particular models of financial calculators to perform linear regression.

Additional statistical measures, for instance t-statistics and F-statistics, can be computed with little difficulty from the intermediate sums of squares available on many calculator models. The *HP-17B II* and *HP-19B II* are also able to fit models to exponential, logarithmic and power curves.

## III. CONCLUSIONS

Financial calculators can be a useful tool in the introductory finance curriculum provided students and instructors understand their applicability and limitations. However, it does not necessarily follow that the mere availability of the time-value-of money functions on a particular model will increase students' problem-solving abilities. First, there is a strong tendency on the part of many students to treat financial calculators as mysterious black boxes. Instructors should be careful to explain the financial logic used by calculators in arriving at a solution and caution students to avoid simply punching buttons. Second, modern financial calculators are *not* simple machines. Different models implement similar functions in different fashions, and these differences can lead to significant confusion in the classroom setting. Telling students to "look it up in the manual" is inappropriate, as most manuals provide rote solutions with little or no exposition of underlying financial concepts.

There is a trend to incorporate the use of microcomputers in the introductory financial management course, generally using spreadsheet programs such as Excel or Lotus 1-2-3. It is quite rare, however, for instructors *not* to provide some sort of spreadsheet-specific guidance.

Financial calculators provide similar and more convenient opportunities for learning at a fraction of the cost, but they, too, can be complex and mystifying to beginning students, who can benefit from brief lectures on their use and abuse. Most students never fully realize the potential of their financial calculators.

This paper provides *comparative* pedagogical material for ten major financial calculator models. It describes keystroke solutions for problems typically encountered in the introductory finance course, emphasizes operational differences and recognizes the strengths and weaknesses of particular makes and models. Aids are provided to identify appropriate keystroke sequences on unfamiliar calculator models, and an introduction is provided for calculator novices unfamiliar with the use of their newly-acquired tool. Mastery of a financial calculator, like the mastery of any tool, enhances self-confidence and inspires one to continue the learning process. Today's students hold the power of ENIAC in the palms of their hands. They should be encouraged to learn to use it wisely and well.

## References

1.  W. S. Bauman, J. Komarynsky and J. C. Siska Goytre, Investment Securities Program Guide Using the HP-12C,. New York, McGraw-Hill, 1987.

2.  B. Bhandari, "Compounding/Discounting of Intrayear Cash Flows: Principles, Pedagogy and Practices," Financial Practice and Education (Spring 1991), pp. 87-89.

3.  E. F. Brigham, Fundamentals of Financial Management, 4th ed., Chicago, IL, The Dryden Press, 1986, Chapter 4.

4.  E. F. Brigham and L. C. Gapenski, Financial Management: and Practice, 5th ed., Chicago, IL, The Dryden Press, 1988, Chapter 4.

5.  P. Carr, "A Calculator Program for Option Values and Implied Standard Deviations," Journal of Financial Education (Fall 1988), pp. 89-93.

6.  P. L Cooley and P. F. Roden. Business Financial Management, Chicago, IL, The Dryden Press, 1988, Chapter 4.

7.  E. B. Greynolds, Jr., J. S. Aronofsky, Julius and R. J. Frame, Financial Analysis Using Calculators, New York, McGraw-Hill, 1980.

8.  R. C. Moyer, J. R. McGuigan and W. J. Kretlow, Contemporary Financial Management, 4th ed, St. Paul, MN, West Publishing Company, 1990, Chapter 5.

9.  G. E. Pinches, Essentials of Financial Management, 3rd ed., New York, Harper and Row, 1990, Chapter 5.

10. R. K. S. Rao, Fundamentals of Financial Management, New York, Macmillan, 1989, Chapter 2.

11. S. P. Rich and J. T. Rose, "A Note on Finance Principles, Bond Valuation, and the Appropriate Discount Rate," Financial Practice and Education (Fall 1991), pp. 99-101.

12. S. A. Ross, R. W. Westerfield and B. D. Jordan, Fundamentals of Corporate Finance, Homewood, IL, Richard D. Irwin, Inc., 1991, Chapter 5.

13. J. M. Smith, Financial Analysis and Business Decisions on the Pocket Calculator, New York, John Wiley & Sons, 1976.

14. R. W. Taylor, "Portfolio Management with a Hand-Held Calculator," Journal of Portfolio Management (Summer 1984), pp. 27-31.

15. _____, "Bond Duration Analysis: A Pedagogical Note," Financial Analyst's Journal (July/August 1987), pp. 71-72.

16. _____, "Option Valuation for Alternative Instruments with the Black-Scholes Model: A Pedagogical Note," Journal of Financial Education (Fall 1987), pp. 73-77.

17. M. A. White, "Financial Calculators in the Classroom: A Comparative Analysis," Journal of Financial Education, forthcoming.

## APPENDIX A

*The following pages contain templates containing keystroke solutions to the problems presented in the text. Instructors may want to use a different color of paper for each financial calculator model. This makes it very easy to identify the appropriate templates and distribute it to the student in need of a little extra help.*

# Financial Problem-Solving with an Electronic Calculator -- Mark A. White

## *Texas Instruments BA-II*

The *Texas Instruments BA-II* calculator incorporates basic financial and statistical functions into an affordable calculator for student use. This brochure provides illustrative keystroke solutions for problems commonly encountered in the introductory financial management course.

The *BA-II* operates in "modes." Before solving a financial problem, users must enter financial mode by pressing [2nd] {MODE}. Housekeeping functions needed to perform basic operations such as setting display formats, clearing calculator memory and adjusting for annuties due are summarized below.

### Housekeeping Functions

| | |
|---|---|
| Set Display Format to Two Decimal Places | [FIX] 2 |
| Set Financial Mode | [2nd] {MODE} |
| Clear Display | [ON/C] |
| Clear TVM Registers | [2nd] {CMR} |
| Adjust for payments at Beginning of Period | [DUE] * |

* Press the [DUE] key just prior to the last keystroke needed to solve the problem.

### Future Value of a Present Sum

Harry has just deposited $1000 into a savings account paying 6 percent, compounded annually. How much will he have in the account at the end of five years?

| | | |
|---|---|---|
| 1000.00 | [PV] | |
| 6.00 | [%i] | |
| 5.00 | [ N ] | |
| [2nd] [FV] | 1338.23 | |

*Harry will have accumulated $1,338.23 at the end of five years.*

### Present Value of an Annuity

Nancy had obtained an $11,000 bank loan to finance the purchase of a new car. The loan is for 48 months at an interest rate of 12 percent, compounded monthly. What is the amount of her monthly payment?

| | | |
|---|---|---|
| 11000.00 | [PV] | |
| 1.00 | [%i] | |
| 48.00 | [ N ] | |
| [2nd] [PMT] | 289.67 | |

*Nancy's monthly payment is $289.67.*

### Finding an Unknown Interest Rate

Exactly five years ago, Dave and Cindy purchased 100 shares of Gro-Tex Corporation at $45 per share. They now wish to sell their holdings at the current market price of $75 per share. What was their average annual rate of return over this period?

| | |
|---|---|
| 45.00 | [PV] |
| 5.00 | [N] |
| 75.00 | [FV] |
| [2nd] [%i] | 10.76 |

*Dave and Cindy earned a 10.76 percent holding period rate of return.*

### Finding an Unknown Number of Periods

Stacy received her retirement pension in a lump sum, and has invested it in an account which guarantees her a 10 percent annual rate of return. She wishes to make annual withdrawals of $35,000 beginning at the end of this year. If her current account balance is $250,000, how long will it be until she exhausts her account?

| | |
|---|---|
| 250000.00 | [PV] |
| 10.00 | [%i] |
| 35000.00 | [PMT] |
| [2nd] [N] | 13 14 |

*Her account balance will be exhausted in 13.14 periods; her last withdrawal (which will be smaller than her earlier ones) will be made 14 years from today.*

### Simple Bond Pricing

What is the price of an 8 percent semiannual coupon bond maturing EXACTLY six years from now? It has a par value of $1000, and bonds of similar risk are yielding 10 percent.

| | |
|---|---|
| 40.00 | [PMT] |
| 12.00 | [N] |
| 5.00 | [%i] |
| [2nd] [PV] | 354.53 |

| | |
|---|---|
| 1000.00 | [FV] |
| 12.00 | [N] |
| 5.00 | [%i] |
| [2nd] [PV] | 556.84 |

*The bond should sell for $354.53 + $556.84 = $911.37.*

### Simple Bond Yields to Maturity

What is the yield to maturity on a 10 percent annual coupon bond currently selling for $1,038.31? It matures in exactly three years.

| | |
|---|---|
| 1038.31 | [PV] |
| 100.00 | [PMT] |
| 1000.00 | [FV] |
| 3.00 | [N] |
| [2nd] [%i] | Error |

*Unfortunately, the BA-II cannot compute bond yields-to-maturity in a single step. The correct answer is 8.50 percent and must be obtained using a "trial and error" approach.*

# Financial Problem Solving with an Electronic Calculator
## *Mark A. White*

## *Texas Instruments BA-35*

The *Texas Instruments BA-35* financial calculator provides basic financial functions at an attractive price. This brochure provides illustrative keystroke solutions for problems commonly encountered in the introductory financial management course.

The *BA-35* operates in "modes". Before solving a financial problem, users must enter financial mode by pressing [2nd] {FIN}. Housekeeping functions needed to perform basic operations such as setting display formats, clearing calculator memory and adjusting for annuities due are summarized below.

### Housekeeping Functions

| | |
|---|---|
| Set Display Format to Two Decimal Places | [2nd] {Decimal} |
| Set Financial Mode | [2nd] {FIN} |
| Clear Display | [ON/C] |
| Clear TVM Registers | [2nd] {FIN} |
| Adust for Payments at Beginning of Period | [DUE ] * |

* Press the [DUE] key just prior to the last keystroke needed to solve problem

### Future Value of a Present Sum

Harry just deposited $1000 into a savings account paying 6 percent counpounded annually. How much will he have in the account at the end of five years?

| | |
|---|---|
| 1000.00 | [PV] |
| 6.00 | [%i] |
| 5.00 | [N] |
| [CPT] [FV] | 1338.23 |

*Harry will have accumulated $1,338.23 at the end of five years.*

### Present Value of an Annuity

Nancy has obtained an $11,000 bank loan to finance the purchase of a new car. The loan is for 48 months at an interest rate of 12 percent, compounded monthly. What is the amount of her monthly payment?

| | |
|---|---|
| 11000.00 | [PV] |
| 1.00 | [%i] |
| 48.00 | [N] |
| [CPT] [PMT] | 289.67 |

*Nancy's monthly payment is $289.67.*

### Finding an Unknown Interest Rate

Exactly five years ago, Dave and Cindy purchased 100 shares of Gro-Tex Corporation at $45 per share. They now wish to sell their holdings at the current market price of $75 per share. What was their average annual rate of return over this period?

| | |
|---|---|
| 45.00 | [PV] |
| 5.00 | [N] |
| 75.00 | [FV] |
| [CPT] [%i] | 10.76 |

*Dave and Cindy earned a 10.76 percent holding period rate of return.*

### Finding an Unknown Number of Periods

Stacy received her retirement pension in a lump sum, and has invested it in an account which guarantees her a 10 percent annual rate of return. She wishes to make annual withdrawals of $35,000 beginning at the end of this year. If her current account balance is $250,000, how long will it be until she exhausts her account?

| | |
|---|---|
| 250000.00 | [PV] |
| 10.00 | [%i] |
| 35000.00 | [PMT] |
| [CPT] [N] | 13.14 |

*Her account balance will be exhausted in 13.14 periods; her last withdrawal (which will be smaller than her earlier ones) will be made 14 years from today.*

### Simple Bond Pricing

What is the price of an 8 percent semiannual coupon bond maturing EXACTLY six years from now? It has a par value of $1000, and bonds of similar risk are yielding 10 percent.

| | |
|---|---|
| 40.00 | [PMT] |
| 12.00 | [N] |
| 5.00 | [%i] |
| 1000.00 | [FV] |
| [CPT] [PV] | -911.37 |

*The bond should sell for $354.53 + 556.84 = $911.37*

### Simple Bond Yields to Maturity

What is the yield to maturity on a 10 percent annual coupon bond currently selling for $1,038.31? It matures in exactly three years.

| | |
|---|---|
| 1038.31 | [PV] |
| 100.00 | [PMT] |
| 1000.00 | [FV] |
| 3.00 | [N] |
| [CPT] [%i] | 8.50 |

*The bond is priced to yield 8.50 percent per year.*

### Loan Amortization

Prepare an amortization schedule for a one-year, $2,000 computrer loan at 12 percent annual interest, compounded monthly. Monthly payments are $177.70.

| | |
|---|---|
| 2000.00 | [PV] |
| 1.00 | [%i] |
| 177.70 | [PMT] |
| 1 [2nd] [INT] | 20.00 |
| [STO] [2nd] [RCL] [PMT] [ - ] [RCL] [=] | 157.70 |
| 1 [2nd] [BAL] | 1842.30 |
| 2 [2nd] [INT] | 18.42 |
| [STO] [2nd] [RCL] [PMT] [ - ] [RCL] [=] | 159.28 |
| 2 [2nd] [BAL] | 1683.02 |

Interest portion of 1st payment = $20.00
Principal portion of 1st payment = $157.70
Loan balance after 1st payment = $1,842.30
Interest portion of 2nd payment = $18.42
Principal portion of 2nd payment = $159.28
Loan balance after 2nd payment = $1,683.02

### Interest Rate Conversions

A furniture store offers loan terms of 18 percent, compounded monthly. What is the loan's effective annual rate?

| | |
|---|---|
| 12.00 | [2nd] {APR> >} |
| 18.00 [ ≡ ] | 19.56 |

*The effective annual rate is 19.56 percent.*

*Example Continues*

335

## Financial Problem Solving with an Electronic Calculator - Mark A. White

### Texas Instruments - Financial Investment Analyst

Texas Instruments' *Financial Investment Analyst* is an advanced financial calculator offering a wide variety of basic and advanced financial functions accessed through a nested menu system. This brochure provides illustrative keystroke solutions for problems commonly encountered in the introductory financial management course.

Housekeeping functions needed to perform basic operations such as setting display formats, clearing calculator memory and adjusting for annuities due are summarized below.

### Housekeeping Functions

| | |
|---|---|
| Set Display Format to 2 Decimal Places | [2nd] {FORMAT} 2 [DEC] |
| Set Financial Mode | [TVM] |
| Clear Display | [CE/C] |
| Clear TVM Registers | [2nd] {CLR COL} |
| Adjust for Payments at Beginning of Period | [BGN], [END] |
| Set Compounding Frequency to 1x per Period | 1 [P/Y] |

### Future Value of a Present Sum

Harry has just deposited $1000 into a saving account paying 6 percent, compounded annually. How much will he have in the account at the end of five years?

| | |
|---|---|
| -1,000.00 | [PV] |
| 6.00 | [I/Y] |
| 5.00 | [N] |
| [Compute] [FV] | 1,338.23 |

*Harry will have accumulated $1,338.23 at the end of five years.*

### Present Value of an Annuity

Nancy has obtained an $11,000 bank loan to finance the purchase of a new car. The loan is for 48 months at an interest rate of 12 percent, compounded monthly. What is the amount of her monthly payment?

| | |
|---|---|
| 11,000.00 | [PV] |
| 1.00 | [I/Y] |
| 48.00 | [N] |
| [Compute] [PMT] | -289.67 |

*Nancy's monthly payment is $289.67.*

### Finding an Unknown Interest Rate

Exactly five years ago, Dave and Cindy purchased 100 shares of Gro-Tex Corporation at $45 per share. They now wish to sell their holding at the current market price of $75 per share. What was their average annual rate of return over this period?

| | |
|---|---|
| -45.00 | [PV] |
| 5.00 | [N] |
| 75.00 | [FV] |
| [Compute] [I/YR] | 10.76 |

### Finding an Unknown Number of Periods

Stacy received her retirement pension in a lump sum, and has invested it in an account which guarantees her a 10 percent annual rate of return. She wishes to make annual withdrawals of $35,000 beginning at the end of this year. If her current account balance is $250,000, how long will it be until she exhausts her account?

| | |
|---|---|
| -250,000.00 | [PV] |
| 10.00 | [I/YR] |
| 35,000.00 | [PMT] |
| [Compute] [N] | 13.14 |

*Her account balance will be exhausted in 13.14 periods; her last withdrawal (which will be smaller than her earlier ones) will be made 14 years from today.*

### Simple Bond Pricing

What is the price of an 8 percent semiannual coupon bond maturing EXACTLY six years from now? It has a par value of $1000, and bonds of similar risk are yielding 10 percent.

| | |
|---|---|
| 40.00 | [PMT] |
| 12.00 | [N] |
| 5.00 | [I/YR] |
| 1,000.00 | [FV] |
| [Compute] [PV] | -911.37 |

*The bond should sell for $911.37.*

### Simple Bond Yields to Maturity

What is the yield to maturity on a 10 percent annual coupon bond currently selling for $1,038.31? It matures in exactly three years.

| | |
|---|---|
| -1,038.31 | [PV] |
| 100.00 | [PMT] |
| 1,000.00 | [FV] |
| 3.00 | [N] |
| [Compute] [I/YR] | 8.50 |

*The bond is priced to yield 8.50 percent per year.*

### Cash Flow Analysis

An investment project promises the following schedule of cash flows. The project's initial outlay is -$100,000 and the appropriate discount rate is 10%. Use the NPV and IRR criteria to determine acceptance or rejection of this project.

| | |
|---|---|
| Year 1: | $15,000 |
| Year 2: | $20,000 |
| Year 3: | $20,000 |
| Year 4: | $20,000 |
| Year 5: | $20,000 |
| Year 6: | $60,000 |

| | |
|---|---|
| -100,000.00 | [CF 0] |
| [↓] | |
| 15,000.00 | [CF n] |
| 20,000.00 | [CF n] |

| | |
|---|---|
| 4 | [FRQ] |
| [↓] | |
| 60,000.00 | [CF n] |
| 10.00 | [I] |
| [CashF] | |
| [Compute] [NPV] | 5,138.72 |
| [Compute] [IRR] | 11.42 |

The project should be accepted because its NPV of $5,138.72 is greater than zero and its IRR of 11.42% is greater than the discount rate of 10 percent.

### Loan Amortization

Prepare an amortization schedule for a one-year, $2,000 computer loan at 12 percent annual interest, compounded monthly. Monthly payments are $177.70.

| | |
|---|---|
| 2,000.00 | [PV] |
| 1.00 | [I/Y] |
| -177.70 | [PMT] |
| [↓] [Compute] | 1,842.30 |
| | -157.70 |
| | -20.00 |

| | |
|---|---|
| 2 [P1] 2 [P2] | 1,683.02 |
| [Compute] | -159.28 |
| | -18.42 |

Interest portion of 1st payment = $20.00
Principal portion of 1st payment = $157.70
Loan balance after 1st payment = $1,842.30

Interest portion of 2nd payment = $18.42
Principal portion of 2nd payment = $159.28
Loan balance after 2nd payment = $1,683.02

### Interest Rate Conversions

A furniture store offers loan terms of 18 percent, compounded monthly. What is the loan's effective annual rate?

| | |
|---|---|
| 12.00 | [C/Y] |
| 18.00 | [APR] |
| [Compute] [AER] | 19.56 |

*The effective annual rate is 19.56 percent.*

# Financial Problem Solving using an Electronic Calculator - Mark A. White

## Sharp Electronics EL-731

The *Sharp Electronics EL-731* financial calculator provides basic financial functions at an affordable price. This brochure provides illustrative keystroke solutions for problems commonly encountered in the introductory financial management course.

The *EL-731* operates in "modes." Before solving a financial problem, users must enter financial mode by pressing [2ndF] {MODE}. Housekeeping functions needed to perform basic operations such as setting display formats, clearing calculator memory and adjusting for annuities due are summarized below.

### Housekeeping Functions

| | |
|---|---|
| Set Display Format to Two Decimal Places | [2ndF] {TAB} 2 |
| Set Financial Mode | [2ndF] {MODE} |
| Clear Display | [C-CE] |
| Clear TVM Registers | [2ndF] {CA} |
| Adjust for Payments at Beginning of Period | [BGN] |

### Future Value of a Present Sum

Harry has just deposited $1000 into a savings account paying 6 percent, compounded annually. How much will he have in the acccount at the end of five years?

| | | |
|---|---|---|
| -1'000.00 | [PV] | |
| 6.00 | [i] | |
| 5.00 | [n] | |
| [COMP] [FV] | 1'338.23 | |

*Harry will have accumulated $1,338.23 at the end of five years.*

### Present Value of an Annuity

Nancy has obtained an $11,000 bank loan to finance the purchase of a new car. The loan is for 48 months at an interest rate of 12 percent, compounded monthly. What is the amount of her monthly payment?

| | | |
|---|---|---|
| 11'000 | [PV] | |
| 1.00 | [i] | |
| 48.00 | [n] | |
| [COMP] [PMT] | -289.67 | |

*Nancy's monthly payment is $289.67.*

### Finding an Unknown Interest Rate

Exactly five years ago, Dave and Cindy purchased 100 shares of Gro-Tex Corporation at $45 per share. They now wish to sell their holdings at the current market price of $75 per share. What was their average annual rate of return over this period?

| | | |
|---|---|---|
| -45.00 | [PV] | |
| 5.00 | [n] | |
| 75.00 | [FV] | |
| [COMP] [i] | 10.76 | |

*Dave and Cindy earned a 10.76 percent holding rate of return.*

### Finding an Unknown Number of Periods

Stacy received her retirement pension in a lump sum, and has invested it in an account which guarantees her a 10 percent annual rate of return. She wishes to make annual withdrawals of $35,000 beginning at the end of this year. If her current account balance is $250,000, how long will it be until she exhausts her account?

| | | |
|---|---|---|
| -250'000.00 | [PV] | |
| 10.00 | [i] | |
| 35'000.00 | [PMT] | |
| [COMP] [n] | 13.14 | |

*Her account balance will be exhausted in 13.14 periods; her last withdrawal (which will be smaller than her earlier ones) will be made 14 years from today.*

### Simple Bond Pricing

What is the price of an 8 percent semiannual coupon bond maturing EXACTLY six years from now? It has a par value of $1000, and bonds of similar risk are yielding 10 percent.

| | | |
|---|---|---|
| 40.00 | [PMT] | |
| 12.00 | [n] | |
| 5.00 | [i] | |
| 1'000.00 | [FV] | |
| [COMP] [PV] | -911.37 | |

*The bond should sell for $911.37.*

### Simple Bond Yields to Maturity

What is the yield to maturity on a 10 percent annual coupon bond currently selling for $1,038.31? It matures in exactly three years.

| | | |
|---|---|---|
| -1'038.31 | [PV] | |
| 100.00 | [PMT] | |
| 1'000.00 | [FV] | |
| 3.00 | [n] | |
| [COMP] [i] | 8.50 | |

*The bond is priced to yield 8.50 percent per year.*

### Loan Amortization

Prepare an amortization schedule for a one-year, $2,000 computer loan at 12 percent annual interest, compounded monthly. Monthly payments are $177.70.

| | | |
|---|---|---|
| 2'000.00 | [PV] | |
| 1.00 | [i] | |
| -177.70 | [PMT] | |
| 1 [AMRT] | -157.70 | |
| [AMRT] | -20.00 | |
| [AMRT] | 1'842.30 | |
| | | |
| 2 [AMRT] | -159.28 | |
| [AMRT] | -18.42 | |
| [AMRT] | 1'683.02 | |

Interest portion of 1st payment = $20.00
Principal portion of 1st payment = $157.70
Loan balance after 1st payment = $1,842.30

Interest portion of 2nd payment = $18.42
Principal portion of 2nd payment =$159.28
Loan balance after 2nd payment = $1,638.02

### Interest Rate Conversions

A furniture store offers loan terms of 18 percent, compounded monthly. What is the loan's effective annual rate?

| | | |
|---|---|---|
| 12.00 | [ 2ndF] {>>EFF } | |
| 18.00 [ ≡ ] | 19.56 | |

*The effective annual rate is 19.56 percent.*

## Financial Problem Solving using an Electronic Calculator - Mark A. White

## Sharp Electronics EL-733. EL-735

The *Sharp Electronics EL-733* and *EL-735* financial calculators offer basic and advanced financial functions, including the ability to perform cash flow analysis. This brochure provides illustrative keystroke solutions for problems commonly encountered in the introductory financial management course.

Users of the *EL-733* must first enter financial mode by pressing [2ndF] {MODE} before solving financial problems. Housekeeping functions needed to perform basic operations such as setting display formats, clearing calculator memory and adjusting for annuities due are summarized below.

### Housekeeping Functions

| | |
|---|---|
| Set Display Format to Two Decimal Places | [2ndF] {TAB} 2 |
| Set Financial Mode | [2ndF] {MODE} |
| Clear Display | [C-CE] |
| Clear TVM Registers | [2ndF] {CA} |
| Adjust for Payments at Beginning of Period | [BGN] |

### Future Value of a Present Sum

Harry has just deposited $1000 into a savings account paying 6 percent, compounded annually. How much will he have in the account at the end of five years?

| | |
|---|---|
| -1'000.00 | [PV] |
| 6.00 | [ ⊥ ] |
| 5.00 | [ n ] |
| [COMP] [FV] | 1'338.23 |

*Harry will have accumulated $1,338.23 at the end of five years.*

### Present Value of an Annuity

Nancy has obtained an $11,000 bank loan to finance the purchase of a new car. The loan is for 48 months at an interest rate of 12 percent, compounded monthly. What is the amount of her monthly payment?

| | |
|---|---|
| 11'000 | [PV] |
| 1.00 | [ i ] |
| 48.00 | [ n ] |
| [COMP] [PMT] | -289.67 |

*Nancy's monthly payment is $289.67.*

### Finding an Unknown Interest Rate

Exactly five years ago, Dave and Cindy purchased 100 shares of Gro-Tex Corporation at $45 per share. They now wish to sell their holdings at the current market price of $75 per share. What was their average annual rate of return over this period?

| | |
|---|---|
| -45.00 | [PV] |
| 5.00 | [ n ] |
| 75.00 | [FV] |
| [COMP] [ i ] | 10.76 |

*Dave and Cindy earned a 10.76 percent holding rate of return.*

### Finding an Unknown Number of Periods

Stacy received her retirement pension in a lump sum, and has invested it in an account which guarantees her a 10 percent annual rate of return. She wishes to make annual withdrawals of $35,000 beginning at the end of this year. If her current account balance is $250,000, how long will it be until she exhausts her account?

| | |
|---|---|
| -250'000 | [PV] |
| 10.00 | [ i ] |
| 35'000 | [PMT] |
| [COMP] [ n ] | 13.14 |

*Her account balance will be exhausted in 13.14 periods; her last withdrawal (which will be smaller than her earlier ones) will be made 14 years from today.*

### Simple Bond Pricing

What is the price of an 8 percent semiannual coupon bond maturing EXACTLY six years from now? It has a par value of $1000, and bonds of similar risk are yielding 10 percent.

| | |
|---|---|
| 40.00 | [PMT] |
| 12.00 | [ n ] |
| 5.00 | [ i ] |
| 1'000.00 | [FV] |
| [COMP] [PV] | -911.37 |

*The bond should sell for $911.37.*

### Simple Bond Yields to Maturity

What is the yield to maturity on a 10 percent annual coupon bond currently selling for $1,038.31? It matures in exactly three years.

| | |
|---|---|
| -1'038.31 | [PV] |
| 100.00 | [PMT] |
| 1'000.00 | [FV] |
| 3.00 | [ n ] |
| [COMP] [ i ] | 8.50 |

*The bond is priced to yield 8.50 percent per year.*

### Cash Flow Analysis

An investment project promises the following schedule of cash flows. The project's initial outlay is -$100,000 and the appropriate discount rate is 10%. Use the NPV and the IRR criteria to determine acceptance or rejection of this project.

| | |
|---|---|
| Year 1: | $15,000 |
| Year 2: | $20,000 |
| Year 3: | $20,000 |
| Year 4: | $20,000 |
| Year 5: | $20,000 |
| Year 6: | $60,000 |

| | |
|---|---|
| -100'000.00 | [CFi] |
| 15'000.00 | [CFi] |
| 4 | [2ndF] {Ni} |
| 20'000.00 | [CFi] |
| 60'000.00 | [CFi] |
| 10.00 | [ ⊥ ] |
| [NPV] | 5'138.72 |
| [IRR] | 11.42 |

*The project should be accepted because its NPV of $5,138.72 is greater than zero and its IRR of 11.42 percent is greater than the discount rate of 10 percent.*

### Loan Amortization

Prepare an amortization schedule for a one-year, $2,000 computer loan at 12 percent annual interest, compounded monthly. Monthly payments are $177.70.

| | | |
|---|---|---|
| 2'000.00 | [PV] | |
| 1.00 | [ i ] | |
| -177.70 | [PMT] | |
| 1 [AMRT] | | -157.70 |
| [AMRT] | | -20.00 |
| [AMRT] | | 1'842.30 |
| | | |
| 2 [AMRT] | | -159.28 |
| [AMRT] | | -18.42 |
| [AMRT] | | 1'683.02 |

Interest portion of 1st payment = $20.00
Principal portion of 1st payment = $157.70
Loan balance after 1st payment = $1,842.30

Interest portion of 2nd payment = $18.42
Principal portion of 2nd payment =$159.28
Loan balance after 2nd payment = $1,638.02

### Interest Rate Conversions

A furniture store offers loan terms of 18 percent, compounded monthly. What is the loan's effective annual rate?

| | |
|---|---|
| 12.00 | [2ndF] {> > EFF} |
| 18.00 [ ≡ ] | 19.56 |

*The effective annual rate is 19.56 percent.*

## Financial Problem Solving with an Electronic Calculator - Mark A. White

### *Hewlett-Packard HP-10B*

The *Hewlett-Packard HP-10B* is a powerful, easy-to-use financial calculator capable of solving both basic and advanced financial problems. This brochure provides illustrative keystroke solutions for problems commonly encountered in the introductory financial management course.

By default, the *HP-10B* assumes monthly compounding, or 12 times per period. Beginning students should change this setting to once per period by pressing 1 [_] {P/YR}. Additional housekeeping functions needed to perform basic operations such as setting display formats, clearing calculator memory and adjusting for annuities due are summarized below.

#### Housekeeping Functions

| | |
|---|---|
| Set Display Format to Two Decimal Places | [_] [DSP] 2 |
| Clear Display | [C] |
| Clear TVM Registers | [_] {CLEAR ALL} |
| Adjust for Payments at Beginning of Period | [ _ ] {BEG/END} |
| Set Compounding Frequency to 1x per Period | 1 [_] {P/YR} |

#### Future Value of a Present Sum

Harry has just deposited $1000 into a savings account paying 6 percent, compounded annually. How much will he have in the acccount at the end of five years?

| | | |
|---|---|---|
| -1,000.00 | [PV] | |
| 6.00 | [I/YR] | |
| 5.00 | [N] | |
| [FV] | 1,338.23 | |

*Harry will have accumulated $1,338.23 at the end of five years.*

#### Present Value of an Annuity

Nancy has obtained an $11,000 bank loan to finance the purchase of a new car. The loan is for 48 months at an interest rate of 12 percent, compounded monthly. What is the amount of her monthly payment?

| | | |
|---|---|---|
| 11,0000.00 | [PV] | |
| 1.00 | [I/YR] | |
| 48.00 | [N] | |
| [PMT] | -289.67 | |

*Nancy's monthly payment is $289.67.*

#### Finding an Unknown Interest Rate

Exactly five years ago, Dave and Cindy purchased 100 shares of Gro-Tex Corporation at $45 per share. They now wish to sell their holdings at the current market price of $75 per share. What was their ~~average~~ annual rate of return over this period?

Compound

| | | |
|---|---|---|
| -45.00 | [PV] | |
| 5.00 | [N] | |
| 75.00 | [FV] | |
| [I/YR] | 10.76 | |

*Dave and Cindy earned a 10.76 percent holding period rate of return.*

#### Finding an Unknown Number of Periods

Stacy received her retirement pension in a lump sum, and has invested it in an account which guarantees her a 10 percent annual rate of return. She wishes to make annual withdrawals of $35,000 beginning at the end of this year. If her current account balance is $250,000, how long will it be until she exhausts her account?

| | | |
|---|---|---|
| -250,000.00 | [PV] | |
| 10.00 | [I/YR] | |
| 35,000.00 | [PMT] | |
| [N] | 13.14 | |

*Her account balance will be exhausted in 13.14 periods; her last withdrawal (which will be smaller than her earlier ones) will be made 14 years from today.*

#### Simple Bond Pricing

What is the price of an 8 percent semiannual coupon bond maturing EXACTLY six years from now? It has a par value of $1000, and bonds of similar risk are yielding 10 percent.

| | | |
|---|---|---|
| 40.00 | [PMT] | |
| 12.00 | [N] | |
| 5.00 | [I/YR] | |
| 1,000.00 | [FV] | |
| [PV] | -911.37 | |

*The bond should sell for $911.37.*

#### Simple Bond Yields to Maturity

What is the yield to maturity on a 10 percent annual coupon bond currently selling for $1,038.31? It matures in exactly three years.

| | | |
|---|---|---|
| -1,038.31 | [PV] | |
| 100.00 | [PMT] | |
| 1,000.00 | [FV] | |
| 3.00 | [N] | |
| [I/YR] | 8.50 | |

*The bond is priced to yield 8.50 percent per year.*

#### Cash Flow Analysis

An investment project promises the following schedule of cash flows. The project's initial outlay is -$100,000 and the appropriate discount rate is 10%. Use the NPV and the IRR criteria to determine acceptance or rejection of this project.

| | |
|---|---|
| Year 1: | $15,000 |
| Year 2: | $20,000 |
| Year 3: | $20,000 |
| Year 4: | $20,000 |
| Year 5: | $20,000 |
| Year 6: | $60,000 |

| | | |
|---|---|---|
| -100,000.00 | [CFj] | |
| 15,000.00 | [CFj] | |
| 20,000.00 | [CFj] | |
| 4.00 | [_] [ Nj ] | |
| 60,000.00 | [CFj] | |
| 10.00 | [I/YR] | |
| [_] {NPV} | 5,138.72 | |
| [_] {IRR/YR} | 11.42 | |

The project should be accepted because its NPV of $5,138.72 is greater than zero and its IRR of 11.42 percent is greater than the discount rate of 10 percent.

#### Loan Amortization

Prepare an amortization schedule for a one-year, $2,000 computer loan at 12 percent annual interest, compounded monthly. Monthly payments are $177.70.

| | | |
|---|---|---|
| 2,000.00 | [PV] | |
| 1.00 | [I/YR] | |
| -177.70 | [PMT] | |

| | | | |
|---|---|---|---|
| 1[INPUT][ ][AMORT] | [=] | -20.00 | |
| | [=] | -157.70 | |
| | [=] | 1,842.30 | |
| 2[INPUT][ ][AMORT] | [=] | -18.42 | |
| | [=] | -159.28 | |
| | [=] | 1,683.02 | |

Interest portion of 1st payment = $20.00
Principal portion of 1st payment = $157.70
Loan balance after 1st payment = $1,842.30

Interest portion of 2nd payment = $18.42
Principal portion of 2nd payment = $159.28
Loan balance after 2nd payment = 1,683.02

#### Interest Rate Conversions

A furniture store offers loan terms of 18 percent, compounded monthly. What is the loan's effective annual rate?

| | | |
|---|---|---|
| 12.00 | [_] {P/YR} | |
| 18.00 | [_] {NOM%} | |
| [_] {EFF%} | 19.56 | |

*The effective annual rate is 19.56 percent.*

# Financial Problem Solving using an Electronic Calculator - Mark A. White

## Hewlett-Packard HP-12C

The *Hewlett-Packard HP-12C* incorporates numerous financial problem-solving functions and can be programmed to determine many more. This brochure provides illustrative keystroke solutions for problems commonly encountered in the introductory financial management course.

Some users may find the *HP-12C* difficult to operate because it evaluates arithmetic expressions using RPN logic. The *HP-12C* Owner's Handbook provides instructions in the use ot this method of data entry. Housekeeping functions needed to perform basic operations such as setting display formats, clearing calculator memory and adjusting for annuites due are summarized below.

### Housekeeping Functions

Set Display Format to [ f ] 2
Two Decimal Places

Display Numbers in [ f ] [ ⌐ ]
Scientific Notation

Clear Display [CLX]

Clear TVM Registers [ f ] CLEAR {FIN}

Adjust for Payments at [ g ] {BEG}, [ g ] {END}
Beginning of Period

### Future Value of a Present Sum

Harry has just deposited $1000 into a savings account paying 6 percent, compounded annually. How much will he have in the account at the end of five years?

| | | |
|---|---|---|
| -1,000.00 | [PV] | |
| 6.00 | [ i ] | |
| 5.00 | [ n ] | |
| [FV] | 1,338.23 | |

*Harry will have accumulated $1,338.23 at the end of five years.*

### Present Value of an Annuity

Nancy has obtained an $11,000 bank loan to finance the purchase of a new car. The loan is for 48 months at an interest rate of 12 percent, compounded monthly. What is the amount of her monthly payment?

| | | |
|---|---|---|
| 11,0000.00 | [PV] | |
| 1.00 | [ i ] | |
| 48.00 | [ n ] | |
| [PMT] | -289.67 | |

*Nancy's monthly payment is $289.67.*

### Finding an Unknown Interest Rate

Exactly five years ago, Dave and Cindy purchased 100 shares of Gro-Tex Corporation at $45 per share. They now wish to sell their holdings at the current market price of $75 per share. What was their ~~average~~ annual rate of return over this period?

*Compound*

| | | |
|---|---|---|
| -45.00 | [PV] | |
| 5.00 | [ n ] | |
| 75.00 | [FV] | |
| [ i ] | 10.76 | |

*Dave and Cindy earned a 10.76 percent holding period rate of return.*

### Finding an Unknown Number of Periods

Stacy received her retirement pension in a lump sum, and has invested it in an account which guarantees her a 10 percent annual rate of return. She wishes to make annual withdrawals of $35,000 beginning at the end of this year. If her current account balance is $250,000, how long will it be until she exhausts her account?

| | | |
|---|---|---|
| -250,000.00 | [PV] | |
| 10.00 | [ i ] | |
| 35,000.00 | [PMT] | |
| [ n ] | 14.00 | |

*Her account balance will be exhausted in 13.14 periods; her last withdrawal (which will be smaller than her earlier ones) will be made 14 years from today.*

### Simple Bond Pricing

What is the price of an 8 percent semiannual coupon bond maturing EXACTLY six years from now? It has a par value of $1000, and bonds of similar risk are yielding 10 percent.

| | | |
|---|---|---|
| 40.00 | [PMT] | |
| 12.00 | [ n ] | |
| 5.00 | [ i ] | |
| 1,000.00 | [FV] | |
| [PV] | -911.37 | |

*The bond should sell for $911.37.*

### Simple Bond Yields to Maturity

What is the yield to maturity on a 10 percent annual coupon bond currently selling for $1,038.31? It matures in exactly three years.

| | | |
|---|---|---|
| -1,038.31 | [PV] | |
| 100.00 | [PMT] | |
| 1,000.00 | [FV] | |
| 3.00 | [ n ] | |
| [ i ] | 8.50 | |

*The bond is priced to yield 8.50 percent per year.*

### Cash Flow Analysis

An investment project promises the following schedule of cash flows. The project's initial outlay is -$100,000 and the appropriate discount rate is 10%. Use the NPV and the IRR criteria to determine acceptance or rejection of this project.

| | |
|---|---|
| Year 1: | $15,000 |
| Year 2: | $20,000 |
| Year 3: | $20,000 |
| Year 4: | $20,000 |
| Year 5: | $20,000 |
| Year 6: | $60,000 |

| | | |
|---|---|---|
| -100,000.00 | [ g ] {CF$_o$} | |
| 15,000.00 | [ g ] {CF$_j$} | |
| 20,000.00 | [ g ] {CF$_j$} | |
| 4.00 | [ g ] {Nj} | |
| 60,000.00 | [ g ] {CF$_j$} | |
| 10.00 | [ i ] | |
| [ f ] {NPV} | 5,138.72 | |
| [ f ] {IRR} | 11.42 | |

*The project should be accepted because its NPV of $5,138.72 is greater than zero and its IRR of 11.42 percent is greater than the discount rate of 10 percent.*

### Loan Amortization

Prepare an amortization schedule for a one-year, $2,000 computer loan at 12 percent annual interest, compounded monthly. Monthly payments are $177.70.

| | | |
|---|---|---|
| 2,000.00 | [PV] | |
| 1.00 | [ i ] | |
| -177.70 | [PMT] | |

| | | |
|---|---|---|
| 1 [f] {AMORT} | -20.00 | |
| [ x≷y ] | -157.70 | |
| [RCL] [PV] | 1,842.30 | |

| | | |
|---|---|---|
| 1 [f] {AMORT} | -18.42 | |
| [ x≷y ] | -159.28 | |
| [RCL] [PV] | 1,683.02 | |

| | |
|---|---|
| Interest portion of 1st payment = | $20.00 |
| Principal portion of 1st payment = | $157.70 |
| Loan balance after 1st payment = | $1,842.30 |

| | |
|---|---|
| Interest portion of 2nd payment = | $18.42 |
| Principal portion of 2nd payment = | $159.28 |
| Loan balance after 2nd payment = | $1,683.02 |

### Miscellany

- To perform a calculator self-test, turn the calculator on while holding down the [ x ] key.
- To change between American and European display formats, turn the calculator on while holding down the [ . ] key.
- Press [STO] {EEX} to toggle the 'c' annunciator, which determines whether intra-period interest is calculated on a simple or compound basis.

# Financial Problem Solving using an Electronic Calculator - Mark A. White

## Hewlett-Packard HP-17B II, HP-19B II

*Hewlett-Packard's HP-17B II and HP-19B II are highly sophisticated financial calculators incorporating numerous analytical problem-solving functions which are assessed using a nested menu system. For instance, the financial functions are located with the [FIN] menu. This brochure provides illustrative keystroke solutions for problems commonly encountered in the introductory financial management course. Housekeeping functions needed to perform basic operations such as setting display formats, clearing calculator memory and adjusting for annuities due are summarized below.*

### Housekeeping Functions

| | |
|---|---|
| Set Display Format to Two Decimal Places | [DSP] [FIX] 2 [INPUT] |
| Clear Display | [_] {CLEAR} |
| Clear TVM Registers | [_] {CLEAR DATA} |
| Adjust for Payments at Beginning of Period | [BEG], [END] * |
| Set Compounding Frequency to 1x per Period | 1 [P/YR] * |

\* *Press [FIN] [TVM] [OTHER] to access the menus needed to change these options.*

### Future Value of a Present Sum

Harry has just deposited $1000 into a savings account paying 6 percent, compounded annually. How much will he have in the account at the end of five years?

| | | |
|---|---|---|
| -1,000.00 | [PV] | |
| 6.00 | [I%YR] | |
| 5.00 | [n] | |
| | [FV] | 1,338.23 |

*Harry will have accumulated $1,338.23 at the end of five years.*

### Present Value of an Annuity

Nancy has obtained an $11,000 bank loan to finance the purchase of a new car. The loan is for 48 months at an interest rate of 12 percent, compounded monthly. What is the amount of her monthly payment?

| | | |
|---|---|---|
| 11,0000.00 | [PV] | |
| 1.00 | [I%YR] | |
| 48.00 | [N] | |
| | [PMT] | -289.67 |

*Nancy's monthly payment is $289.67.*

---

### Finding an Unknown Interest Rate

Exactly five years ago, Dave and Cindy purchased 100 shares of Gro-Tex Corporation at $45 per share. They now wish to sell their holdings at the current market price of $75 per share. What was their ~~average~~ compound annual rate of return over this period?

| | | |
|---|---|---|
| -45.00 | [PV] | |
| 5.00 | [N] | |
| 75.00 | [FV] | |
| | [I%YR] | 10.76 |

*Dave and Cindy earned a 10.76 percent holding rate of return.*

### Finding an Unknown Number of Periods

Stacy received her retirement pension in a lump sum, and has invested it in an account which guarantees her a 10 percent annual rate of return. She wishes to make annual withdrawals of $35,000 beginning at the end of this year. If her current account balance is $250,000, how long will it be until she exhausts her account?

| | | |
|---|---|---|
| -250,000.00 | [PV] | |
| 10.00 | [I%YR] | |
| 35,000.00 | [PMT] | |
| | [N] | 13.14 |

*Her account balance will be exhausted in 13.14 periods; her last withdrawal (which will be smaller than her earlier ones) will be made 14 years from today.*

### Simple Bond Pricing

What is the price of an 8 percent semiannual coupon bond maturing EXACTLY six years from now? It has a par value of $1000, and bonds of similar risk are yielding 10 percent.

| | | |
|---|---|---|
| 40.00 | [PMT] | |
| 12.00 | [N] | |
| 5.00 | [I%YR] | |
| 1,000.00 | [FV] | |
| | [PV] | -911.37 |

*The bond should sell for $911.37.*

### Simple Bond Yields to Maturity

What is the yield to maturity on a 10 percent annual coupon bond currently selling for $1,038.31? It matures in exactly three years.

| | | |
|---|---|---|
| -1,038.31 | [PV] | |
| 100.00 | [PMT] | |
| 1,000.00 | [FV] | |
| 3.00 | [N] | |
| | [I%YR] | 8.50 |

*The bond is priced to yield 8.50 percent per year.*

### Cash Flow Analysis

An investment project promises the following schedule of cash flows. The project's initial outlay is -$100,000 and the appropriate discount rate is 10%. Use the NPV and the IRR criteria to determine acceptance or rejection of this project.

| | |
|---|---|
| Year 1: | $15,000 |
| Year 2: | $20,000 |
| Year 3: | $20,000 |
| Year 4: | $20,000 |
| Year 5: | $20,000 |
| Year 6: | $60,000 |

| | | |
|---|---|---|
| -100,000.00 | [INPUT] | |
| 15,000.00 | [INPUT] | |
| 1.00 | [INPUT] | |
| 20,000.00 | [INPUT] | |
| 4.00 | [INPUT] | |
| 60,000.00 | [INPUT] | |
| 1.00 | [INPUT] | |
| [CALC] | | |
| 10.00 | [I%] | |
| [NPV] | | 5,138.72 |
| [IRR%] | | 11.42 |

*The project should be accepted because its NPV of $5,138.72 is greater than zero and its IRR of 11.42 percent is greater than the discount rate of 10 percent.*

### Loan Amortization

Prepare an amortization schedule for a one-year, $2,000 computer loan at 12 percent annual interest, compounded monthly. Monthly payments are $177.70.

| | | |
|---|---|---|
| 2,000.00 | [PV] | |
| 1.00 | [I%YR] | |
| -177.70 | [PMT] | |

| | | |
|---|---|---|
| [OTHER] [AMRT] | | |
| 1 [#P] [INT] | -20.00 | |
| [PRIN] | -157.70 | |
| [BAL] | 1,842.30 | |
| [NEXT] [INT] | -18.42 | |
| [PRIN] | -159.28 | |
| [BAL] | 1,683.02 | |

| | |
|---|---|
| Interest portion of 1st payment = | $20.00 |
| Principal portion of 1st payment = | $157.70 |
| Loan balance after 1st payment = | $1,842.30 |
| Interest portion of 2nd payment = | $18.42 |
| Principal portion of 2nd payment = | $159.28 |
| Loan balance after 2nd payment = | $1,683.02 |

### Interest Rate Conversions

A furniture store offers loan terms of 18 percent, compounded monthly. What is the loan's effective annual rate?

| | | |
|---|---|---|
| 12.00 | [P] | |
| 18.00 | [NOM%] | |
| | [EFF%] | 19.56 |

*The effective annual rate is 19.56 percent.*

# ANSWERS TO SELF TESTS

## Chapter 1

### True-False

| | | | | | | | | | |
|---|---|---|---|---|---|---|---|---|---|
| 1. | F | 2. | T | 3. | F | 4. | T | 5. | T |
| 6. | F | 7. | F | 8. | F | 9. | T | 10. | F |
| 11. | T | | | | | | | | |

### Multiple Choice

| | | | | | | | | | |
|---|---|---|---|---|---|---|---|---|---|
| 1. | d | 2. | e | 3. | e | 4. | e | 5. | d |
| 6. | d | 7. | c | 8. | d | | | | |

## Chapter 2

### True-False

| | | | | | | | | | |
|---|---|---|---|---|---|---|---|---|---|
| 1. | F | 2. | T | 3. | F | 4. | F | 5. | F |
| 6. | F | 7. | T | 8. | T | 9. | F | 10. | T |
| 11. | T | 12. | F | 13. | T | 14. | F | 15. | F |
| 16. | T | 17. | T | 18. | F | 19. | F | 20. | T |
| 21. | F | 22. | T | 23. | F | 24. | F | 25. | T |
| 26. | F | 27. | T | 28. | T | 29. | F | | |

### Multiple Choice

| | | | | | | | | | |
|---|---|---|---|---|---|---|---|---|---|
| 1. | c | 2. | d | 3. | e | 4. | b | 5. | b |
| 6. | a | 7. | c | 8. | d | 9. | c | 10. | c |
| 11. | d | 12. | b | 13. | b | 14. | c | 15. | c |
| 16. | d | 17. | d | 18. | b | 19. | d | 20. | c |
| 21. | c | 22. | c | 23. | c | 24. | b | 25. | c |

# Chapter 3

## True-False

| | | | | | | | | | |
|---|---|---|---|---|---|---|---|---|---|
| 1. | F | 2. | T | 3. | F | 4. | T | 5. | T |
| 6. | F | 7. | F | 8. | F | 9. | F | 10. | T |
| 11. | F | 12. | F | 13. | T | 14. | F | 15. | F |

## Multiple Choice

| | | | | | | | | | |
|---|---|---|---|---|---|---|---|---|---|
| 1. | d | 2. | a | 3. | d | 4. | d | 5. | b |
| 6. | b | 7. | c | 8. | b | 9. | a | 10. | d |

# Chapter 4

## True-False

| | | | | | | | | | |
|---|---|---|---|---|---|---|---|---|---|
| 1. | T | 2. | T | 3. | F | 4. | T | 5. | F |
| 6. | T | 7. | F | 8. | F | 9. | T | 10. | F |

## Multiple Choice

| | | | | | | | | | |
|---|---|---|---|---|---|---|---|---|---|
| 1. | c | 2. | d | 3. | e | 4. | c | 5. | e |
| 6. | c | | | | | | | | |

# Chapter 5

## True-False

| | | | | | | | | | |
|---|---|---|---|---|---|---|---|---|---|
| 1. | T | 2. | T | 3. | F | 4. | T | 5. | T |
| 6. | T | 7. | T | 8. | F | 9. | T | 10. | F |

## Multiple Choice

| | | | | | | | | | |
|---|---|---|---|---|---|---|---|---|---|
| 1. | a | 2. | c | 3. | d | 4. | c | 5. | a |

# Chapter 6

## True-False

| | | | | | | | | | |
|---|---|---|---|---|---|---|---|---|---|
| 1. | T | 2. | T | 3. | T | 4. | T | 5. | F |
| 6. | T | 7. | F | 8. | T | 9. | T | 10. | F |
| 11. | F | 12. | F | 13. | F | 14. | F | 15. | F |
| 16. | T | 17. | F | 18. | T | | | | |

## Multiple Choice

| | | | | | | | | | |
|---|---|---|---|---|---|---|---|---|---|
| 1. | a | 2. | c | 3. | a | 4. | b | 5. | b |
| 6. | c | 7. | c | 8. | a | 9. | b | 10. | d |
| 11. | b | 12. | a | 13. | b | 14. | b | 15. | D |
| 16. | c | 17. | e | | | | | | |

# Chapter 7

## True-False

| | | | | | | | | | |
|---|---|---|---|---|---|---|---|---|---|
| 1. | T | 2. | T | 3. | F | 4. | F | 5. | F |
| 6. | F | 7. | F | 8. | F | 9. | F | 10. | F |
| 11. | T | 12. | F | 13. | F | 14. | F | 15. | T |

## Multiple Choice

| | | | | | | | | | |
|---|---|---|---|---|---|---|---|---|---|
| 1. | a | 2. | b | 3. | d | 4. | c | 5. | a |
| 6. | c | 7. | a | 8. | b | 9. | c | 10. | d |
| 11. | d | 12. | b | | | | | | |

# Chapter 8

## True-False

| | | | | | | | | | |
|---|---|---|---|---|---|---|---|---|---|
| 1. | T | 2. | T | 3. | T | 4. | F | 5. | F |
| 6. | F | 7. | T | 8. | T | 9. | F | 10. | F |
| 11. | F | 12. | F | | | | | | |

## Multiple Choice

| 1. | b | 2. | d | 3. | c | 4. | d | 5. | b |
|----|---|----|---|----|---|----|---|----|---|
| 6. | d | 7. | b | 8. | b | 9. | a | | |

## Chapter 9

## True-False

| 1. | T | 2. | T | 3. | T | 4. | T | 5. | F |
|----|---|----|---|----|---|----|---|----|---|
| 6. | T | 7. | T | 8. | F | 9. | T | 10. | T |

## Multiple Choice

| 1. | c | 2. | a | 3. | c | 4. | b |
|----|---|----|---|----|---|----|---|

## Chapter 10

## True-False

| 1. | T | 2. | T | 3. | F | 4. | F | 5. | F |
|----|---|----|---|----|---|----|---|----|---|
| 6. | T | 7. | T | 8. | T | | | | |

## Multiple Choice

| 1. | c | 2. | d | 3. | e | 4. | d |
|----|---|----|---|----|---|----|---|

## Chapter 11

## True-False

| 1. | F | 2. | F | 3. | T | 4. | F | 5. | T |
|----|---|----|---|----|---|----|---|----|---|
| 6. | F | 7. | T | 8. | T | 9. | T | 10. | T |

## Multiple Choice

| 1. | d | 2. | d | 3. | d | 4. | b | 5. | b |
|----|---|----|---|----|---|----|---|----|---|
| 6. | b | | | | | | | | |

# Chapter 12

<u>**True-False**</u>

| | | | | | | | | | |
|---|---|---|---|---|---|---|---|---|---|
| 1. | F | 2. | F | 3. | T | 4. | T | 5. | F |
| 6. | T | 7. | F | 8. | T | 9. | F | 10. | F |
| 11. | F | 12. | F | 13. | F | 14. | F | 15. | T |
| 16. | T | 17. | T | 18. | T | 19. | T | 20. | T |
| 21. | F | 22. | F | 23. | T | 24. | F | 25. | F |
| 26. | T | 27. | T | 28. | T | 29. | F | 30. | T |
| 31. | F | 32. | F | 33. | T | 34. | F | 35. | F |
| 36. | F | 37. | F | 38. | T | 39. | T | 40. | F |
| 41. | F | 42. | F | 43. | T | 44. | T | 45. | F |
| 46. | F | 47. | F | 48. | F | 49. | T | 50. | F |
| 51. | T | | | | | | | | |

<u>**Multiple Choice**</u>

| | | | | | | | | | |
|---|---|---|---|---|---|---|---|---|---|
| 1. | c | 2. | c | 3. | c | 4. | c | 5. | b |
| 6. | b | 7. | b | 8. | b | 9. | b | 10. | d |
| 11. | b | 12. | c | 13. | a | 14. | b | 15. | c |
| 16. | d | 17. | b | 18. | d | 19. | c | 20. | a |
| 21. | b | 22. | b | 23. | c | 24. | e | 25. | b |
| 26. | d | 27. | b | 28. | b | 29. | a | 30. | d |
| 31. | b | 32. | d | 33. | e | 34. | c | 35. | b |
| 36. | e | 37. | a | | | | | | |

# Chapter 13

<u>**True-False**</u>

| | | | | | | | | | |
|---|---|---|---|---|---|---|---|---|---|
| 1. | T | 2. | F | 3. | F | 4. | F | 5. | T |
| 6. | F | 7. | T | 8. | T | 9. | F | 10. | T |
| 11. | T | 12. | F | 13. | F | 14. | F | 15. | F |

## Multiple Choice

| | | | | | | | | | |
|---|---|---|---|---|---|---|---|---|---|
| 1. | b | 2. | d | 3. | d | 4. | c | 5. | d |
| 6. | d | 7. | d | 8. | d | 9. | e | 10. | f |
| 11. | b | 12. | b | 13. | d | | | | |

## Chapter 14

### True-False

| | | | | | | | | | |
|---|---|---|---|---|---|---|---|---|---|
| 1. | F | 2. | F | 3. | T | 4. | F | 5. | T |
| 6. | T | 7. | F | 8. | T | 9. | F | 10. | T |
| 11. | F | 12. | F | 13. | T | 14. | F | 15. | F |
| 16. | T | 17. | F | 18. | F | 19. | T | | |

### Multiple Choice

| | | | | | | | | | |
|---|---|---|---|---|---|---|---|---|---|
| 1. | d | 2. | f | 3. | c | 4. | a | 5. | c |
| 6. | e | 7. | c | 8. | b | 9. | a | 10. | c |
| 11. | b | | | | | | | | |

## Chapter 15

### True-False

| | | | | | | | | | |
|---|---|---|---|---|---|---|---|---|---|
| 1. | F | 2. | F | 3. | T | 4. | F | 5. | T |
| 6. | F | 7. | T | 8. | F | 9. | F | 10. | F |
| 11. | F | 12. | F | 13. | F | 14. | F | 15. | F |
| 16. | F | 17. | T | 18. | T | 19. | F | 20. | F |
| 21. | T | 22. | T | 23. | F | 24. | F | 25. | T |
| 26. | T | 27. | T | 28. | F | 29. | T | 30. | F |
| 31. | T | 32. | F | 33. | F | 34. | T | 35. | F |
| 36. | F | 37. | F | 38. | F | 39. | F | 40. | T |
| 41. | T | 42. | T | 43. | F | 44. | T | 45. | T |
| 46. | F | 47. | T | 48. | F | | | | |

## Multiple Choice

| | | | | | | | | | |
|---|---|---|---|---|---|---|---|---|---|
| 1. | a | 2. | d | 3. | c | 4. | a | 5. | d |
| 6. | c | 7. | d | 8. | e | 9. | c | 10. | d |
| 11. | e | 12. | d | 13. | c | 14. | b | 15. | b |
| 16. | d | 17. | c | 18. | c | 19. | d | 20. | e |
| 21. | c | 22. | c | 23. | e | 24. | d | 25. | d |
| 26. | b | 27. | a | 28. | d | | | | |

## Chapter 16

### True-False

| | | | | | | | | | |
|---|---|---|---|---|---|---|---|---|---|
| 1. | T | 2. | F | 3. | F | 4. | F | 5. | T |
| 6. | T | 7. | F | 8. | F | 9. | T | 10. | T |
| 11. | T | 12. | T | 13. | T | 14. | F | 15. | T |
| 16. | F | | | | | | | | |

### Multiple Choice

| | | | | | | | | | |
|---|---|---|---|---|---|---|---|---|---|
| 1. | d | 2. | e | 3. | c | 4. | c | 5. | a |
| 6. | e | 7. | e | 8. | b | 9. | d | 10. | e |

## Chapter 17

### True-False

| | | | | | | | | | |
|---|---|---|---|---|---|---|---|---|---|
| 1. | T | 2. | F | 3. | T | 4. | T | 5. | F |
| 6. | T | 7. | T | | | | | | |

### Multiple Choice

| | | | |
|---|---|---|---|
| 1. | c | 2. | a |

# USING THE CALCULATOR TO COMPUTE TABLE VALUES

Note: See that the memory is cleared; you are in the correct mode for financial calculations; and have adequate decimal places.

## Appendix B (Compound sum of $1): $FVIF_{i,n} = \$1(1+i)^n$

**Hewlett-Packard HP-12C**

1 [CHS] [PV] ( No. of periods / Days, mths., or yrs. ) [n] ( Interest rate / per period ) [i] 0 [PMT] [FV] → ANSWER

**Hewlett-Packard HP-17B II, HP-19B II**

1 [+/-] [PV] ( No. of periods / Days, mths., or yrs. ) [N] ( Interest rate / per period ) [I%YR] 0 [PMT] [FV] → ANSWER

**Texas Instruments BA-35**

1 [+/-] [PV] ( No. of periods / Days, mths., or yrs. ) [N] ( Interest rate / per period ) [%i] 0 [PMT] [CPT] [FV] → ANSWER

**Texas Instruments BAII**

1 [+/-] [PV] ( No. of periods / Days, mths., or yrs. ) [N] ( Interest rate / per period ) [%i] 0 [PMT] [2nd] [FV] → ANSWER

**Texas Instruments BAII Plus**

1 [+/-] [PV] ( No. of periods / Days, mths., or yrs. ) [N] ( Interest rate / per period ) [I/Y] 0 [PMT] [CPT] [FV] → ANSWER

## Appendix C (Present value of $1): $PVIF_{i,n} = \dfrac{\$1}{(1+i)^n}$

**Hewlett-Packard HP-12C**

1 [CHS] [FV] ( No. of periods / Days, mths., or yrs. ) [n] ( Interest rate / per period ) [i] 0 [PMT] [PV] → ANSWER

**Hewlett-Packard HP-17B II, HP-19B II**

1 [+/-] [FV] ( No. of periods / Days, mths., or yrs. ) [N] ( Interest rate / per period ) [I%YR] 0 [PMT] [PV] → ANSWER

**Texas Instruments BA-35**

1 [+/-] [FV] ( No. of periods / Days, mths., or yrs. ) [N] ( Interest rate / per period ) [%i] 0 [PMT] [CPT] [PV] → ANSWER

**Texas Instruments BAII**

1 [+/-] [FV] ( No. of periods / Days, mths., or yrs. ) [N] ( Interest rate / per period ) [%i] 0 [PMT] [2nd] [PV] → ANSWER

**Texas Instruments BAII Plus**

1 [+/-] [FV] ( No. of periods / Days, mths., or yrs. ) [N] ( Interest rate / per period ) [I/Y] 0 [PMT] [CPT] [PV] → ANSWER

## Appendix D (Sum of an annuity of $1):

$$FVIFA_{i,n} = \$1 \sum_{t=0}^{n-1} (1+i)^t$$

**Hewlett-Packard HP-12C**

1 [CHS] [PMT] ( No. of periods (Days, mths., or yrs.) ) [n] ( Interest rate per period ) [i] 0 [PV] [FV] → ANSWER

**Hewlett-Packard HP-17B II, HP-19B II**

1 [+/-] [PMT] ( No. of periods (Days, mths., or yrs.) ) [N] ( Interest rate per period ) [I%YR] 0 [PV] [FV] → ANSWER

**Texas Instruments BA-35**

1 [+/-] [PMT] ( No. of periods (Days, mths., or yrs.) ) [N] ( Interest rate per period ) [%i] 0 [PV] [CPT] [FV] → ANSWER

**Texas Instruments BAII**

1 [+/-] [PMT] ( No. of periods (Days, mths., or yrs.) ) [N] ( Interest rate per period ) [%i] 0 [PV] [2nd] [FV] → ANSWER

**Texas Instruments BAII Plus**

1 [+/-] [PMT] ( No. of periods (Days, mths., or yrs.) ) [N] ( Interest rate per period ) [I/Y] 0 [PV] [CPT] [FV] → ANSWER

## Appendix E (Present value of an annuity of $1):

$$PVIFA_{i,n} = \left( \sum_{t=1}^{n} \frac{\$1}{(1+i)^t} \right)$$

**Hewlett-Packard HP-12C**

1 [CHS] [PMT] ( No. of periods (Days, mths., or yrs.) ) [n] ( Interest rate per period ) [i] 0 [FV] [PV] → ANSWER

**Hewlett-Packard HP-17B II, HP-19B II**

1 [+/-] [PMT] ( No. of periods (Days, mths., or yrs.) ) [N] ( Interest rate per period ) [I%YR] 0 [FV] [PV] → ANSWER

**Texas Instruments BA-35**

1 [+/-] [PMT] ( No. of periods (Days, mths., or yrs.) ) [N] ( Interest rate per period ) [%i] 0 [FV] [CPT] [PV] → ANSWER

**Texas Instruments BAII**

1 [+/-] [PMT] ( No. of periods (Days, mths., or yrs.) ) [N] ( Interest rate per period ) [%i] 0 [FV] [2nd] [PV] → ANSWER

**Texas Instruments BAII Plus**

1 [+/-] [PMT] ( No. of periods (Days, mths., or yrs.) ) [N] ( Interest rate per period ) [I/Y] 0 [FV] [CPT] [PV] → ANSWER

# APPENDIX B: COMPOUND SUM OF $1

| n | 1% | 2% | 3% | 4% | 5% | 6% | 7% | 8% | 9% | 10% |
|---|-----|-----|-----|-----|-----|-----|-----|-----|-----|------|
| 1 | 1.010 | 1.020 | 1.030 | 1.040 | 1.050 | 1.060 | 1.070 | 1.080 | 1.090 | 1.100 |
| 2 | 1.020 | 1.040 | 1.061 | 1.082 | 1.103 | 1.124 | 1.145 | 1.166 | 1.188 | 1.210 |
| 3 | 1.030 | 1.061 | 1.093 | 1.125 | 1.158 | 1.191 | 1.225 | 1.260 | 1.295 | 1.331 |
| 4 | 1.041 | 1.082 | 1.126 | 1.170 | 1.216 | 1.262 | 1.311 | 1.360 | 1.412 | 1.464 |
| 5 | 1.051 | 1.104 | 1.159 | 1.217 | 1.276 | 1.338 | 1.403 | 1.469 | 1.539 | 1.611 |
| 6 | 1.062 | 1.126 | 1.194 | 1.265 | 1.340 | 1.419 | 1.501 | 1.587 | 1.677 | 1.772 |
| 7 | 1.072 | 1.149 | 1.230 | 1.316 | 1.407 | 1.504 | 1.606 | 1.714 | 1.828 | 1.949 |
| 8 | 1.083 | 1.172 | 1.267 | 1.369 | 1.477 | 1.594 | 1.718 | 1.851 | 1.993 | 2.144 |
| 9 | 1.094 | 1.195 | 1.305 | 1.423 | 1.551 | 1.689 | 1.838 | 1.999 | 2.172 | 2.358 |
| 10 | 1.105 | 1.219 | 1.344 | 1.480 | 1.629 | 1.791 | 1.967 | 2.159 | 2.367 | 2.594 |
| 11 | 1.116 | 1.243 | 1.384 | 1.539 | 1.710 | 1.898 | 2.105 | 2.332 | 2.580 | 2.853 |
| 12 | 1.127 | 1.268 | 1.426 | 1.601 | 1.796 | 2.012 | 2.252 | 2.518 | 2.813 | 3.138 |
| 13 | 1.138 | 1.294 | 1.469 | 1.665 | 1.886 | 2.133 | 2.410 | 2.720 | 3.066 | 3.452 |
| 14 | 1.149 | 1.319 | 1.513 | 1.732 | 1.980 | 2.261 | 2.579 | 2.937 | 3.342 | 3.797 |
| 15 | 1.161 | 1.346 | 1.558 | 1.801 | 2.079 | 2.397 | 2.759 | 3.172 | 3.642 | 4.177 |
| 16 | 1.173 | 1.373 | 1.605 | 1.873 | 2.183 | 2.540 | 2.952 | 3.426 | 3.970 | 4.595 |
| 17 | 1.184 | 1.400 | 1.653 | 1.948 | 2.292 | 2.693 | 3.159 | 3.700 | 4.328 | 5.054 |
| 18 | 1.196 | 1.428 | 1.702 | 2.026 | 2.407 | 2.854 | 3.380 | 3.996 | 4.717 | 5.560 |
| 19 | 1.208 | 1.457 | 1.754 | 2.107 | 2.527 | 3.026 | 3.617 | 4.316 | 5.142 | 6.116 |
| 20 | 1.220 | 1.486 | 1.806 | 2.191 | 2.653 | 3.207 | 3.870 | 4.661 | 5.604 | 6.727 |
| 21 | 1.232 | 1.516 | 1.860 | 2.279 | 2.786 | 3.400 | 4.141 | 5.034 | 6.109 | 7.400 |
| 22 | 1.245 | 1.546 | 1.916 | 2.370 | 2.925 | 3.604 | 4.430 | 5.437 | 6.659 | 8.140 |
| 23 | 1.257 | 1.577 | 1.974 | 2.465 | 3.072 | 3.820 | 4.741 | 5.871 | 7.258 | 8.954 |
| 24 | 1.270 | 1.608 | 2.033 | 2.563 | 3.225 | 4.049 | 5.072 | 6.341 | 7.911 | 9.850 |
| 25 | 1.282 | 1.641 | 2.094 | 2.666 | 3.386 | 4.292 | 5.427 | 6.848 | 8.623 | 10.835 |
| 30 | 1.348 | 1.811 | 2.427 | 3.243 | 4.322 | 5.743 | 7.612 | 10.063 | 13.268 | 17.449 |
| 40 | 1.489 | 2.208 | 3.262 | 4.801 | 7.040 | 10.286 | 14.974 | 21.725 | 31.409 | 45.259 |
| 50 | 1.645 | 2.692 | 4.384 | 7.107 | 11.467 | 18.420 | 29.457 | 46.902 | 74.358 | 117.391 |

| n | 11% | 12% | 13% | 14% | 15% | 16% | 17% | 18% | 19% | 20% |
|---|---|---|---|---|---|---|---|---|---|---|
| 1 | 1.110 | 1.120 | 1.130 | 1.140 | 1.150 | 1.160 | 1.170 | 1.180 | 1.190 | 1.200 |
| 2 | 1.232 | 1.254 | 1.277 | 1.300 | 1.323 | 1.346 | 1.369 | 1.392 | 1.416 | 1.440 |
| 3 | 1.368 | 1.405 | 1.443 | 1.482 | 1.521 | 1.561 | 1.602 | 1.643 | 1.685 | 1.728 |
| 4 | 1.518 | 1.574 | 1.630 | 1.689 | 1.749 | 1.811 | 1.874 | 1.939 | 2.005 | 2.074 |
| 5 | 1.685 | 1.762 | 1.842 | 1.925 | 2.011 | 2.100 | 2.192 | 2.288 | 2.386 | 2.488 |
| 6 | 1.870 | 1.974 | 2.082 | 2.195 | 2.313 | 2.436 | 2.565 | 2.700 | 2.840 | 2.986 |
| 7 | 2.076 | 2.211 | 2.353 | 2.502 | 2.660 | 2.826 | 3.001 | 3.185 | 3.379 | 3.583 |
| 8 | 2.305 | 2.476 | 2.658 | 2.853 | 3.059 | 3.278 | 3.511 | 3.759 | 4.021 | 4.300 |
| 9 | 2.558 | 2.773 | 3.004 | 3.252 | 3.518 | 3.803 | 4.108 | 4.435 | 4.785 | 5.160 |
| 10 | 2.839 | 3.106 | 3.395 | 3.707 | 4.046 | 4.411 | 4.807 | 5.234 | 5.695 | 6.192 |
| 11 | 3.152 | 3.479 | 3.836 | 4.226 | 4.652 | 5.117 | 5.624 | 6.176 | 6.777 | 7.430 |
| 12 | 3.498 | 3.896 | 4.335 | 4.818 | 5.350 | 5.936 | 6.580 | 7.288 | 8.064 | 8.916 |
| 13 | 3.883 | 4.363 | 4.898 | 5.492 | 6.153 | 6.886 | 7.699 | 8.599 | 9.596 | 10.699 |
| 14 | 4.310 | 4.887 | 5.535 | 6.261 | 7.076 | 7.988 | 9.007 | 10.147 | 11.420 | 12.839 |
| 15 | 4.785 | 5.474 | 6.254 | 7.138 | 8.137 | 9.266 | 10.539 | 11.974 | 13.590 | 15.407 |
| 16 | 5.311 | 6.130 | 7.067 | 8.137 | 9.358 | 10.748 | 12.330 | 14.129 | 16.172 | 18.488 |
| 17 | 5.895 | 6.866 | 7.986 | 9.276 | 10.761 | 12.468 | 14.426 | 16.672 | 19.244 | 22.186 |
| 18 | 6.544 | 7.690 | 9.024 | 10.575 | 12.375 | 14.463 | 16.879 | 19.673 | 22.901 | 26.623 |
| 19 | 7.263 | 8.613 | 10.197 | 12.056 | 14.232 | 16.777 | 19.748 | 23.214 | 27.252 | 31.948 |
| 20 | 8.062 | 9.646 | 11.523 | 13.743 | 16.367 | 19.461 | 23.106 | 27.393 | 32.429 | 38.338 |
| 21 | 8.949 | 10.804 | 13.021 | 15.668 | 18.822 | 22.574 | 27.034 | 32.324 | 38.591 | 46.005 |
| 22 | 9.934 | 12.100 | 14.714 | 17.861 | 21.645 | 26.186 | 31.629 | 38.142 | 45.923 | 55.206 |
| 23 | 11.026 | 13.552 | 16.627 | 20.362 | 24.891 | 30.376 | 37.006 | 45.008 | 54.649 | 66.247 |
| 24 | 12.239 | 15.179 | 18.788 | 23.212 | 28.625 | 35.236 | 43.297 | 53.109 | 65.032 | 79.497 |
| 25 | 13.585 | 17.000 | 21.231 | 26.462 | 32.919 | 40.874 | 50.658 | 62.669 | 77.388 | 95.396 |
| 30 | 22.892 | 29.960 | 39.116 | 50.950 | 66.212 | 85.850 | 111.065 | 143.371 | 184.675 | 237.376 |
| 40 | 65.001 | 93.051 | 132.782 | 188.884 | 267.864 | 378.721 | 533.869 | 750.378 | 1051.668 | 1469.772 |

APPENDIX B: COMPOUND SUM OF $1 (Continued)

| n | 21% | 22% | 23% | 24% | 25% | 26% | 27% | 28% | 29% | 30% |
|---|---|---|---|---|---|---|---|---|---|---|
| 1 | 1.210 | 1.220 | 1.230 | 1.240 | 1.250 | 1.260 | 1.270 | 1.280 | 1.290 | 1.300 |
| 2 | 1.464 | 1.488 | 1.513 | 1.538 | 1.563 | 1.588 | 1.613 | 1.638 | 1.664 | 1.690 |
| 3 | 1.772 | 1.816 | 1.861 | 1.907 | 1.953 | 2.000 | 2.048 | 2.097 | 2.147 | 2.197 |
| 4 | 2.144 | 2.215 | 2.289 | 2.364 | 2.441 | 2.520 | 2.601 | 2.684 | 2.769 | 2.856 |
| 5 | 2.594 | 2.703 | 2.815 | 2.932 | 3.052 | 3.176 | 3.304 | 3.436 | 3.572 | 3.713 |
| 6 | 3.138 | 3.297 | 3.463 | 3.635 | 3.815 | 4.002 | 4.196 | 4.398 | 4.608 | 4.827 |
| 7 | 3.797 | 4.023 | 4.259 | 4.508 | 4.768 | 5.042 | 5.329 | 5.629 | 5.945 | 6.275 |
| 8 | 4.595 | 4.908 | 5.239 | 5.590 | 5.960 | 6.353 | 6.768 | 7.206 | 7.669 | 8.157 |
| 9 | 5.560 | 5.987 | 6.444 | 6.931 | 7.451 | 8.005 | 8.595 | 9.223 | 9.893 | 10.604 |
| 10 | 6.727 | 7.305 | 7.926 | 8.594 | 9.313 | 10.086 | 10.915 | 11.806 | 12.761 | 13.786 |
| 11 | 8.140 | 8.912 | 9.749 | 10.657 | 11.642 | 12.708 | 13.862 | 15.112 | 16.462 | 17.922 |
| 12 | 9.850 | 10.872 | 11.991 | 13.215 | 14.552 | 16.012 | 17.605 | 19.343 | 21.236 | 23.298 |
| 13 | 11.918 | 13.264 | 14.749 | 16.386 | 18.190 | 20.175 | 22.359 | 24.759 | 27.395 | 30.288 |
| 14 | 14.421 | 16.182 | 18.141 | 20.319 | 22.737 | 25.421 | 28.396 | 31.691 | 35.339 | 39.374 |
| 15 | 17.449 | 19.742 | 22.314 | 25.196 | 28.422 | 32.030 | 36.062 | 40.565 | 45.587 | 51.186 |
| 16 | 21.114 | 24.086 | 27.446 | 31.243 | 35.527 | 40.358 | 45.799 | 51.923 | 58.808 | 66.542 |
| 17 | 25.548 | 29.384 | 33.759 | 38.741 | 44.409 | 50.851 | 58.165 | 66.461 | 75.862 | 86.504 |
| 18 | 30.913 | 35.849 | 41.523 | 48.039 | 55.511 | 64.072 | 73.870 | 85.071 | 97.862 | 112.455 |
| 19 | 37.404 | 43.736 | 51.074 | 59.568 | 69.389 | 80.731 | 93.815 | 108.890 | 126.242 | 146.192 |
| 20 | 45.259 | 53.358 | 62.821 | 73.864 | 86.736 | 101.721 | 119.145 | 139.380 | 162.852 | 190.050 |
| 21 | 54.764 | 65.096 | 77.269 | 91.592 | 108.420 | 128.169 | 151.314 | 178.406 | 210.080 | 247.065 |
| 22 | 66.264 | 79.418 | 95.041 | 113.574 | 135.525 | 161.492 | 192.168 | 228.360 | 271.003 | 321.184 |
| 23 | 80.180 | 96.889 | 116.901 | 140.831 | 169.407 | 203.480 | 244.054 | 292.300 | 349.593 | 417.539 |
| 24 | 97.017 | 118.205 | 143.788 | 174.631 | 211.758 | 256.385 | 309.948 | 374.144 | 450.976 | 542.801 |
| 25 | 117.391 | 144.210 | 176.859 | 216.542 | 264.698 | 323.045 | 393.634 | 478.905 | 581.759 | 705.641 |
| 30 | 304.482 | 389.758 | 497.913 | 634.820 | 807.794 | 1025.927 | 1300.504 | 1645.505 | 2078.219 | 2619.996 |
| 40 | 2048.400 | 2847.038 | 3946.430 | 5455.913 | 7523.164 | 10347.175 | 14195.439 | 19426.689 | 26520.909 | 36118.865 |

APPENDIX B: COMPOUND SUM OF $1 (Continued)

| n | 31% | 32% | 33% | 34% | 35% | 36% | 37% | 38% | 39% | 40% |
|---|---|---|---|---|---|---|---|---|---|---|
| 1 | 1.310 | 1.320 | 1.330 | 1.340 | 1.350 | 1.360 | 1.370 | 1.380 | 1.390 | 1.400 |
| 2 | 1.716 | 1.742 | 1.769 | 1.796 | 1.823 | 1.850 | 1.877 | 1.904 | 1.932 | 1.960 |
| 3 | 2.248 | 2.300 | 2.353 | 2.406 | 2.460 | 2.515 | 2.571 | 2.628 | 2.686 | 2.744 |
| 4 | 2.945 | 3.036 | 3.129 | 3.224 | 3.322 | 3.421 | 3.523 | 3.627 | 3.733 | 3.842 |
| 5 | 3.858 | 4.007 | 4.162 | 4.320 | 4.484 | 4.653 | 4.826 | 5.005 | 5.189 | 5.378 |
| 6 | 5.054 | 5.290 | 5.535 | 5.789 | 6.053 | 6.328 | 6.612 | 6.907 | 7.213 | 7.530 |
| 7 | 6.621 | 6.983 | 7.361 | 7.758 | 8.172 | 8.605 | 9.058 | 9.531 | 10.025 | 10.541 |
| 8 | 8.673 | 9.217 | 9.791 | 10.395 | 11.032 | 11.703 | 12.410 | 13.153 | 13.935 | 14.758 |
| 9 | 11.362 | 12.166 | 13.022 | 13.930 | 14.894 | 15.917 | 17.001 | 18.151 | 19.370 | 20.661 |
| 10 | 14.884 | 16.060 | 17.319 | 18.666 | 20.107 | 21.647 | 23.292 | 25.049 | 26.925 | 28.925 |
| 11 | 19.498 | 21.199 | 23.034 | 25.012 | 27.144 | 29.439 | 31.910 | 34.568 | 37.425 | 40.496 |
| 12 | 25.542 | 27.983 | 30.635 | 33.516 | 36.644 | 40.037 | 43.717 | 47.703 | 52.021 | 56.694 |
| 13 | 33.460 | 36.937 | 40.745 | 44.912 | 49.470 | 54.451 | 59.892 | 65.831 | 72.309 | 79.371 |
| 14 | 43.833 | 48.757 | 54.190 | 60.182 | 66.784 | 74.053 | 82.052 | 90.846 | 100.510 | 111.120 |
| 15 | 57.421 | 64.359 | 72.073 | 80.644 | 90.158 | 100.713 | 112.411 | 125.368 | 139.708 | 155.568 |
| 16 | 75.221 | 84.954 | 95.858 | 108.063 | 121.714 | 136.969 | 154.003 | 173.008 | 194.194 | 217.795 |
| 17 | 98.540 | 112.139 | 127.491 | 144.804 | 164.314 | 186.278 | 210.984 | 238.751 | 269.930 | 304.913 |
| 18 | 129.087 | 148.024 | 169.562 | 194.038 | 221.824 | 253.338 | 289.048 | 329.476 | 375.203 | 426.879 |
| 19 | 169.104 | 195.391 | 225.518 | 260.011 | 299.462 | 344.540 | 395.996 | 454.677 | 521.532 | 597.630 |
| 20 | 221.527 | 257.916 | 299.939 | 348.414 | 404.274 | 468.574 | 542.514 | 627.454 | 724.930 | 836.683 |
| 21 | 290.200 | 340.449 | 398.919 | 466.875 | 545.769 | 637.261 | 743.245 | 865.886 | 1007.653 | 1171.356 |
| 22 | 380.162 | 449.393 | 530.562 | 625.613 | 736.789 | 866.674 | 1018.245 | 1194.923 | 1400.637 | 1639.898 |
| 23 | 498.012 | 593.199 | 705.647 | 838.321 | 994.665 | 1178.677 | 1394.996 | 1648.994 | 1946.885 | 2295.857 |
| 24 | 652.396 | 783.023 | 938.511 | 1123.350 | 1342.797 | 1603.001 | 1911.145 | 2275.611 | 2706.171 | 3214.200 |
| 25 | 854.638 | 1033.590 | 1248.220 | 1505.289 | 1812.776 | 2180.081 | 2618.268 | 3140.344 | 3761.577 | 4499.880 |
| 30 | 3297.151 | 4142.075 | 5194.566 | 6503.452 | 8128.550 | 10143.019 | 12636.215 | 15717.106 | 19518.391 | 24201.432 |
| 40 | 49074.04 | 66520.77 | 89963.35 | 121392.52 | 163437.13 | 219561.57 | 294321.97 | 393698.22 | 525523.34 | 700037.70 |

# APPENDIX C: PRESENT VALUE OF $1

| n | 1% | 2% | 3% | 4% | 5% | 6% | 7% | 8% | 9% | 10% |
|---|-----|-----|-----|-----|-----|-----|-----|-----|-----|-----|
| 1 | 0.990 | 0.980 | 0.971 | 0.962 | 0.952 | 0.943 | 0.935 | 0.926 | 0.917 | 0.909 |
| 2 | 0.980 | 0.961 | 0.943 | 0.925 | 0.907 | 0.890 | 0.873 | 0.857 | 0.842 | 0.826 |
| 3 | 0.971 | 0.942 | 0.915 | 0.889 | 0.864 | 0.840 | 0.816 | 0.794 | 0.772 | 0.751 |
| 4 | 0.961 | 0.924 | 0.888 | 0.855 | 0.823 | 0.792 | 0.763 | 0.735 | 0.708 | 0.683 |
| 5 | 0.951 | 0.906 | 0.863 | 0.822 | 0.784 | 0.747 | 0.713 | 0.681 | 0.650 | 0.621 |
| 6 | 0.942 | 0.888 | 0.837 | 0.790 | 0.746 | 0.705 | 0.666 | 0.630 | 0.596 | 0.564 |
| 7 | 0.933 | 0.871 | 0.813 | 0.760 | 0.711 | 0.665 | 0.623 | 0.583 | 0.547 | 0.513 |
| 8 | 0.923 | 0.853 | 0.789 | 0.731 | 0.677 | 0.627 | 0.582 | 0.540 | 0.502 | 0.467 |
| 9 | 0.914 | 0.837 | 0.766 | 0.703 | 0.645 | 0.592 | 0.544 | 0.500 | 0.460 | 0.424 |
| 10 | 0.905 | 0.820 | 0.744 | 0.676 | 0.614 | 0.558 | 0.508 | 0.463 | 0.422 | 0.386 |
| 11 | 0.896 | 0.804 | 0.722 | 0.650 | 0.585 | 0.527 | 0.475 | 0.429 | 0.388 | 0.350 |
| 12 | 0.887 | 0.788 | 0.701 | 0.625 | 0.557 | 0.497 | 0.444 | 0.397 | 0.356 | 0.319 |
| 13 | 0.879 | 0.773 | 0.681 | 0.601 | 0.530 | 0.469 | 0.415 | 0.368 | 0.326 | 0.290 |
| 14 | 0.870 | 0.758 | 0.661 | 0.577 | 0.505 | 0.442 | 0.388 | 0.340 | 0.299 | 0.263 |
| 15 | 0.861 | 0.743 | 0.642 | 0.555 | 0.481 | 0.417 | 0.362 | 0.315 | 0.275 | 0.239 |
| 16 | 0.853 | 0.728 | 0.623 | 0.534 | 0.458 | 0.394 | 0.339 | 0.292 | 0.252 | 0.218 |
| 17 | 0.844 | 0.714 | 0.605 | 0.513 | 0.436 | 0.371 | 0.317 | 0.270 | 0.231 | 0.198 |
| 18 | 0.836 | 0.700 | 0.587 | 0.494 | 0.416 | 0.350 | 0.296 | 0.250 | 0.212 | 0.180 |
| 19 | 0.828 | 0.686 | 0.570 | 0.475 | 0.396 | 0.331 | 0.277 | 0.232 | 0.194 | 0.164 |
| 20 | 0.820 | 0.673 | 0.554 | 0.456 | 0.377 | 0.312 | 0.258 | 0.215 | 0.178 | 0.149 |
| 21 | 0.811 | 0.660 | 0.538 | 0.439 | 0.359 | 0.294 | 0.242 | 0.199 | 0.164 | 0.135 |
| 22 | 0.803 | 0.647 | 0.522 | 0.422 | 0.342 | 0.278 | 0.226 | 0.184 | 0.150 | 0.123 |
| 23 | 0.795 | 0.634 | 0.507 | 0.406 | 0.326 | 0.262 | 0.211 | 0.170 | 0.138 | 0.112 |
| 24 | 0.788 | 0.622 | 0.492 | 0.390 | 0.310 | 0.247 | 0.197 | 0.158 | 0.126 | 0.102 |
| 25 | 0.780 | 0.610 | 0.478 | 0.375 | 0.295 | 0.233 | 0.184 | 0.146 | 0.116 | 0.092 |
| 30 | 0.742 | 0.552 | 0.412 | 0.308 | 0.231 | 0.174 | 0.131 | 0.099 | 0.075 | 0.057 |
| 40 | 0.672 | 0.453 | 0.307 | 0.208 | 0.142 | 0.097 | 0.067 | 0.046 | 0.032 | 0.022 |
| 50 | 0.608 | 0.372 | 0.228 | 0.141 | 0.087 | 0.054 | 0.034 | 0.021 | 0.013 | 0.009 |

357

# APPENDIX C: PRESENT VALUE OF $1 (Continued)

| n | 11% | 12% | 13% | 14% | 15% | 16% | 17% | 18% | 19% | 20% |
|---|-----|-----|-----|-----|-----|-----|-----|-----|-----|-----|
| 1 | 0.901 | 0.893 | 0.885 | 0.877 | 0.870 | 0.862 | 0.855 | 0.847 | 0.840 | 0.833 |
| 2 | 0.812 | 0.797 | 0.783 | 0.769 | 0.756 | 0.743 | 0.731 | 0.718 | 0.706 | 0.694 |
| 3 | 0.731 | 0.712 | 0.693 | 0.675 | 0.658 | 0.641 | 0.624 | 0.609 | 0.593 | 0.579 |
| 4 | 0.659 | 0.636 | 0.613 | 0.592 | 0.572 | 0.552 | 0.534 | 0.516 | 0.499 | 0.482 |
| 5 | 0.593 | 0.567 | 0.543 | 0.519 | 0.497 | 0.476 | 0.456 | 0.437 | 0.419 | 0.402 |
| 6 | 0.535 | 0.507 | 0.480 | 0.456 | 0.432 | 0.410 | 0.390 | 0.370 | 0.352 | 0.335 |
| 7 | 0.482 | 0.452 | 0.425 | 0.400 | 0.376 | 0.354 | 0.333 | 0.314 | 0.296 | 0.279 |
| 8 | 0.434 | 0.404 | 0.376 | 0.351 | 0.327 | 0.305 | 0.285 | 0.266 | 0.249 | 0.233 |
| 9 | 0.391 | 0.361 | 0.333 | 0.308 | 0.284 | 0.263 | 0.243 | 0.225 | 0.209 | 0.194 |
| 10 | 0.352 | 0.322 | 0.295 | 0.270 | 0.247 | 0.227 | 0.208 | 0.191 | 0.176 | 0.162 |
| 11 | 0.317 | 0.287 | 0.261 | 0.237 | 0.215 | 0.195 | 0.178 | 0.162 | 0.148 | 0.135 |
| 12 | 0.286 | 0.257 | 0.231 | 0.208 | 0.187 | 0.168 | 0.152 | 0.137 | 0.124 | 0.112 |
| 13 | 0.258 | 0.229 | 0.204 | 0.182 | 0.163 | 0.145 | 0.130 | 0.116 | 0.104 | 0.093 |
| 14 | 0.232 | 0.205 | 0.181 | 0.160 | 0.141 | 0.125 | 0.111 | 0.099 | 0.088 | 0.078 |
| 15 | 0.209 | 0.183 | 0.160 | 0.140 | 0.123 | 0.108 | 0.095 | 0.084 | 0.074 | 0.065 |
| 16 | 0.188 | 0.163 | 0.141 | 0.123 | 0.107 | 0.093 | 0.081 | 0.071 | 0.062 | 0.054 |
| 17 | 0.170 | 0.146 | 0.125 | 0.108 | 0.093 | 0.080 | 0.069 | 0.060 | 0.052 | 0.045 |
| 18 | 0.153 | 0.130 | 0.111 | 0.095 | 0.081 | 0.069 | 0.059 | 0.051 | 0.044 | 0.038 |
| 19 | 0.138 | 0.116 | 0.098 | 0.083 | 0.070 | 0.060 | 0.051 | 0.043 | 0.037 | 0.031 |
| 20 | 0.124 | 0.104 | 0.087 | 0.073 | 0.061 | 0.051 | 0.043 | 0.037 | 0.031 | 0.026 |
| 21 | 0.112 | 0.093 | 0.077 | 0.064 | 0.053 | 0.044 | 0.037 | 0.031 | 0.026 | 0.022 |
| 22 | 0.101 | 0.083 | 0.068 | 0.056 | 0.046 | 0.038 | 0.032 | 0.026 | 0.022 | 0.018 |
| 23 | 0.091 | 0.074 | 0.060 | 0.049 | 0.040 | 0.033 | 0.027 | 0.022 | 0.018 | 0.015 |
| 24 | 0.082 | 0.066 | 0.053 | 0.043 | 0.035 | 0.028 | 0.023 | 0.019 | 0.015 | 0.013 |
| 25 | 0.074 | 0.059 | 0.047 | 0.038 | 0.030 | 0.024 | 0.020 | 0.016 | 0.013 | 0.010 |
| 30 | 0.044 | 0.033 | 0.026 | 0.020 | 0.015 | 0.012 | 0.009 | 0.007 | 0.005 | 0.004 |
| 40 | 0.015 | 0.011 | 0.008 | 0.005 | 0.004 | 0.003 | 0.002 | 0.001 | 0.001 | 0.001 |
| 50 | 0.005 | 0.003 | 0.002 | 0.001 | 0.001 | 0.001 | 0.000 | 0.000 | 0.000 | 0.000 |

# APPENDIX C: PRESENT VALUE OF $1 (Continued)

| n | 21% | 22% | 23% | 24% | 25% | 26% | 27% | 28% | 29% | 30% |
|---|---|---|---|---|---|---|---|---|---|---|
| 1 | 0.826 | 0.820 | 0.813 | 0.806 | 0.800 | 0.794 | 0.787 | 0.781 | 0.775 | 0.769 |
| 2 | 0.683 | 0.672 | 0.661 | 0.650 | 0.640 | 0.630 | 0.620 | 0.610 | 0.601 | 0.592 |
| 3 | 0.564 | 0.551 | 0.537 | 0.524 | 0.512 | 0.500 | 0.488 | 0.477 | 0.466 | 0.455 |
| 4 | 0.467 | 0.451 | 0.437 | 0.423 | 0.410 | 0.397 | 0.384 | 0.373 | 0.361 | 0.350 |
| 5 | 0.386 | 0.370 | 0.355 | 0.341 | 0.328 | 0.315 | 0.303 | 0.291 | 0.280 | 0.269 |
| 6 | 0.319 | 0.303 | 0.289 | 0.275 | 0.262 | 0.250 | 0.238 | 0.227 | 0.217 | 0.207 |
| 7 | 0.263 | 0.249 | 0.235 | 0.222 | 0.210 | 0.198 | 0.188 | 0.178 | 0.168 | 0.159 |
| 8 | 0.218 | 0.204 | 0.191 | 0.179 | 0.168 | 0.157 | 0.148 | 0.139 | 0.130 | 0.123 |
| 9 | 0.180 | 0.167 | 0.155 | 0.144 | 0.134 | 0.125 | 0.116 | 0.108 | 0.101 | 0.094 |
| 10 | 0.149 | 0.137 | 0.126 | 0.116 | 0.107 | 0.099 | 0.092 | 0.085 | 0.078 | 0.073 |
| 11 | 0.123 | 0.112 | 0.103 | 0.094 | 0.086 | 0.079 | 0.072 | 0.066 | 0.061 | 0.056 |
| 12 | 0.102 | 0.092 | 0.083 | 0.076 | 0.069 | 0.062 | 0.057 | 0.052 | 0.047 | 0.043 |
| 13 | 0.084 | 0.075 | 0.068 | 0.061 | 0.055 | 0.050 | 0.045 | 0.040 | 0.037 | 0.033 |
| 14 | 0.069 | 0.062 | 0.055 | 0.049 | 0.044 | 0.039 | 0.035 | 0.032 | 0.028 | 0.025 |
| 15 | 0.057 | 0.051 | 0.045 | 0.040 | 0.035 | 0.031 | 0.028 | 0.025 | 0.022 | 0.020 |
| 16 | 0.047 | 0.042 | 0.036 | 0.032 | 0.028 | 0.025 | 0.022 | 0.019 | 0.017 | 0.015 |
| 17 | 0.039 | 0.034 | 0.030 | 0.026 | 0.023 | 0.020 | 0.017 | 0.015 | 0.013 | 0.012 |
| 18 | 0.032 | 0.028 | 0.024 | 0.021 | 0.018 | 0.016 | 0.014 | 0.012 | 0.010 | 0.009 |
| 19 | 0.027 | 0.023 | 0.020 | 0.017 | 0.014 | 0.012 | 0.011 | 0.009 | 0.008 | 0.007 |
| 20 | 0.022 | 0.019 | 0.016 | 0.014 | 0.012 | 0.010 | 0.008 | 0.007 | 0.006 | 0.005 |
| 21 | 0.018 | 0.015 | 0.013 | 0.011 | 0.009 | 0.008 | 0.007 | 0.006 | 0.005 | 0.004 |
| 22 | 0.015 | 0.013 | 0.011 | 0.009 | 0.007 | 0.006 | 0.005 | 0.004 | 0.004 | 0.003 |
| 23 | 0.012 | 0.010 | 0.009 | 0.007 | 0.006 | 0.005 | 0.004 | 0.003 | 0.003 | 0.002 |
| 24 | 0.010 | 0.008 | 0.007 | 0.006 | 0.005 | 0.004 | 0.003 | 0.003 | 0.002 | 0.002 |
| 25 | 0.009 | 0.007 | 0.006 | 0.005 | 0.004 | 0.003 | 0.003 | 0.002 | 0.002 | 0.001 |
| 30 | 0.003 | 0.003 | 0.002 | 0.002 | 0.001 | 0.001 | 0.001 | 0.001 | 0.000 | 0.000 |
| 40 | 0.000 | 0.000 | 0.000 | 0.000 | 0.000 | 0.000 | 0.000 | 0.000 | 0.000 | 0.000 |
| 50 | 0.000 | 0.000 | 0.000 | 0.000 | 0.000 | 0.000 | 0.000 | 0.000 | 0.000 | 0.000 |

# APPENDIX C: PRESENT VALUE OF $1 (Continued)

| n | 31% | 32% | 33% | 34% | 35% | 36% | 37% | 38% | 39% | 40% |
|---|-----|-----|-----|-----|-----|-----|-----|-----|-----|-----|
| 1 | 0.763 | 0.758 | 0.752 | 0.746 | 0.741 | 0.735 | 0.730 | 0.725 | 0.719 | 0.714 |
| 2 | 0.583 | 0.574 | 0.565 | 0.557 | 0.549 | 0.541 | 0.533 | 0.525 | 0.518 | 0.510 |
| 3 | 0.445 | 0.435 | 0.425 | 0.416 | 0.406 | 0.398 | 0.389 | 0.381 | 0.372 | 0.364 |
| 4 | 0.340 | 0.329 | 0.320 | 0.310 | 0.301 | 0.292 | 0.284 | 0.276 | 0.268 | 0.260 |
| 5 | 0.259 | 0.250 | 0.240 | 0.231 | 0.223 | 0.215 | 0.207 | 0.200 | 0.193 | 0.186 |
| 6 | 0.198 | 0.189 | 0.181 | 0.173 | 0.165 | 0.158 | 0.151 | 0.145 | 0.139 | 0.133 |
| 7 | 0.151 | 0.143 | 0.136 | 0.129 | 0.122 | 0.116 | 0.110 | 0.105 | 0.100 | 0.095 |
| 8 | 0.115 | 0.108 | 0.102 | 0.096 | 0.091 | 0.085 | 0.081 | 0.076 | 0.072 | 0.068 |
| 9 | 0.088 | 0.082 | 0.077 | 0.072 | 0.067 | 0.063 | 0.059 | 0.055 | 0.052 | 0.048 |
| 10 | 0.067 | 0.062 | 0.058 | 0.054 | 0.050 | 0.046 | 0.043 | 0.040 | 0.037 | 0.035 |
| 11 | 0.051 | 0.047 | 0.043 | 0.040 | 0.037 | 0.034 | 0.031 | 0.029 | 0.027 | 0.025 |
| 12 | 0.039 | 0.036 | 0.033 | 0.030 | 0.027 | 0.025 | 0.023 | 0.021 | 0.019 | 0.018 |
| 13 | 0.030 | 0.027 | 0.025 | 0.022 | 0.020 | 0.018 | 0.017 | 0.015 | 0.014 | 0.013 |
| 14 | 0.023 | 0.021 | 0.018 | 0.017 | 0.015 | 0.014 | 0.012 | 0.011 | 0.010 | 0.009 |
| 15 | 0.017 | 0.016 | 0.014 | 0.012 | 0.011 | 0.010 | 0.009 | 0.008 | 0.007 | 0.006 |
| 16 | 0.013 | 0.012 | 0.010 | 0.009 | 0.008 | 0.007 | 0.006 | 0.006 | 0.005 | 0.005 |
| 17 | 0.010 | 0.009 | 0.008 | 0.007 | 0.006 | 0.005 | 0.005 | 0.004 | 0.004 | 0.003 |
| 18 | 0.008 | 0.007 | 0.006 | 0.005 | 0.005 | 0.004 | 0.003 | 0.003 | 0.003 | 0.002 |
| 19 | 0.006 | 0.005 | 0.004 | 0.004 | 0.003 | 0.003 | 0.003 | 0.002 | 0.002 | 0.002 |
| 20 | 0.005 | 0.004 | 0.003 | 0.003 | 0.002 | 0.002 | 0.002 | 0.002 | 0.001 | 0.001 |
| 21 | 0.003 | 0.003 | 0.003 | 0.002 | 0.002 | 0.002 | 0.001 | 0.001 | 0.001 | 0.001 |
| 22 | 0.003 | 0.002 | 0.002 | 0.002 | 0.001 | 0.001 | 0.001 | 0.001 | 0.001 | 0.001 |
| 23 | 0.002 | 0.002 | 0.001 | 0.001 | 0.001 | 0.001 | 0.001 | 0.001 | 0.001 | 0.000 |
| 24 | 0.002 | 0.001 | 0.001 | 0.001 | 0.001 | 0.001 | 0.001 | 0.000 | 0.000 | 0.000 |
| 25 | 0.001 | 0.001 | 0.001 | 0.001 | 0.001 | 0.000 | 0.000 | 0.000 | 0.000 | 0.000 |
| 30 | 0.000 | 0.000 | 0.000 | 0.000 | 0.000 | 0.000 | 0.000 | 0.000 | 0.000 | 0.000 |
| 40 | 0.000 | 0.000 | 0.000 | 0.000 | 0.000 | 0.000 | 0.000 | 0.000 | 0.000 | 0.000 |
| 50 | 0.000 | 0.000 | 0.000 | 0.000 | 0.000 | 0.000 | 0.000 | 0.000 | 0.000 | 0.000 |

# APPENDIX D: SUM OF AN ANNUITY OF $1 FOR N PERIODS

| n | 1% | 2% | 3% | 4% | 5% | 6% | 7% | 8% | 9% | 10% |
|---|------|------|------|------|------|------|------|------|------|------|
| 1 | 1.000 | 1.000 | 1.000 | 1.000 | 1.000 | 1.000 | 1.000 | 1.000 | 1.000 | 1.000 |
| 2 | 2.010 | 2.020 | 2.030 | 2.040 | 2.050 | 2.060 | 2.070 | 2.080 | 2.090 | 2.100 |
| 3 | 3.030 | 3.060 | 3.091 | 3.122 | 3.153 | 3.184 | 3.215 | 3.246 | 3.278 | 3.310 |
| 4 | 4.060 | 4.122 | 4.184 | 4.246 | 4.310 | 4.375 | 4.440 | 4.506 | 4.573 | 4.641 |
| 5 | 5.101 | 5.204 | 5.309 | 5.416 | 5.526 | 5.637 | 5.751 | 5.867 | 5.985 | 6.105 |
| 6 | 6.152 | 6.308 | 6.468 | 6.633 | 6.802 | 6.975 | 7.153 | 7.336 | 7.523 | 7.716 |
| 7 | 7.214 | 7.434 | 7.662 | 7.898 | 8.142 | 8.394 | 8.654 | 8.923 | 9.200 | 9.487 |
| 8 | 8.286 | 8.583 | 8.892 | 9.214 | 9.549 | 9.897 | 10.260 | 10.637 | 11.028 | 11.436 |
| 9 | 9.369 | 9.755 | 10.159 | 10.583 | 11.027 | 11.491 | 11.978 | 12.488 | 13.021 | 13.579 |
| 10 | 10.462 | 10.950 | 11.464 | 12.006 | 12.578 | 13.181 | 13.816 | 14.487 | 15.193 | 15.937 |
| 11 | 11.567 | 12.169 | 12.808 | 13.486 | 14.207 | 14.972 | 15.784 | 16.645 | 17.560 | 18.531 |
| 12 | 12.683 | 13.412 | 14.192 | 15.026 | 15.917 | 16.870 | 17.888 | 18.977 | 20.141 | 21.384 |
| 13 | 13.809 | 14.680 | 15.618 | 16.627 | 17.713 | 18.882 | 20.141 | 21.495 | 22.953 | 24.523 |
| 14 | 14.947 | 15.974 | 17.086 | 18.292 | 19.599 | 21.015 | 22.550 | 24.215 | 26.019 | 27.975 |
| 15 | 16.097 | 17.293 | 18.599 | 20.024 | 21.579 | 23.276 | 25.129 | 27.152 | 29.361 | 31.772 |
| 16 | 17.258 | 18.639 | 20.157 | 21.825 | 23.657 | 25.673 | 27.888 | 30.324 | 33.003 | 35.950 |
| 17 | 18.430 | 20.012 | 21.762 | 23.698 | 25.840 | 28.213 | 30.840 | 33.750 | 36.974 | 40.545 |
| 18 | 19.615 | 21.412 | 23.414 | 25.645 | 28.132 | 30.906 | 33.999 | 37.450 | 41.301 | 45.599 |
| 19 | 20.811 | 22.841 | 25.117 | 27.671 | 30.539 | 33.760 | 37.379 | 41.446 | 46.018 | 51.159 |
| 20 | 22.019 | 24.297 | 26.870 | 29.778 | 33.066 | 36.786 | 40.995 | 45.762 | 51.160 | 57.275 |
| 21 | 23.239 | 25.783 | 28.676 | 31.969 | 35.719 | 39.993 | 44.865 | 50.423 | 56.765 | 64.002 |
| 22 | 24.472 | 27.299 | 30.537 | 34.248 | 38.505 | 43.392 | 49.006 | 55.457 | 62.873 | 71.403 |
| 23 | 25.716 | 28.845 | 32.453 | 36.618 | 41.430 | 46.996 | 53.436 | 60.893 | 69.532 | 79.543 |
| 24 | 26.973 | 30.422 | 34.426 | 39.083 | 44.502 | 50.816 | 58.177 | 66.765 | 76.790 | 88.497 |
| 25 | 28.243 | 32.030 | 36.459 | 41.646 | 47.727 | 54.865 | 63.249 | 73.106 | 84.701 | 98.347 |
| 30 | 34.785 | 40.568 | 47.575 | 56.085 | 66.439 | 79.058 | 94.461 | 113.283 | 136.308 | 164.494 |
| 40 | 48.886 | 60.402 | 75.401 | 95.026 | 120.800 | 154.762 | 199.635 | 259.057 | 337.882 | 442.593 |
| 50 | 64.463 | 84.579 | 112.797 | 152.667 | 209.348 | 290.336 | 406.529 | 573.770 | 815.084 | 1163.909 |

# APPENDIX D: SUM OF AN ANNUITY OF $1 FOR N PERIODS (Continued)

| n | 11% | 12% | 13% | 14% | 15% | 16% | 17% | 18% | 19% | 20% |
|---|---|---|---|---|---|---|---|---|---|---|
| 1 | 1.000 | 1.000 | 1.000 | 1.000 | 1.000 | 1.000 | 1.000 | 1.000 | 1.000 | 1.000 |
| 2 | 2.110 | 2.120 | 2.130 | 2.140 | 2.150 | 2.160 | 2.170 | 2.180 | 2.190 | 2.200 |
| 3 | 3.342 | 3.374 | 3.407 | 3.440 | 3.473 | 3.506 | 3.539 | 3.572 | 3.606 | 3.640 |
| 4 | 4.710 | 4.779 | 4.850 | 4.921 | 4.993 | 5.066 | 5.141 | 5.215 | 5.291 | 5.368 |
| 5 | 6.228 | 6.353 | 6.480 | 6.610 | 6.742 | 6.877 | 7.014 | 7.154 | 7.297 | 7.442 |
| 6 | 7.913 | 8.115 | 8.323 | 8.536 | 8.754 | 8.977 | 9.207 | 9.442 | 9.683 | 9.930 |
| 7 | 9.783 | 10.089 | 10.405 | 10.730 | 11.067 | 11.414 | 11.772 | 12.142 | 12.523 | 12.916 |
| 8 | 11.859 | 12.300 | 12.757 | 13.233 | 13.727 | 14.240 | 14.773 | 15.327 | 15.902 | 16.499 |
| 9 | 14.164 | 14.776 | 15.416 | 16.085 | 16.786 | 17.519 | 18.285 | 19.086 | 19.923 | 20.799 |
| 10 | 16.722 | 17.549 | 18.420 | 19.337 | 20.304 | 21.321 | 22.393 | 23.521 | 24.709 | 25.959 |
| 11 | 19.561 | 20.655 | 21.814 | 23.045 | 24.349 | 25.733 | 27.200 | 28.755 | 30.404 | 32.150 |
| 12 | 22.713 | 24.133 | 25.650 | 27.271 | 29.002 | 30.850 | 32.824 | 34.931 | 37.180 | 39.581 |
| 13 | 26.212 | 28.029 | 29.985 | 32.089 | 34.352 | 36.786 | 39.404 | 42.219 | 45.244 | 48.497 |
| 14 | 30.095 | 32.393 | 34.883 | 37.581 | 40.505 | 43.672 | 47.103 | 50.818 | 54.841 | 59.196 |
| 15 | 34.405 | 37.280 | 40.417 | 43.842 | 47.580 | 51.660 | 56.110 | 60.965 | 66.261 | 72.035 |
| 16 | 39.190 | 42.753 | 46.672 | 50.980 | 55.717 | 60.925 | 66.649 | 72.939 | 79.850 | 87.442 |
| 17 | 44.501 | 48.884 | 53.739 | 59.118 | 65.075 | 71.673 | 78.979 | 87.068 | 96.022 | 105.931 |
| 18 | 50.396 | 55.750 | 61.725 | 68.394 | 75.836 | 84.141 | 93.406 | 103.740 | 115.266 | 128.117 |
| 19 | 56.939 | 63.440 | 70.749 | 78.969 | 88.212 | 98.603 | 110.285 | 123.414 | 138.166 | 154.740 |
| 20 | 64.203 | 72.052 | 80.947 | 91.025 | 102.444 | 115.380 | 130.033 | 146.628 | 165.418 | 186.688 |
| 21 | 72.265 | 81.699 | 92.470 | 104.768 | 118.810 | 134.841 | 153.139 | 174.021 | 197.847 | 225.026 |
| 22 | 81.214 | 92.503 | 105.491 | 120.436 | 137.632 | 157.415 | 180.172 | 206.345 | 236.438 | 271.031 |
| 23 | 91.148 | 104.603 | 120.205 | 138.297 | 159.276 | 183.601 | 211.801 | 244.487 | 282.362 | 326.237 |
| 24 | 102.174 | 118.155 | 136.831 | 158.659 | 184.168 | 213.978 | 248.808 | 289.494 | 337.010 | 392.484 |
| 25 | 114.413 | 133.334 | 155.620 | 181.871 | 212.793 | 249.214 | 292.105 | 342.603 | 402.042 | 471.981 |
| 30 | 199.021 | 241.333 | 293.199 | 356.787 | 434.745 | 530.312 | 647.439 | 790.948 | 966.712 | 1181.882 |
| 40 | 581.826 | 767.091 | 1013.704 | 1342.025 | 1779.090 | 2360.757 | 3134.522 | 4163.213 | 5529.829 | 7343.858 |

# APPENDIX D: SUM OF AN ANNUITY OF $1 FOR N PERIODS (Continued)

| n | 21% | 22% | 23% | 24% | 25% | 26% | 27% | 28% | 29% | 30% |
|---|------|------|------|------|------|------|------|------|------|------|
| 1 | 1.000 | 1.000 | 1.000 | 1.000 | 1.000 | 1.000 | 1.000 | 1.000 | 1.000 | 1.000 |
| 2 | 2.210 | 2.220 | 2.230 | 2.240 | 2.250 | 2.260 | 2.270 | 2.280 | 2.290 | 2.300 |
| 3 | 3.674 | 3.708 | 3.743 | 3.778 | 3.813 | 3.848 | 3.883 | 3.918 | 3.954 | 3.990 |
| 4 | 5.446 | 5.524 | 5.604 | 5.684 | 5.766 | 5.848 | 5.931 | 6.016 | 6.101 | 6.187 |
| 5 | 7.589 | 7.740 | 7.893 | 8.048 | 8.207 | 8.368 | 8.533 | 8.700 | 8.870 | 9.043 |
| 6 | 10.183 | 10.442 | 10.708 | 10.980 | 11.259 | 11.544 | 11.837 | 12.136 | 12.442 | 12.756 |
| 7 | 13.321 | 13.740 | 14.171 | 14.615 | 15.073 | 15.546 | 16.032 | 16.534 | 17.051 | 17.583 |
| 8 | 17.119 | 17.762 | 18.430 | 19.123 | 19.842 | 20.588 | 21.361 | 22.163 | 22.995 | 23.858 |
| 9 | 21.714 | 22.670 | 23.669 | 24.712 | 25.802 | 26.940 | 28.129 | 29.369 | 30.664 | 32.015 |
| 10 | 27.274 | 28.657 | 30.113 | 31.643 | 33.253 | 34.945 | 36.723 | 38.593 | 40.556 | 42.619 |
| 11 | 34.001 | 35.962 | 38.039 | 40.238 | 42.566 | 45.031 | 47.639 | 50.398 | 53.318 | 56.405 |
| 12 | 42.142 | 44.874 | 47.788 | 50.895 | 54.208 | 57.739 | 61.501 | 65.510 | 69.780 | 74.327 |
| 13 | 51.991 | 55.746 | 59.779 | 64.110 | 68.760 | 73.751 | 79.107 | 84.853 | 91.016 | 97.625 |
| 14 | 63.909 | 69.010 | 74.528 | 80.496 | 86.949 | 93.926 | 101.465 | 109.612 | 118.411 | 127.913 |
| 15 | 78.330 | 85.192 | 92.669 | 100.815 | 109.687 | 119.347 | 129.861 | 141.303 | 153.750 | 167.286 |
| 16 | 95.780 | 104.935 | 114.983 | 126.011 | 138.109 | 151.377 | 165.924 | 181.868 | 199.337 | 218.472 |
| 17 | 116.894 | 129.020 | 142.430 | 157.253 | 173.636 | 191.735 | 211.723 | 233.791 | 258.145 | 285.014 |
| 18 | 142.441 | 158.405 | 176.188 | 195.994 | 218.045 | 242.585 | 269.888 | 300.252 | 334.007 | 371.518 |
| 19 | 173.354 | 194.254 | 217.712 | 244.033 | 273.556 | 306.658 | 343.758 | 385.323 | 431.870 | 483.973 |
| 20 | 210.758 | 237.989 | 268.785 | 303.601 | 342.945 | 387.389 | 437.573 | 494.213 | 558.112 | 630.165 |
| 21 | 256.018 | 291.347 | 331.606 | 377.465 | 429.681 | 489.110 | 556.717 | 633.593 | 720.964 | 820.215 |
| 22 | 310.781 | 356.443 | 408.875 | 469.056 | 538.101 | 617.278 | 708.031 | 811.999 | 931.044 | 1067.280 |
| 23 | 377.045 | 435.861 | 503.917 | 582.630 | 673.626 | 778.771 | 900.199 | 1040.358 | 1202.047 | 1388.464 |
| 24 | 457.225 | 532.750 | 620.817 | 723.461 | 843.033 | 982.251 | 1144.253 | 1332.659 | 1551.640 | 1806.003 |
| 25 | 554.242 | 650.955 | 764.605 | 898.092 | 1054.791 | 1238.636 | 1454.201 | 1706.803 | 2002.616 | 2348.803 |
| 30 | 1445.151 | 1767.081 | 2160.491 | 2640.916 | 3227.174 | 3942.026 | 4812.977 | 5873.231 | 7162.824 | 8729.985 |

363

# APPENDIX D: SUM OF AN ANNUITY OF $1 FOR N PERIODS (Continued)

| n | 31% | 32% | 33% | 34% | 35% | 36% | 37% | 38% | 39% | 40% |
|---|---|---|---|---|---|---|---|---|---|---|
| 1 | 1.000 | 1.000 | 1.000 | 1.000 | 1.000 | 1.000 | 1.000 | 1.000 | 1.000 | 1.000 |
| 2 | 2.310 | 2.320 | 2.330 | 2.340 | 2.350 | 2.360 | 2.370 | 2.380 | 2.390 | 2.400 |
| 3 | 4.026 | 4.062 | 4.099 | 4.136 | 4.173 | 4.210 | 4.247 | 4.284 | 4.322 | 4.360 |
| 4 | 6.274 | 6.362 | 6.452 | 6.542 | 6.633 | 6.725 | 6.818 | 6.912 | 7.008 | 7.104 |
| 5 | 9.219 | 9.398 | 9.581 | 9.766 | 9.954 | 10.146 | 10.341 | 10.539 | 10.741 | 10.946 |
| 6 | 13.077 | 13.406 | 13.742 | 14.086 | 14.438 | 14.799 | 15.167 | 15.544 | 15.930 | 16.324 |
| 7 | 18.131 | 18.696 | 19.277 | 19.876 | 20.492 | 21.126 | 21.779 | 22.451 | 23.142 | 23.853 |
| 8 | 24.752 | 25.678 | 26.638 | 27.633 | 28.664 | 29.732 | 30.837 | 31.982 | 33.168 | 34.395 |
| 9 | 33.425 | 34.895 | 36.429 | 38.029 | 39.696 | 41.435 | 43.247 | 45.135 | 47.103 | 49.153 |
| 10 | 44.786 | 47.062 | 49.451 | 51.958 | 54.590 | 57.352 | 60.248 | 63.287 | 66.473 | 69.814 |
| 11 | 59.670 | 63.122 | 66.769 | 70.624 | 74.697 | 78.998 | 83.540 | 88.336 | 93.398 | 98.739 |
| 12 | 79.168 | 84.320 | 89.803 | 95.637 | 101.841 | 108.437 | 115.450 | 122.904 | 130.823 | 139.235 |
| 13 | 104.710 | 112.303 | 120.439 | 129.153 | 138.485 | 148.475 | 159.167 | 170.607 | 182.844 | 195.929 |
| 14 | 138.170 | 149.240 | 161.183 | 174.065 | 187.954 | 202.926 | 219.059 | 236.438 | 255.153 | 275.300 |
| 15 | 182.003 | 197.997 | 215.374 | 234.247 | 254.738 | 276.979 | 301.111 | 327.284 | 355.662 | 386.420 |
| 16 | 239.423 | 262.356 | 287.447 | 314.891 | 344.897 | 377.692 | 413.522 | 452.652 | 495.370 | 541.988 |
| 17 | 314.645 | 347.309 | 383.305 | 422.954 | 466.611 | 514.661 | 567.524 | 625.659 | 689.565 | 759.784 |
| 18 | 413.185 | 459.449 | 510.795 | 567.758 | 630.925 | 700.939 | 778.509 | 864.410 | 959.495 | 1064.697 |
| 19 | 542.272 | 607.472 | 680.358 | 761.796 | 852.748 | 954.277 | 1067.557 | 1193.886 | 1334.698 | 1491.576 |
| 20 | 711.376 | 802.863 | 905.876 | 1021.807 | 1152.210 | 1298.817 | 1463.553 | 1648.563 | 1856.230 | 2089.206 |
| 21 | 932.903 | 1060.779 | 1205.814 | 1370.221 | 1556.484 | 1767.391 | 2006.067 | 2276.016 | 2581.160 | 2925.889 |
| 22 | 1223.103 | 1401.229 | 1604.733 | 1837.096 | 2102.253 | 2404.651 | 2749.312 | 3141.902 | 3588.813 | 4097.245 |
| 23 | 1603.264 | 1850.622 | 2135.295 | 2462.709 | 2839.042 | 3271.326 | 3767.557 | 4336.825 | 4989.450 | 5737.142 |
| 24 | 2101.276 | 2443.821 | 2840.943 | 3301.030 | 3833.706 | 4450.003 | 5162.554 | 5985.819 | 6936.335 | 8032.999 |
| 25 | 2753.672 | 3226.844 | 3779.454 | 4424.380 | 5176.504 | 6053.004 | 7073.699 | 8261.430 | 9642.506 | 11247.199 |

# APPENDIX E: PRESENT VALUE OF AN ANNUITY OF $1 FOR N PERIODS

| n | 1% | 2% | 3% | 4% | 5% | 6% | 7% | 8% | 9% | 10% |
|---|---|---|---|---|---|---|---|---|---|---|
| 1 | 0.990 | 0.980 | 0.971 | 0.962 | 0.952 | 0.943 | 0.935 | 0.926 | 0.917 | 0.909 |
| 2 | 1.970 | 1.942 | 1.913 | 1.886 | 1.859 | 1.833 | 1.808 | 1.783 | 1.759 | 1.736 |
| 3 | 2.941 | 2.884 | 2.829 | 2.775 | 2.723 | 2.673 | 2.624 | 2.577 | 2.531 | 2.487 |
| 4 | 3.902 | 3.808 | 3.717 | 3.630 | 3.546 | 3.465 | 3.387 | 3.312 | 3.240 | 3.170 |
| 5 | 4.853 | 4.713 | 4.580 | 4.452 | 4.329 | 4.212 | 4.100 | 3.993 | 3.890 | 3.791 |
| 6 | 5.795 | 5.601 | 5.417 | 5.242 | 5.076 | 4.917 | 4.767 | 4.623 | 4.486 | 4.355 |
| 7 | 6.728 | 6.472 | 6.230 | 6.002 | 5.786 | 5.582 | 5.389 | 5.206 | 5.033 | 4.868 |
| 8 | 7.652 | 7.325 | 7.020 | 6.733 | 6.463 | 6.210 | 5.971 | 5.747 | 5.535 | 5.335 |
| 9 | 8.566 | 8.162 | 7.786 | 7.435 | 7.108 | 6.802 | 6.515 | 6.247 | 5.995 | 5.759 |
| 10 | 9.471 | 8.983 | 8.530 | 8.111 | 7.722 | 7.360 | 7.024 | 6.710 | 6.418 | 6.145 |
| 11 | 10.368 | 9.787 | 9.253 | 8.760 | 8.306 | 7.887 | 7.499 | 7.139 | 6.805 | 6.495 |
| 12 | 11.255 | 10.575 | 9.954 | 9.385 | 8.863 | 8.384 | 7.943 | 7.536 | 7.161 | 6.814 |
| 13 | 12.134 | 11.348 | 10.635 | 9.986 | 9.394 | 8.853 | 8.358 | 7.904 | 7.487 | 7.103 |
| 14 | 13.004 | 12.106 | 11.296 | 10.563 | 9.899 | 9.295 | 8.745 | 8.244 | 7.786 | 7.367 |
| 15 | 13.865 | 12.849 | 11.938 | 11.118 | 10.380 | 9.712 | 9.108 | 8.559 | 8.061 | 7.606 |
| 16 | 14.718 | 13.578 | 12.561 | 11.652 | 10.838 | 10.106 | 9.447 | 8.851 | 8.313 | 7.824 |
| 17 | 15.562 | 14.292 | 13.166 | 12.166 | 11.274 | 10.477 | 9.763 | 9.122 | 8.544 | 8.022 |
| 18 | 16.398 | 14.992 | 13.754 | 12.659 | 11.690 | 10.828 | 10.059 | 9.372 | 8.756 | 8.201 |
| 19 | 17.226 | 15.678 | 14.324 | 13.134 | 12.085 | 11.158 | 10.336 | 9.604 | 8.950 | 8.365 |
| 20 | 18.046 | 16.351 | 14.877 | 13.590 | 12.462 | 11.470 | 10.594 | 9.818 | 9.129 | 8.514 |
| 21 | 18.857 | 17.011 | 15.415 | 14.029 | 12.821 | 11.764 | 10.836 | 10.017 | 9.292 | 8.649 |
| 22 | 19.660 | 17.658 | 15.937 | 14.451 | 13.163 | 12.042 | 11.061 | 10.201 | 9.442 | 8.772 |
| 23 | 20.456 | 18.292 | 16.444 | 14.857 | 13.489 | 12.303 | 11.272 | 10.371 | 9.580 | 8.883 |
| 24 | 21.243 | 18.914 | 16.936 | 15.247 | 13.799 | 12.550 | 11.469 | 10.529 | 9.707 | 8.985 |
| 25 | 22.023 | 19.523 | 17.413 | 15.622 | 14.094 | 12.783 | 11.654 | 10.675 | 9.823 | 9.077 |
| 30 | 25.808 | 22.396 | 19.600 | 17.292 | 15.372 | 13.765 | 12.409 | 11.258 | 10.274 | 9.427 |
| 40 | 32.835 | 27.355 | 23.115 | 19.793 | 17.159 | 15.046 | 13.332 | 11.925 | 10.757 | 9.779 |
| 50 | 39.196 | 31.424 | 25.730 | 21.482 | 18.256 | 15.762 | 13.801 | 12.233 | 10.962 | 9.915 |

## APPENDIX E: PRESENT VALUE OF AN ANNUITY OF $1 FOR N PERIODS (Cont.)

| n | 11% | 12% | 13% | 14% | 15% | 16% | 17% | 18% | 19% | 20% |
|---|---|---|---|---|---|---|---|---|---|---|
| 1 | 0.901 | 0.893 | 0.885 | 0.877 | 0.870 | 0.862 | 0.855 | 0.847 | 0.840 | 0.833 |
| 2 | 1.713 | 1.690 | 1.668 | 1.647 | 1.626 | 1.605 | 1.585 | 1.566 | 1.547 | 1.528 |
| 3 | 2.444 | 2.402 | 2.361 | 2.322 | 2.283 | 2.246 | 2.210 | 2.174 | 2.140 | 2.106 |
| 4 | 3.102 | 3.037 | 2.974 | 2.914 | 2.855 | 2.798 | 2.743 | 2.690 | 2.639 | 2.589 |
| 5 | 3.696 | 3.605 | 3.517 | 3.433 | 3.352 | 3.274 | 3.199 | 3.127 | 3.058 | 2.991 |
| 6 | 4.231 | 4.111 | 3.998 | 3.889 | 3.784 | 3.685 | 3.589 | 3.498 | 3.410 | 3.326 |
| 7 | 4.712 | 4.564 | 4.423 | 4.288 | 4.160 | 4.039 | 3.922 | 3.812 | 3.706 | 3.605 |
| 8 | 5.146 | 4.968 | 4.799 | 4.639 | 4.487 | 4.344 | 4.207 | 4.078 | 3.954 | 3.837 |
| 9 | 5.537 | 5.328 | 5.132 | 4.946 | 4.772 | 4.607 | 4.451 | 4.303 | 4.163 | 4.031 |
| 10 | 5.889 | 5.650 | 5.426 | 5.216 | 5.019 | 4.833 | 4.659 | 4.494 | 4.339 | 4.192 |
| 11 | 6.207 | 5.938 | 5.687 | 5.453 | 5.234 | 5.029 | 4.836 | 4.656 | 4.486 | 4.327 |
| 12 | 6.492 | 6.194 | 5.918 | 5.660 | 5.421 | 5.197 | 4.988 | 4.793 | 4.611 | 4.439 |
| 13 | 6.750 | 6.424 | 6.122 | 5.842 | 5.583 | 5.342 | 5.118 | 4.910 | 4.715 | 4.533 |
| 14 | 6.982 | 6.628 | 6.302 | 6.002 | 5.724 | 5.468 | 5.229 | 5.008 | 4.802 | 4.611 |
| 15 | 7.191 | 6.811 | 6.462 | 6.142 | 5.847 | 5.575 | 5.324 | 5.092 | 4.876 | 4.675 |
| 16 | 7.379 | 6.974 | 6.604 | 6.265 | 5.954 | 5.668 | 5.405 | 5.162 | 4.938 | 4.730 |
| 17 | 7.549 | 7.120 | 6.729 | 6.373 | 6.047 | 5.749 | 5.475 | 5.222 | 4.990 | 4.775 |
| 18 | 7.702 | 7.250 | 6.840 | 6.467 | 6.128 | 5.818 | 5.534 | 5.273 | 5.033 | 4.812 |
| 19 | 7.839 | 7.366 | 6.938 | 6.550 | 6.198 | 5.877 | 5.584 | 5.316 | 5.070 | 4.843 |
| 20 | 7.963 | 7.469 | 7.025 | 6.623 | 6.259 | 5.929 | 5.628 | 5.353 | 5.101 | 4.870 |
| 21 | 8.075 | 7.562 | 7.102 | 6.687 | 6.312 | 5.973 | 5.665 | 5.384 | 5.127 | 4.891 |
| 22 | 8.176 | 7.645 | 7.170 | 6.743 | 6.359 | 6.011 | 5.696 | 5.410 | 5.149 | 4.909 |
| 23 | 8.266 | 7.718 | 7.230 | 6.792 | 6.399 | 6.044 | 5.723 | 5.432 | 5.167 | 4.925 |
| 24 | 8.348 | 7.784 | 7.283 | 6.835 | 6.434 | 6.073 | 5.746 | 5.451 | 5.182 | 4.937 |
| 25 | 8.422 | 7.843 | 7.330 | 6.873 | 6.464 | 6.097 | 5.766 | 5.467 | 5.195 | 4.948 |
| 30 | 8.694 | 8.055 | 7.496 | 7.003 | 6.566 | 6.177 | 5.829 | 5.517 | 5.235 | 4.979 |
| 40 | 8.951 | 8.244 | 7.634 | 7.105 | 6.642 | 6.233 | 5.871 | 5.548 | 5.258 | 4.997 |
| 50 | 9.042 | 8.304 | 7.675 | 7.133 | 6.661 | 6.246 | 5.880 | 5.554 | 5.262 | 4.999 |

# APPENDIX E: PRESENT VALUE OF AN ANNUITY OF $1 FOR N PERIODS (Cont.)

| n | 21% | 22% | 23% | 24% | 25% | 26% | 27% | 28% | 29% | 30% |
|---|-----|-----|-----|-----|-----|-----|-----|-----|-----|-----|
| 1 | 0.826 | 0.820 | 0.813 | 0.806 | 0.800 | 0.794 | 0.787 | 0.781 | 0.775 | 0.769 |
| 2 | 1.509 | 1.492 | 1.474 | 1.457 | 1.440 | 1.424 | 1.407 | 1.392 | 1.376 | 1.361 |
| 3 | 2.074 | 2.042 | 2.011 | 1.981 | 1.952 | 1.923 | 1.896 | 1.868 | 1.842 | 1.816 |
| 4 | 2.540 | 2.494 | 2.448 | 2.404 | 2.362 | 2.320 | 2.280 | 2.241 | 2.203 | 2.166 |
| 5 | 2.926 | 2.864 | 2.803 | 2.745 | 2.689 | 2.635 | 2.583 | 2.532 | 2.483 | 2.436 |
| 6 | 3.245 | 3.167 | 3.092 | 3.020 | 2.951 | 2.885 | 2.821 | 2.759 | 2.700 | 2.643 |
| 7 | 3.508 | 3.416 | 3.327 | 3.242 | 3.161 | 3.083 | 3.009 | 2.937 | 2.868 | 2.802 |
| 8 | 3.726 | 3.619 | 3.518 | 3.421 | 3.329 | 3.241 | 3.156 | 3.076 | 2.999 | 2.925 |
| 9 | 3.905 | 3.786 | 3.673 | 3.566 | 3.463 | 3.366 | 3.273 | 3.184 | 3.100 | 3.019 |
| 10 | 4.054 | 3.923 | 3.799 | 3.682 | 3.571 | 3.465 | 3.364 | 3.269 | 3.178 | 3.092 |
| 11 | 4.177 | 4.035 | 3.902 | 3.776 | 3.656 | 3.543 | 3.437 | 3.335 | 3.239 | 3.147 |
| 12 | 4.278 | 4.127 | 3.985 | 3.851 | 3.725 | 3.606 | 3.493 | 3.387 | 3.286 | 3.190 |
| 13 | 4.362 | 4.203 | 4.053 | 3.912 | 3.780 | 3.656 | 3.538 | 3.427 | 3.322 | 3.223 |
| 14 | 4.432 | 4.265 | 4.108 | 3.962 | 3.824 | 3.695 | 3.573 | 3.459 | 3.351 | 3.249 |
| 15 | 4.489 | 4.315 | 4.153 | 4.001 | 3.859 | 3.726 | 3.601 | 3.483 | 3.373 | 3.268 |
| 16 | 4.536 | 4.357 | 4.189 | 4.033 | 3.887 | 3.751 | 3.623 | 3.503 | 3.390 | 3.283 |
| 17 | 4.576 | 4.391 | 4.219 | 4.059 | 3.910 | 3.771 | 3.640 | 3.518 | 3.403 | 3.295 |
| 18 | 4.608 | 4.419 | 4.243 | 4.080 | 3.928 | 3.786 | 3.654 | 3.529 | 3.413 | 3.304 |
| 19 | 4.635 | 4.442 | 4.263 | 4.097 | 3.942 | 3.799 | 3.664 | 3.539 | 3.421 | 3.311 |
| 20 | 4.657 | 4.460 | 4.279 | 4.110 | 3.954 | 3.808 | 3.673 | 3.546 | 3.427 | 3.316 |
| 21 | 4.675 | 4.476 | 4.292 | 4.121 | 3.963 | 3.816 | 3.679 | 3.551 | 3.432 | 3.320 |
| 22 | 4.690 | 4.488 | 4.302 | 4.130 | 3.970 | 3.822 | 3.684 | 3.556 | 3.436 | 3.323 |
| 23 | 4.703 | 4.499 | 4.311 | 4.137 | 3.976 | 3.827 | 3.689 | 3.559 | 3.438 | 3.325 |
| 24 | 4.713 | 4.507 | 4.318 | 4.143 | 3.981 | 3.831 | 3.692 | 3.562 | 3.441 | 3.327 |
| 25 | 4.721 | 4.514 | 4.323 | 4.147 | 3.985 | 3.834 | 3.694 | 3.564 | 3.442 | 3.329 |
| 30 | 4.746 | 4.534 | 4.339 | 4.160 | 3.995 | 3.842 | 3.701 | 3.569 | 3.447 | 3.332 |
| 40 | 4.760 | 4.544 | 4.347 | 4.166 | 3.999 | 3.846 | 3.703 | 3.571 | 3.448 | 3.333 |
| 50 | 4.762 | 4.545 | 4.348 | 4.167 | 4.000 | 3.846 | 3.704 | 3.571 | 3.448 | 3.333 |

# APPENDIX E: PRESENT VALUE OF AN ANNUITY OF $1 FOR N PERIODS (Cont.)

| n | 31% | 32% | 33% | 34% | 35% | 36% | 37% | 38% | 39% | 40% |
|---|-----|-----|-----|-----|-----|-----|-----|-----|-----|-----|
| 1 | 0.763 | 0.758 | 0.752 | 0.746 | 0.741 | 0.735 | 0.730 | 0.725 | 0.719 | 0.714 |
| 2 | 1.346 | 1.331 | 1.317 | 1.303 | 1.289 | 1.276 | 1.263 | 1.250 | 1.237 | 1.224 |
| 3 | 1.791 | 1.766 | 1.742 | 1.719 | 1.696 | 1.673 | 1.652 | 1.630 | 1.609 | 1.589 |
| 4 | 2.130 | 2.096 | 2.062 | 2.029 | 1.997 | 1.966 | 1.935 | 1.906 | 1.877 | 1.849 |
| 5 | 2.390 | 2.345 | 2.302 | 2.260 | 2.220 | 2.181 | 2.143 | 2.106 | 2.070 | 2.035 |
| 6 | 2.588 | 2.534 | 2.483 | 2.433 | 2.385 | 2.339 | 2.294 | 2.251 | 2.209 | 2.168 |
| 7 | 2.739 | 2.677 | 2.619 | 2.562 | 2.508 | 2.455 | 2.404 | 2.355 | 2.308 | 2.263 |
| 8 | 2.854 | 2.786 | 2.721 | 2.658 | 2.598 | 2.540 | 2.485 | 2.432 | 2.380 | 2.331 |
| 9 | 2.942 | 2.868 | 2.798 | 2.730 | 2.665 | 2.603 | 2.544 | 2.487 | 2.432 | 2.379 |
| 10 | 3.009 | 2.930 | 2.855 | 2.784 | 2.715 | 2.649 | 2.587 | 2.527 | 2.469 | 2.414 |
| 11 | 3.060 | 2.978 | 2.899 | 2.824 | 2.752 | 2.683 | 2.618 | 2.555 | 2.496 | 2.438 |
| 12 | 3.100 | 3.013 | 2.931 | 2.853 | 2.779 | 2.708 | 2.641 | 2.576 | 2.515 | 2.456 |
| 13 | 3.129 | 3.040 | 2.956 | 2.876 | 2.799 | 2.727 | 2.658 | 2.592 | 2.529 | 2.469 |
| 14 | 3.152 | 3.061 | 2.974 | 2.892 | 2.814 | 2.740 | 2.670 | 2.603 | 2.539 | 2.478 |
| 15 | 3.170 | 3.076 | 2.988 | 2.905 | 2.825 | 2.750 | 2.679 | 2.611 | 2.546 | 2.484 |
| 16 | 3.183 | 3.088 | 2.999 | 2.914 | 2.834 | 2.757 | 2.685 | 2.616 | 2.551 | 2.489 |
| 17 | 3.193 | 3.097 | 3.007 | 2.921 | 2.840 | 2.763 | 2.690 | 2.621 | 2.555 | 2.492 |
| 18 | 3.201 | 3.104 | 3.012 | 2.926 | 2.844 | 2.767 | 2.693 | 2.624 | 2.557 | 2.494 |
| 19 | 3.207 | 3.109 | 3.017 | 2.930 | 2.848 | 2.770 | 2.696 | 2.626 | 2.559 | 2.496 |
| 20 | 3.211 | 3.113 | 3.020 | 2.933 | 2.850 | 2.772 | 2.698 | 2.627 | 2.561 | 2.497 |
| 21 | 3.215 | 3.116 | 3.023 | 2.935 | 2.852 | 2.773 | 2.699 | 2.629 | 2.562 | 2.498 |
| 22 | 3.217 | 3.118 | 3.025 | 2.936 | 2.853 | 2.775 | 2.700 | 2.629 | 2.562 | 2.498 |
| 23 | 3.219 | 3.120 | 3.026 | 2.938 | 2.854 | 2.775 | 2.701 | 2.630 | 2.563 | 2.499 |
| 24 | 3.221 | 3.121 | 3.027 | 2.939 | 2.855 | 2.776 | 2.701 | 2.630 | 2.563 | 2.499 |
| 25 | 3.222 | 3.122 | 3.028 | 2.939 | 2.856 | 2.777 | 2.702 | 2.631 | 2.563 | 2.499 |
| 30 | 3.225 | 3.124 | 3.030 | 2.941 | 2.857 | 2.778 | 2.702 | 2.631 | 2.564 | 2.500 |
| 40 | 3.226 | 3.125 | 3.030 | 2.941 | 2.857 | 2.778 | 2.703 | 2.632 | 2.564 | 2.500 |
| 50 | 3.226 | 3.125 | 3.030 | 2.941 | 2.857 | 2.778 | 2.703 | 2.632 | 2.564 | 2.500 |